Step into the Magical World of the Andean People

If you are drawn to the mystic beauty of the Andes, Machu Picchu and ancient Peruvian culture, *Journey to Machu Picchu* will connect you intimately with the people who have lived there for thousands of years. As you traverse these pages, you will discover a side of the Peruvian experience that often is overlooked and undervalued. And you will absorb the energy of Machu Picchu, one of the greatest spiritual centers in the world, in a unique spiritual metamorphosis.

This is the first book written about the traditions and spirituality of the gentle Quechua (ketch-uwa) people of Qosqo and Machu Picchu. It is the only written testament to the rich heritage of today's Quechua, who believe they emerged from the depths of Pachamama, Mother Earth. As you submerge into the inexplicable realities of the Andean people, their world of dignity, self-respect, and self-love will steal into your soul.

Journey to Machu Picchu sounds the warnings of Mother Earth—as spoken by ancient Andeans to today's modern farmer. Follow along as *Journey to Machu Picchu* transports you to a place of hope, respite, and healing that will in turn energize your commitment to yourself and to the world around you.

"*Journey to Machu Picchu* is a penetrating, wise, and wonderful personal account of the spiritual wisdom of the Quechua people, their history and their love affair with Pachamama—the earth which is their mother. This book is filled with passion. The authors' words are clear and honest and their love for Machu Picchu and the land around her is unbounded. The mythology of the Andes, the shamanic practices that form the basis of the union between people and the land, and the consistent respect that the authors have for their subject is truely inspiring."

—Leslie Kenton
Bestselling writer, teacher, and broadcaster

About the Authors

Carol Cumes was born in South Africa. After living in California for twenty years, Cumes established Magical Journey, a travel company for tourists all over the world interested in spiritual visits to Peru. She traveled extensively in the Andes, lived with the Quechua people, and studied South American shamanism with *curanderos* and Andean *pakkos* in the jungles, deserts, and mountains of Peru. In 1995, Cumes moved to the Sacred Valley near Machu Picchu, where she built Willka T'ika, a garden guest house and spiritual retreat for special interest groups. In addition to conducting tours through Magical Journey, Cumes is continuing her work with Andean medicinal plants and herbal teas.

Rómulo Lizárraga Valencia is Quechua. Lizárraga studied languages at the University of Qosqo, and has a post-graduate degree in tourism. He has been lecturing to university students and leading excursions as a professional Andean trail guide for fifteen years. He has a wife and two daughters.

About the Chief Photographer

Teryl Matkins' skills as a photographer began with a desire to record the lives of her two sons. She later used this talent to document the scenery and wildlife of Africa. *Journey to Machu Picchu* is a perfect melding of her talents as both portrait and landscape photographer.

This book also includes several photographs taken by Carol Cumes.

To Write to the Authors

If you wish to contact the authors or would like more information about this book, please write to the authors in care of Llewellyn Worldwide, and we will forward your request. Both the authors and publisher appreciate hearing from you and learning of your enjoyment of this book and how it has helped you. Llewellyn Worldwide cannot guarantee that every letter written to the authors can be answered, but all will be forwarded. Please write:

Carol Cumes and Rómulo Lizárraga Valencia
% Llewellyn Worldwide
P.O. Box 64383, K186-4, St. Paul, MN 55164-0383, U.S.A.

Please enclose a self-addressed, stamped envelope for reply, or $1.00 to cover costs. If outside the U.S.A., enclose international postal reply coupon.

About Willka T'ika

For more information on Willka T'ika and sacred journeys to Peru, check their web page: www.travelperu.com; e-mail: info@travelperu.com; or contact the Magical Journey office:

Magical Journey
915 Cole St., Suite 236, San Francisco, CA 94117 • 888-PERU-070

Journey to Machu Picchu

Spiritual Wisdom from the Andes

Carol Cumes

Rómulo Lizárraga Valencia

Second Edition, revised and expanded

1999
Llewellyn Publications
St. Paul, MN 55164-0383, U.S.A.

SECOND EDITION, revised and expanded
Second printing, 1999
(previously titled *Pachamama's Children*)

First edition, one printing, 1995

Cover photo: Carol Cumes
Cover design: Michael Matheny
Color insert design: Anne Marie Garrison
Chief photographer: Teryl Matkins
Additional photography: Carol Cumes and Beverly Elder
Original book design and editing: Pamela Henkel
Second edition project management and editing: Kimberly Nightingale and
    Christine Snow

Library of Congress Cataloging-in-Publication Data
Cumes, Carol, 1945—
        Journey to Machu Picchu : spiritual wisdom from the Andes / Carol
        Cumes, Rómulo Lizárraga Valencia. — 2nd ed.
            p.   cm.
        Rev. ed. of: Pachamama's children. 1st ed. 1995.
        Includes bibliographical references and index.
        ISBN 1-56718-186-4 (trade paper)
        1. Sacred space—Peru. 2. Quechua Indians—Religion. 3. Machu Picchu
        Site (Peru). I. Cumes, Carol, 1945- Pachamama's children.
        II. Lizárraga Valencia, Rómulo, 1958— . III. Title.
        BL581.P4C86 1998
        299'.883—dc21   98-36032
                                                                            CIP

Llewellyn Publications
A Division of Llewellyn Worldwide, Ltd.
P.O. Box 64383, St. Paul, MN 55164-0383

Printed in the United States of America

Dedicated to Our Children

Lila, Terry, Paul, and Romi Cumes

Indira and Shakti Lizárraga Chicata
and all of Pachamama's Children

With Thanks

My heartfelt thanks to Mark Hennessy for being there for me over the past three years.

To my children in California: Lila, Terry, Paul, and Romi Cumes, and my son-in-law Robert Mosakowski. Thank you for being so supportive and for your help and encouragement to me to continue on my path.

And thank you to Antonia, Fabian, Luchio, Livio, and Rosalio, for the spirit in which they work and live at Willka T'ika.

To Kimberly Nightingale at Llewellyn for her continued belief in this book; Christine Snow, the Llewellyn staff, and Susan Weaver for their assistance; and Teryl Matkins for her beautiful photographs.

For the past 14 years, I have been honored to meet and work with authentic pakkokuna, healers, curanderos, and professional guides from the Andes, Amazon, altiplano, and desert regions of Peru. I thank you all.

Juan Bravo Vizcarra, renowned Peruvian artist, created the painting for the cover of *Pachamama's Children*. The painting shows Pachamama, womb of this earth, whose braid transforms into the female Goddess serpent. From Her hand grows pure white maize, sacred plant of the Andes. The snake represents the inner world, Ukhupacha. Apu *kuntur,* the condor, is a deity and messenger from the Gods. Chokkechinchay is a mythical puma whose tail sweeps the clouds and produces hail, storms, and rain. Behind Pachamama are three steps of the square Andean cross symbolizing the three worlds within Andean cosmology, which stems from the constellation called *chakana* (the Southern Cross). Two stars at the left of chakana are *llamaq ñawikuna,* the eyes of the llama. Inti, revered as the masculine Sun God, appears in Pachamama's portrait in balance with the feminine moon, Mama Killa.

Contents

Preface to the Second Edition

Machu Picchu (Máh-choo Pee-choo), ancient city of light, is a magical journey to those who set forth to explore her secrets. Nestled in the Andean mountains, surrounded by spectacular peaks and green subtropical vegetation, the beauty and majesty of the stone city leaves visitors in awe. Machu Picchu imparts its beauty from the first glimpse of a graceful morning mist, and she lives ever after. She enriches with treasures that touch the soul and offers promises to fulfill the spiritual quest. None who visit this mysterious and sacred site leave unchanged.

In 1984, I first came to Machu Picchu as the culmination of a shamanic journey, during which I was introduced to the methods and ceremonies of healers who worked with the energies of the plants of northern Peru.

On that first visit, a small group of us climbed Waynapicchu, young woman's mountain, to meditate upon a small rock surface at the top. The rest of the group, accompanied by the late Don Eduardo Calderon, a respected healer from Trujillo, sat in meditation at the temple below the Intiwatana, concentrating on us. I closed my eyes, feeling surprisingly relaxed and at peace. I heard a rustling sound and "felt" the huge, feathered wing of a condor gently lifting me on his back. We soared into the gray sky, flying between the Putukusi peak and eastern section of the city, circling south around Machu Picchu peak, gliding slowly west, then back to salute the north, where I was returned to the rock. With a jolt I came back into my body, opened my eyes and shuddered as I peered down a sheer-faced rock cliff that fell hundreds of meters to the river below, just a few inches from where I sat. I had never experienced such a feeling of ecstasy. Later, Eduardo explained that I had encountered the good fortune to be embraced by the condor, guardian of the ancient city that had welcomed me back.

I became connected to the spiritual world of Machu Picchu, and I left Peru wanting to learn and understand more. Each return to Machu Picchu left me in awe of its stillness and beauty, and always I was captivated by the mystery. During each visit I was drawn to a different site where I could sit and absorb the unique energy of the scene. I once was told that pilgrims came from all over the world to experience this share of the purest energy on earth.

My greatest desire was to learn more about the spirituality of the Andes, to understand the beliefs that led to the building of cities like Machu Picchu. I spoke with local "experts" on Andean cosmology and listened to what other spiritual group leaders had to say. I would chat with anyone who would talk about this mysterious antiquity. Nothing rang true to me, and sadly I realized that people simply were creating their own stories and ceremonies to suit their personal objectives. After a few years I realized that, if the truth were to be found, it would lie in the beliefs of those who had lived and cultivated this land over thousands of years, through all the epochs of history. I needed to explore the culture and cosmology of the Quechua (ketch-uwa) *campesinos*, the farmers of the isolated mountain communities.

I journeyed into the villages to meet with these Andean people. There in the mountains, living with the locals and hearing their stories, I began to understand and experience the heartbeat of the land. Their generosity, the earthy texture of their lifestyles, the vibrant colors of their clothes, and their sincere, deep love for Pachamama, the *apukuna*, spirits of the mountains, and all of nature, filled my soul. An ancient and continuous tradition of spirituality was alive and well in the Andes.

Nothing prepared me for the effect Machu Picchu was to have on me, and no one could have predicted how my life would change as a result, or how I was to find myself drawn to the Kkechuwa-speaking people who live in the surrounding areas and their interaction with Pachamama, the Mother Earth.

I began to understand that there were many gateways to the spirituality of this holy city. I entered Machu Picchu in spirit and focused on expanding my consciousness to deepen my innate healing abilities. I received energy by quietly sitting in meditation or I focused on breathing patterns aimed at opening the meridians and energy centers of my body. This, I believed, allowed in the energy for my personal work.

I wrote the original edition of *Pachamama's Children: Mother Earth and Her Children of the Andes* to bring to the reader an authentic account of the simple but profound beliefs and practices of the Quechua people. I began writing about the Quechua and their ancient cosmology in 1990 while still living in the United States and traveling back and forth to Peru. I believed then, as I do today, that in these beliefs lie the true wisdom of the Andes. Since that time, I have been living in the Sacred Valley of Peru and have met and guided spiritual seekers who have journeyed to the Andes from all over the world. I soon came to understand that the Andes were calling to the feminine side in all of us, and Machu Picchu in particular seemed to attract and nurture everyone in some way.

In this new edition, *Journey to Machu Picchu: Spiritual Wisdom of the Andes*, I have added chapters to give voice to new insights and natural occurrences that have recently taken place in the Machu Picchu area. I have also added a chapter concerning my personal experience with Machu Picchu called "Carol's Story." Hopefully, this will be of interest to many others on similar paths, illustrating what it is about Peru that draws souls here and changes lives forever.

The past few years have brought an increase in tourism to Peru, and with it, a corresponding decrease in respect for Pachamama, Mother Earth. In February 1995, the first of a series of natural disasters began around Machu Picchu, and since then, Pachamama has sent similar warnings to the people in the area. Quechua elders explain that the Andean Gods have been offended by those who fail to respect them and who misrepresent the true beliefs of the Andean people. They maintain that both visitors and locals have entered sacred space without asking permission from the apukuna, the powerful mountain deities who have shown their vengeance with the recent natural disasters. Most tourists who visit the ruins at Machu Picchu remain unaware of and unaffected by these tragedies which I describe in this new edition.

Andean *pakkokuna*, healers, are men and women who have dedicated their lives to their profession of healing. They have undergone years of apprenticeship, strenuous physical and mental preparation, and personal sacrifices to follow this calling. Besides working in spiritual dimensions, they provide pragmatic wisdom about everyday matters of their *ayllukuna*, communities. In this edition, I have incorporated the story of Alicia, a young Quechua healer who has stayed close to her own roots, to illustrate clearly what is important to the Quechua people in this region. I believe that from these people we can learn to end our own alienation from nature, not by distorting their traditions and beliefs but by rediscovering our own heritage of respect rooted in the same Mother Earth.

I believe I was led to take some of this essence of Machu Picchu and create my own garden in the Sacred Valley so that others could visit and enjoy its beauties. Visitors to my retreat Willka T'ika have written to say they are starting their own special gardens in Africa, England, Israel, all over the United States and in Europe. As each of these gardeners pays homage or expresses appreciation to Pachamama, so the essence and positive energy of Machu Picchu spreads throughout the planet.

I recognize now just what a continuing inspiration Machu Picchu has been to me. In my early visits, I pondered over the mysteries of the city. I heard guides try to explain what they knew about the sacred city. The more I listened to "experts"—scientists, guides, shamans, and foreign spiritual masters—the more convinced I became that no one knew or would ever know the factual history of Machu Picchu and that it really was not important. The essence of what Machu Picchu was, is, and will always be is what matters, and that it is there for all to see in its terraces and temples, coupled with the beliefs of the Andean people.

In *Journey to Machu Picchu*, I share with you this authentic spiritual wisdom of the Andean people, hoping it will be of value on your own journey to this magical place.

I personally would like to invite you to visit my gardens at Willka T'ika, spend a few days at my garden house, join one of the sacred tours to Machu Picchu, or bring your own special interest group. Advance arrangements are necessary, and further information can be accessed through our web page or by e-mail.

In the U.S.A.:
Magical Journey
915 Cole St., Suite 236
San Francisco, CA 94117
888-PERU-070

Web: www.travelperu.com
E-mail: info@travelperu.com

In Peru:
Casilla Postal 70
Urubamba, Cusco, Peru
Fax: 51 84 201181

—Carol Cumes
May 1998

Preface to the First Edition

It is the presence of the Quechua people, with their beautiful faces and gentle natures, that brings life to the Sacred Valley of the Inkakuna (or Incas), the ruins at Machu Picchu, and the ancient cobblestoned city of Qosqo (or Cusco, pronounced Koos-ko). Visitors from all over the world are drawn to these famous places for their magnificent scenery and graceful civilization.

Few people are aware that the ancestors of today's Quechua society lived in these Andean areas long before the arrival of the Inkakuna, the Children of the Sun. Historians date the Inka dynasty around the years 1200 to 1572 A.D. As the Inkakuna developed their civilization, they dominated the Kkechuwa-speaking Andean people who lived in the countryside, and they incorporated Quechua beliefs and traditions into their own religious practices.

The Andean campesinos (farmers) who lived in the countryside maintained their agricultural way of life, while quietly continuing to observe their ancient rituals. For thousands of years the traditions and spirituality of the Andean people were passed down orally from generation to generation.

These rituals were directed to the Pachamama (Mother Earth) and they embraced special offerings to Her asking for help with their agricultural production. The hope was to produce sufficient food to nurture all Her children, and this is still the objective of the Quechua campesinos living in the Andes today.

We step into the magical world of the Andean people and unearth their traditions and cosmology as we seek to understand how this mysterious past connects to their humble present and promises a future filled with love and harmony. Familiarity with the continuity of life and beliefs under Pachamama's watchful eye can open the door to the spiritual power pervading the area.

This book is a result of our many years of investigation in the countryside, and is a compilation of firsthand knowledge of the world of the Andean Quechua. It includes personal stories gathered from conversations with the campesinos residing in those areas, as well as material gained from extensive reading. We have spent much time living with the Quechua people, where we were able to pool our knowledge, further our research, and verify the information.

Journey to Machu Picchu (Pachamama's Children) is not intended as an academic treatise, as there are many available and we had no desire to duplicate them. The bibliography represents some of the background reading we have distilled for readers, and which was done to confirm some of the anecdotal information gathered from the Quechua people.

We present a side of the Peruvian experience that often is overlooked and undervalued. Within these pages, this view is easily accessible to the average tourist and armchair traveler who desires to learn more about the Quechua people than can be found in the available guide books to Peru.

We dedicate this book to the Kkechuwa-speaking Andean farming families who have survived half a millennium of abuse and degradation. These campesinos believe they emerged from the depths of Mother Earth. They have always lived in harmony with Her. They have fed and nourished Her, and in return have received Her gifts of life.

The guiding tenet of their way of life exemplifies the co-dependence of all elements of the earth, where humans live in harmony with a Nature from which they have never separated. Mountain peaks, rivers, plants, and animals all play an active role in the lives of the Quechua people. They practice *ayni*, the gift of helping each other and sharing tasks.

Quechua campesinos incorporate their spirituality into every aspect of their daily lives. They thus set an example for the rest of humankind on how to work, share, and love one another, all through their connection to Pachamama, Mother Earth.

Carol Cumes   Rómulo Lizárraga Valencia
Willka T'ika   Qosqo, Peru

Introduction:
Andeans, Inkakuna, and 500
Years of Spanish Influence

In order to understand the context in which the modern Quechua live, and the extraordinary resilience of their spiritual beliefs that connect them to the early inhabitants of Machu Picchu, an overview of their history and mythology is helpful. The Spanish invasion in 1532 led to the collapse of the Inka Empire and a deliberate destruction of all Inkan historical records. Only mythology has survived from the period before the arrival of the Spanish and therefore no accurate dating is available.

Long before the Inkakuna (Incas) built their empire, people lived in the Andes in the surrounding areas of Qosqo and Machu Picchu. These people lived closely connected to nature and the earth from which they came. They believed in a Creator God called Wirakkocha or Teksi-wirakkocha, who brought forth the people from the diverse Andean regions, from the caves and the mountains, the rivers, and streams. Offerings and blessings were made to all the tangible and intangible aspects of nature, which were also their deities.

Every action of their lives bore purpose. These gentle people of the Andes would communicate with invisible beings through ritual and ceremony that took place in nature, and the beings would work with them to ensure that all their needs were met. They were in tune with nature and lived in total harmony with her—connected to the earth, the mountains, the cosmos, and to all else in their realm of awareness.

Various manifestations of these nature-worshipping civilizations spanned thousands of years, yet none left written records or codices for historians and scientists to unravel.

According to the most recent mythology of the region, the cosmovision that guided the conquering Inkan people, the Sun God Inti created

1

The city of Qosqo nestled in the Andean mountains.

the first Inkakuna. Mánkko Kkhápakk was the mythical founder of the Inka Empire, which, according to historians, commenced in the thirteenth century.

Several versions exist of the myths of origin. One of the most popular concerns the Sun God Inti, his consort, the moon Killa, and their two children, Mánkko Kkhápakk and his sister Mama Okkllo. According to legend, Inti sent his children to civilize the earth. From their birthplace, the foam of the waters of Lake Titicaca, they were to found the city of Qosqo, which was to become the center of the new Inka Empire.

The Sun gave his children a golden rod and told them that the site would be wherever the rod sank with one thrust into ground as soft and fertile as the human navel. This occurred at Guanacaure Mountain; Qosqo, which means "navel" in the Kkechuwa language, was born. Mánkko Kkhápakk and Mama Okkllo won the local people over by teaching them a more advanced form of civilization. The Kkorikancha Temple was the center of the city and there the Inkan rulers initiated the religion of the Sun.

A second popular myth of origin is that four brothers and four sisters (some myths say three) emerged from caves in a cliff near Pakkarikktámpu, which means "the Inn of the Origins" or "place of birth." The siblings set off to build a new city.

One brave brother, Ayar Kachi, caused the others to be jealous of his strength and wisdom. They tricked him into going back to the cave and walled him up inside. He then was seen flying on feathered wings, whence he urged his brothers and sisters to settle in the Qosqo valley. He would guide their destiny, instructing them in rituals for initiation and sovereignty. Then he and two brothers turned to stone.

The fourth brother, Ayar Mánkko, and his sisters went to Qosqo, where they settled among the local population. Ayar Mánkko prayed to the sun at the sacred rock at Guanacaure Mountain and proclaimed himself the Son of the Sun. He became known as Mánkko Kkhápakk the king, and his palace was called Kkolkkampata. The new city of Qosqo was founded in the name of the creator of the Sun, Teksiwirakkocha.

With the arrival of these children of the Sun in the Qosqo area, the Inka Dynasty was created. Its rulers took over the territory and control of the indigenous people who worshipped Pachamama and all her earthly domain.

They introduced a sophisticated political, religious, and social system that, at least overtly, took precedence over the original religious and social practices of the region. The Inkakuna assured the dominance of their way of life by creating an enduring form of history: they recorded stories, historical data, business transactions, mathematical calculations, tabulations of crops and livestock production, and information about their civilization on *khipukuna*, a complicated system of knots tied on colored ropes.

The temple of Pachakámak, built outside of what is now called Lima, was one of the holiest temples in pre-Inkan times. People made pilgrimages to this pyramid-shaped temple from all over the country. They brought offerings of gold, silver, and magnificent woven cloths when they came to the revered shrine to consult the oracle of Pachakámak (*pacha* means "world" and *kámac* means "creator or giver of life"). Priests attended to the temple and communicated with the oracle.

At the top of the pyramid was the holy room of Pachakámak, the two-faced deity known as the Creator of the World. He cared for and healed human beings and assured the growth of the crops. He was also the destroyer, responsible for causing natural disasters and illness in people. The pre-Inkakuna appreciated the polarities of life. They understood the need for balance of the light and the dark sides, the positive and negative.

But Pachamama was of secondary importance in the Inkan scheme of religious values.

Magnificent temples dedicated to the Sun God Inti were constructed next to the temple of Pachakámak, and both became significant to the

Empire. The Inkakuna lined the temple walls with decorated gold and silver sheets and the rooms were filled with ornaments of the same precious metals. The people continued to worship both the Sun and Pachakámak.

Qosqo became the capital city of the empire now ruled by a masculine deity, and the Kkorikancha in Qosqo was a model for all the temples in the Inkan sovereign territory. It was the most important and splendid religious structure built in Peru, with the finest stonework perfectly set into place without mortar. Some historians say that thin sheets of silver and clamps of gold were placed between the stones. The structure also had temples within it dedicated to the god Wirakkocha, the moon, rainbow, stars, and the weather gods.

The Andean people living in the countryside continued to dedicate themselves to agriculture. However, the Inkakuna reorganized and modernized Andean farming methods and the campesinos became more productive. The Andeans also continued observing their ancient ceremonies and offerings to Pachamama, Mother Earth. Such was the attraction and persistent strength of their traditions and love for nature, that the Inkakuna incorporated these earlier beliefs into the new state religion.

The Inka Empire extended for thousands of miles outside of Qosqo. To the north it reached Ecuador and the frontiers of Colombia. In the south it stretched to Chile and north of Argentina. It met the Pacific Ocean in the west and eastward entered the gateway of the Amazon Jungle at such sites as Willkapampa, known as the last stronghold of the Inka Empire.

For governing purposes it was divided into four regions collectively known as Tawantinsuyo. The Inkan armies conquered many nations whose rich cultures left Peru with ancient cities and temples as well as spectacular figures, and gigantic, mysterious etchings.

The Land of Wiru

From the eighth through the fifteenth centuries, all of Spain's energy was directed toward the persecution and subsequent elimination of non-Christians (Muslims, Arabs, and Jews) living in Spanish territory. By 1492 Spain's Catholic kings had driven out the Moors, mostly Muslims who had occupied Spain since 711. The year 1492 also marked the end of tolerance for the Jews who continued to observe their own laws rather than those of the Catholic Church. With all non-Christian groups eliminated from her land or persecuted within it, Spain turned to missionary work: the conquest and religious conversion of non-Christians in the New World's vast market.

Francisco Pizarro, an illiterate man of illegitimate birth, set off from Spain in search of gold and glory in the newly discovered lands of America. Over the next ten years, he invaded and conquered the Inka Empire of Peru, in the name of Christianity.

There are many renditions of the origin of the name Peru. The following is from an elderly Qosqoruna, a citizen of Qosqo, whose memory of oral stories traces back several generations.

When the Spanish got to what would later be known as Central America, a soldier asked the locals what land lay to the south. He was told "The land of Wiru," and this referred to a landscape covered with stalks of green corn. The Spanish could not pronounce Wiru, called it Viru, and it became Piru which we now know as Peru.

Setting off from the area that is now Panama, the Spanish encountered some Andean men traveling north by boat from Peru with a cargo of exquisite gold and silver beaded ornaments. The Andean men planned to trade these for the *phututu* (Spandolus shell), which had great ritual value in Inkan ceremonies and was also used in fine jewelry. It did not take the Spanish sailors long to become aware of the Inkakuna and their golden treasures, magnificent temples, and sophisticated road systems.

Pizarro entered Inkan territory in 1532 to get the gold. To disguise his greed as legitimate, and in keeping with the Spanish Catholic tradition of demonology, he set out to prove that the god to whom all the treasures were dedicated was not really a god but rather the Devil. He carefully planned the capture and death of the Inka ruler Atawallpa in the northern city of Cajamarca.

Atawallpa was the ruler in the north of Peru who succeeded his father Wayna Kkápakk, the eleventh Inka ruler, when he died from smallpox. The disease, unwittingly brought by the Spanish, quickly spread throughout the empire and killed thousands.

Atawallpa's younger brother Waskar ruled in the Qosqo region of the south. The civil war between the two brothers resulted in the death of Waskar and the weakening of the Inka Empire. Atawallpa was on his way south to Qosqo to be crowned when Pizarro arrived at Cajamarca.

In November 1532, Pizarro and his soldiers rode into Cajamarca. Eighty thousand men from Atawallpa's armies filled the surrounding valley. Pizarro and the Spanish priests lectured Atawallpa about Christianity, the Holy Trinity, and the crucifixion and resurrection of Jesus. They told him about King Charles of Spain and that the pope had "given" to the Spanish the Indies—all of the New World lands.

Atawallpa asked the source of their information. They showed him a Bible, which the Inka king perceived as a "rather minor god with thin square leaves." He placed it next to his ear and said that he could hear nothing and threw it on the ground. For this and other perceived disrespect for Catholicism, the Spanish ruthlessly condemned the Inkan religion. Atawallpa rejected the Spanish demand that he become a Christian. The Inkakuna, of course, had no concept of Christianity, and in all probability never understood what the Spanish in their foreign tongue were talking about.

The Spaniards began to brutally attack the Inkakuna although Atawallpa had told his soldiers not to fight. Legend has it that Atawallpa believed the Spanish were fulfilling the prophecy of the return of the Creator God Wirakkocha, and that the bearded, white-skinned men had returned as gods and were the sons of the Sun, as were the Inkakuna.

The prophecy of the white god returning stems from the Chimu and Mochica cultures. It was based on the arrival of a visitor who later was converted into a deity called Naylamp. He was said to have come from the ocean, which may explain why the Inkakuna reacted as they did to the Spanish arriving from the sea. Naylamp is the little man seen on the Tumi, an artifact commonly sold today in Peru as an ornament or jewelry.

Pizarro took Atawallpa into captivity and a few dozen armed conquistadors were able to slaughter thousands of unarmed Inka warriors in what was to become the biggest massacre in the history of Peru. The Spanish rode on horseback wearing heavy plated armor and brandishing steel swords and, with swift moves, they cut off the heads and hands of the Inka warriors.

The Peruvians had never seen horses or firearms and were terrified, convinced that supernatural forces had fallen upon them. Their sling shots, clubs, spears, and arrows were useless against the onslaught.

Pizarro said Atawallpa could buy his freedom with a room full of gold and two others filled with silver. To expedite the payment, Pizarro sent his half brother, Hernando, with soldiers to collect the treasure and conquer the land.

The soldiers marched on Pachakámak, and, to the horror of the Peruvian holy men, they stormed the pyramid temple and commanded the attending priests to open the sacred room at the pinnacle. There they found a simple wooden pole at the top of which was a carved mask with two faces. This was the altar of Pachakámak.

The simple room of the sacred Pachakámak, with its modest offerings of silver and gold placed on the floor, was ridiculed by the Spaniards. They called it a "filthy chamber" with idols that were "vile, despicable, and worthless." They erected a cross and told the people they had been deceived, that only the Devil lived there.

After the desecration of the temple of Pachaká-mak, the oracle fell silent and public worship came to an end. For the Christians this was confirmation that the oracle had never spoken and that demons had been at work. Just as the Inkan Sun worshippers had incorporated ancient rural beliefs in the Earth Mother, the Creator God Pachakámak became fused with beliefs about the Christian God.

Pachakámak, however, continued to secretly speak to the Andean people through other oracles. Andeans had always spoken to their gods through intermediaries; Atawallpa pressed the Bible next to his ear expecting to hear it speak.

Gold Museum, with permission.

*A wooden carved pole of the two-faced deity
Pachakámak, a god ridiculed by the Spanish.*

Gold, the Sweat of the Sun;
Silver, the Tears of the Moon

As they traveled toward Qosqo, Pizarro's men fought battles with some of Atawallpa's armies. The Inkakuna were no match for the soldiers, whose horses gave them speed and maneuverability on the stone roadways built for Inka runners. Pizarro's men soon arrived in Qosqo for the treasure that supposedly was to earn Atawallpa's release.

Many of the local people in the south welcomed the Spaniards enthusiastically. At that time they supported the brother Waskar rather than Atawallpa, who had conducted a vicious and bloody campaign that

*This Ancient Inka roadway made it easy for the Spanish to ride into
Qosqo on horseback to search for gold.*

resulted in Waskar's death. When the dead brother's followers heard that
Atawallpa had been captured by the Spanish, they were delighted.

Kkorikancha (enclosure of gold), in which the Temple of the Sun
was situated, was among the most sacred places to the Inka. The building
was covered with hundreds of thick sheets of gold to catch the sun's rays
and was dedicated to the mythical ancestors of the Inkakuna. The Spanish
soldiers hacked away the gold as the helpless people of Qosqo watched
while solid gold seats, masks, ornaments, statues, and staves of embalmed
bodies were removed. Within a few months, more than twenty-four tons
of treasure were removed and thrown into the melting fires.

Atawallpa was ultimately killed and Pizarro had Mánkko Inka, one
of Wayna Kkapak's surviving sons, appointed as a puppet Inka and ruler
of Tawantinsuyu.

Hernando Pizarro took the best of the treasures to Toledo, Spain,
to show King Charles V, the king of Spain and emperor of the Holy
Roman Empire. The king immediately ordered the gold to be melted
down for coins.

On Nov. 15, 1533, Pizarro took over the city of Qosqo.

Intic Raymin: The Last Inka Ceremony

In June 1535, the Inkakuna gathered for the major festival of the year, Intic Raymin, to honor the Sun and give thanks for the harvest. They came from all four regions of Tawantisuyo to celebrate this festival. Intic Raymin was the name of the month in which the New Year of the Inkakuna began. It fell on the winter solstice, the shortest day of the year when the sun is situated as far north as it will travel before beginning its journey back to the south.

The Inkakuna prepared themselves by fasting for three days prior to the festival. They brought offerings of gold and silver, which were placed in a special garden at the Kkorikancha temple. The festival was held on the hill of Manturk'alla, which looked toward the rising and setting of the sun.

The Intic Raymin ceremony was performed by Inkakuna of royal blood dressed in their finest tunics, and wearing kkhápakkuna and gold discs on their heads. All sacred figures from the *wakakuna* (holy shrines) were brought out and placed beneath brilliantly colored, feathered canopies.

Akllakuna (the chosen women) prepared the special ceremonial food and drink. As beautiful young girls, they were selected from each community by special officers and brought to Qosqo where they were shut away from society and placed under the care of the *mamakuna*. They were groomed and trained to serve the cult in the temples or become the hostesses or wives to Inka lords or noble warriors.

At sunrise, hundreds of Inka lords under feathered parasols began to move in a procession, chanting hymns to the Sun. As the sun rose, the chanting grew louder and louder and continued until noon when the sun was at its highest. With the setting of the sun the chanting became fainter until it eventually ceased.

The Inkakuna offered the finest coca leaves and gold nuggets to the Sun. The gold nuggets represented his tears. The Inkakuna made a sacrifice of a black and white llama and live llamas were distributed as gifts to the people.

The mamakuna served the Inka lords golden goblets filled with *akkha* (*chicha*, as it is known in Spanish)—a type of beer made from maize. The maize was specially cultivated for this ceremony. As part of a purification ritual they offered the Inka *sankhu*, a dish made of ground toasted corn and mixed with llama blood for this special occasion.

At sunset, the masses joined hands and bowed down in homage to the Sun. The ceremony was repeated over the next eight days and the last sunset signified the close of the harvest season. The Inkakuna brought their gold digging sticks and Mánkko Inka broke the earth with his stick to mark the beginning of the plowing season. The people went back to their land to begin their work.

The Intic Raymin festival of 1535 was the last official ceremony that the Inkakuna were allowed to celebrate. The Spanish now controlled Qosqo and all Inkan ceremonies were prohibited.

Today, the Intic Raymin is one of the most well-known indigenous ceremonies in Peru. Each year in Qosqo it is reenacted on June 24 to coincide with the Catholic holiday of Corpus Christi and Festival of San Juan. Corpus Christi signifies the transfiguration or miracle of converting the bread into the body of Christ. In Qosqo it came to replace the parade of the old Inkan mummies in the plaza, which was done before the festival of the sun, Inti Raymin. San Juan (St. John) was the patron saint of sheep. The *alpaka* was considered the sheep of the land and a gift from God.

Visitors from all over the world attend the festival at the Saksaywaman ruins outside of Qosqo. At that place, Mánkko Inka had made a great effort to drive away the Spanish with an army of 100,000 warriors. There was a violent battle at Saksaywaman, and the Spanish celebrated a narrow win. Mánkko retreated to the fortress of Ollantaytampu, and soon after fled to Willkapampa in the jungle, known today as Vilcabamba, where he lived in exile until his death. With the gold removed, Pizarro had no more interest in Qosqo. Being a sea-faring man, he moved back to the Pacific coast, where he founded the city of Lima in 1535.

Within a few years, Qosqo was no longer an Inkan city. Sacred buildings were torn down and replaced by Christian churches. In 1572 the Spanish Viceroy Toledo captured Mánkko's son, Tupak Amaru I. He was brought to the main square in Qosqo, where thousands of people came to witness his death.

Under great duress he announced that he was now a baptized Christian and was to die according to the law of that belief system's god. He proclaimed that the Inkakuna should no longer worship the Sun, their wakakuna, rocks, rivers, and mountains because belief in them was worthless.

Toledo, a brutal man, forced resettlement of the native people into Spanish-style towns. This system was called *reducciones*. The Andean people had to convert to Christianity, provide the Spanish with labor, and pay tributes to the tax collectors. This was an alien system to the Andean people, who had always worked in an arrangement called ayni, which was a reciprocal form of labor. Prior to the arrival of the Spanish, the Andean people had shared their work and all its benefits.

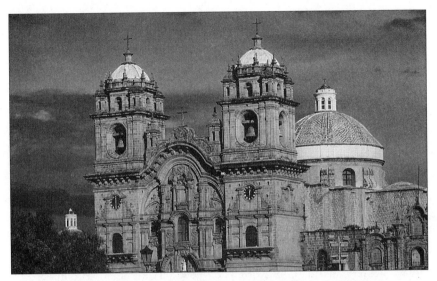

Churches replaced Inkan temples after the Spanish invaded Qosqo.

Toledo declared that every person was to convert to Christianity and that no Inka believer was to remain, dead or alive. Spanish officials took great advantage of the proclamation that all idols were to be seized, and confiscated personal items to enrich themselves. Most of the Andeans were stripped of their ancestral properties when they were resettled in the Spanish villages.

Over the years, the Spanish continued to burn non-Christian objects of worship, and people found in possession of pagan objects were whipped. The Christians preached that their God had condemned all the Inkakuna and their Andean ancestors to everlasting hell as a means to expedite the religious conversion. With all the gold removed, the Spanish assumed that the Andean rituals would end.

But in the Andes, the people worshipped nature rather than gold. Their focus was the Sun, moon, stars and Mother Earth, the Pachamama, who had survived the defeat of the Inkakuna and would live beyond the conquest of the Christians.

The Andean people and their gods proved to be extraordinarily resistant to the Christian preaching. They avoided the Christian God and believed that the painted sticks and saints that the Christians prayed with belonged to the Spanish. They remained convinced their own gods took care of them and brought health and abundance to the people. It was not always possible to avoid the Christians, however, and the Andeans would attend Christian festivities and mass as a pretense; at the same time, they would dance and send offerings to their own deities.

Spanish chroniclers documented information about the Inkakuna from the mid-sixteenth century. Most of the writers were Christian or had converted to Christianity and they all wrote their journals from a Christian perspective. The documents were not intended to preserve the Inkan culture, or to show the remarkable achievements tied to traditional and spiritual Andean practices. They were written from the limited perpective that sought to demonstrate how the Christians perceived the Inkakuna. The Christian authors were convinced that non-believers were influenced by the Devil.

By the 1700s the Spanish colonial system was firmly established in Qosqo and towns throughout the Andes. Stripped of gold and silver, Qosqo was a quiet city that escaped official Spanish notice, and outside of town, the Andeans continued their traditional ceremonies of sowing and harvesting. The now-discredited Inkan religious practices merged with older Andean traditions that had never been connected to the important rituals of the Inkakuna in Qosqo. The Inkakuna had been more interested in celebrating their own mythical origins, worshipping their Sun, and organizing their social and political systems throughout the country.

By contrast, the Andean people living in the countryside were more concerned with rituals that would ensure the success of their crops and provide food for their people. Every rite connected to Pachamama and the ecology of the Andes, the relationship of one thing to another, and the true concept of sharing and cooperation among humans.

There were changes in Andean practices as Spanish missionaries penetrated even the most isolated Andean communities. The people considered themselves Catholics although they still revered the ancient beliefs and superstitions. Despite the influence of the Catholic Church, outside the city of Qosqo, the traditions of the Andeans remained complete and connected to the past.

Today's Quechua

Many traditions and spiritual practices of the ancient Andeans still are celebrated today. Andean healers, specialists, or priests are called by various terms depending on their special abilities: *pampa misayoq, alto misayoq, pakkokuna,* and *curanderos.* They live in Andean villages and conduct rituals and ceremonies while maintaining a strict observance of the ancient ways. They work closely with the deities common to the entire area.

Andean people are now referred to as Quechua* and the ancient language they speak is Kkechuwa. The Quechua people continue to worship

Homes around Qosqo tell of the blend of two faiths. Catholic and traditional Andean religious beliefs are represented in this rooftop arrangement of statues, crosses, and animal figures.

their apukuna, rivers, lakes, trees, plants, and all of Mother Earth. Despite the most terrible pressure from the Church, the Andean Quechua have never wavered in their own beliefs and love for Pachamama.

Modern peasants have adapted Catholic ceremonies of the ruling culture to serve the needs of the Quechua people, and they have a distinct Andean flavor. The community has accepted the existence of a Christian God and they participate in sacraments, matrimony and baptisms. Chapels and parish churches have been constructed on sacred Andean sites in a process of religious synchretism (hybrid joining of beliefs) that is historically typical to this region and others in Latin America, as they are throughout the world.

---

* Modern Kkechuwa words are written in many different forms, and until the Spanish arrived in Peru, Kkechuwa was an oral language. In the sixteenth century, the chroniclers began to write the words using Spanish phonetics, which often distorted their true meanings. In this century, authorities on the Kkechuwa language aspired to establish a written form that would capture this beautiful language accurately. A style is yet to be established that will be uniform and acceptable to all scholars.

For this book, we have selected the spelling method of the late Padre Jorge Lira, the most recognized expert on the Kkechuwa language to date (see Chapter 1). In keeping with his style, *kuna* at the end of a word denotes the plural form. For example: *waka* (holy shrine), *wakakuna* (holy shrines). Inkakuna is the plural of *Inka* (child of the Sun).

In addition, all Kkechuwa and Spanish words are italicized in this book at their first reference only, per standard usage.

View of colonial Plaza de Armas,
main square of Qosqo City.

What's in the Quechua Name?

It is our wish to reveal the fundamental identity of a people who have been poorly understood and even more poorly treated since being conquered by the Inkakuna and then by the Spanish. The Quechua people have been called names that don't correspond to their true identities ever since.

The name "Indian" derives from an error born of geographical ignorance on the part of Columbus, who believed he had arrived in the Indies. Early Spanish chroniclers of the conquest and first years of the colony did not immediately call the natives Indians. They called them natives, barbarians, pagans, *gente gentilica* (Spanish for pagans), or *indigenas*. Gradually, however, the impulse to simplify moved the chroniclers to begin sharing the term *indios*, and forever after it stuck.

The indigenous people of the Andes are reclaiming their original right to their proper name and identity. What's in a name? The essence of each individual culture's chosen way of relating to cosmic forces and the power granted the human species to make its own peace with our essential helplessness before God. To say "Indian" says nothing. To say "Andean," "Quechua," or "Runa" says everything.

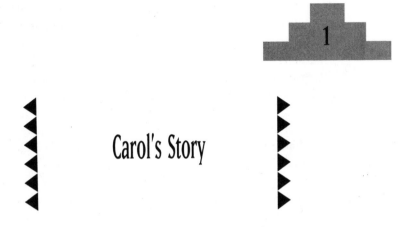

Carol's Story

I moved to Peru in 1995 when *Pachamama's Children: Mother Earth and Her Children of the Andes* first was published.

I had begun writing about the Quechua people and their ancient cosmology in the early 90s while still living in the United States and traveling back and forth to Peru. Since that time, many people have asked me to include more of my own story in this new edition, *Journey to Machu Picchu: Spiritual Wisdom of the Andes*. So much happened during my fifteen years of traveling and living there, that I would need to write a separate book to cover all my adventures. But before I do that, my sense is that readers should first become familiar with the Quechua and their ancient Andean cosmology to illuminate a deeper meaning for their personal journeys.

Included here are highlights of those fifteen years in Peru, which led to major changes in my life. Hopefully, this will enlighten others on similar paths, illustrating what it is about Peru that draws souls here and changes lives forever.

I was living with my husband and four children in a Spanish-style house with a lovely sea view, in the exclusive community of Hope Ranch in Santa Barbara.

One day in 1982, as I gazed at a brilliant orange California sunset over the Pacific, I contemplated on having a private visit with a woman who was a full-bodied trance channel. Our house overlooked the properties of rich and famous celebrities who lived in lavish homes along the bluffs, and I wondered what they would think about my paying one hundred eighty dollars to chat with a spirit. A channeling session was not a typical place to find the wife of a urologist in Santa Barbara.

That afternoon, I visited the well-regarded trance channel at her hillside home. Indira, the spirit, said to me, "I see you sitting at the top of large mountains, wearing white shoes, and leading a group of people."

I pictured myself in the white nurse's shoes I wore while working as an assistant in my husband's medical office. Since I hated those shoes, I thought how unlikely it was that I would ever buy white shoes again. I was a housewife who spent most of my time driving my four children to their daily activities. I certainly was not a mountain person and, moreover, the hills of Santa Barbara did not seem to qualify as "big mountains." I was not convinced.

In 1984, I undertook my first journey to Peru, and my love affair with the country, its people, and its spirituality began—a love affair that refused to wane over the next fifteen years. Nothing would stop me from making annual pilgrimages to the Andes. Later, as my children progressed through high school, I went twice a year. I created opportunities for myself to go back and forth by taking others on sacred and magical journeys to Peru.

The first time I read about journeying to Peru was in an advertisement in *New Age Journal*, and I immediately booked to go. I just told my husband, Dave, we were off to famous Machu Picchu and the mysterious Nazca lines in the desert of Peru. Casually, I mentioned that we might meet some native healers, an experience we had been open to in South Africa, but I did not mention the "other weird stuff" described in the article. I wanted nothing to interfere with my adventure. The people who would be in our group would be well versed in spirituality and holistic healing, and most likely antagonistic to Western doctors. I was certain that the antics of the shamans and participants would be quite a shock to Dave, a serious Stanford Medical School graduate.

Our fellow adventurers came mostly from the east coast of the United States and Europe. They were a little younger than Dave and I, and all hinted at knowledge of ingesting plant medicines. While Americans had been experimenting with marijuana, hallucinogens, and other substances in the 70s, Dave and I were living in South Africa. In those days, there was a penalty of five years in jail and threat of termination to professionals, doctors, and teachers if anyone so much as reported you smoking *dagga*, marijuana. This was enough to deter us from any thought of even sampling the forbidden substances. We did not smoke or drink, not even caffeinated beverages.

Our shamanic group headed to Trujillo in the north, where we worked with the late Don Eduardo Calderon, a respected curandero or healer. He conducted all-night ceremonies in the desert and introduced us to his healing medicine, the San Pedro cactus. I watched Eduardo boil the cactus all day long and throw in some prayers to give it greater potency. The San Pedro healing ceremony in the desert began at ten at night. Dave declined the medicine, but I decided that I was there to try everything and joined in the ceremony.

Eduardo sat at his *mesa*, his altar made up of power objects he used during the ceremony to control the energies. He would chant and sing and shake his rattle throughout the night, periodically dancing around the group, which sat in a circle. He would chant prayers, take a sip from his brew of sickly sweet, perfumed liquid and, with great force, expel it from his mouth and spray it all over each person. The potent smell made me nauseated, yet I drank ceremoniously from a glass filled with Eduardo's cooked San Pedro liquid and proceeded to throw it all up.

Alberto, the leader of the group, shook his head at me and said, "A pity!" I did not understand anything that was going on, but it did not seem to matter. Alberto would translate Eduardo's commentaries to the group and point to luminous figures and shapes in the desert. Happily, I would see them too. I remember saying to Dave, "Look at the man on a horse with a blue dagger in his hand." I was disappointed when he answered, unimpressed, "You're hallucinating!"

I was having a great time, joyously gazing at the southern sky, filled with the same brilliant stars I knew from our African skies, until they and the luminescent figures disappeared with the early rays of dawn.

The city of Qosqo was also one of our stops. On the morning of my first visit to Qosqo, I woke up nauseated and with a bad headache, suffering the effects of the 11,000-foot altitude. I told Dave to go without me on the shamanic group tour to the Saksaywaman ruins outside of Qosqo. But after lying in bed for fifteen minutes, I thought how ridiculous it was having come all this way and with just one day scheduled for the city to waste the time lying in bed. I got up, retrieved my passport and money from the desk, and asked the way to the market.

Before we had emigrated from South Africa to the United States in 1975, Dave and I would spend our family vacations either camping on the white tropical beaches of Mozambique or heading north to the game parks. There, we would gaze in excitement as lions and elephants roamed freely around our tents in the wilds of Zimbabwe, Botswana, and Zululand.

Wherever I went in Africa, my favorite pastime was to wander through local markets, buying handcrafted baskets and beaded necklaces. Living in California, I had missed the color and chaos of Africa, and Peru was a whole new exotic world that beckoned to me. Since I had missed the tour to the ruins that day, I decided to walk to the famous Cusco Market and shop for alpaca wool that a friend had asked me to buy.

I was directed away from the city center, deeper into the masses of crowded stalls piled with goods among sellers who filled the alleyways. I was thrilled by the multitude of tropical fruits and giant vegetables displayed. There were flowers, clothes, pots, pans, and colorfully dressed people everywhere. Joyful music blared and a sense of vibrancy filled the air. I forgot about my headache and proceeded to the wool sellers near the railway station.

I became aware that I had stepped into a seedy area, where glassy-eyed locals dawdled around bags of coca leaves. Vendors hawked plates of steaming hot food and runny-nosed children played in the muddy, garbage-strewn streets. But scenes such as this had never daunted me in Africa. Tourism in Qosqo was not significant in those days, and modern, smartly dressed policemen were nowhere to be found in the crowded and chaotic areas. The city still was a far cry from the neatly organized, renovated Plaza de Armas that visitors see today.

Still suffering the disorienting effects of altitude, I was in somewhat of an altered state of consciousness, feeling disconnected from my body. Suddenly, as I passed through a narrow gap between two stalls, five small women dressed in colorful traditional clothing pushed at me, trapping me against a stall. I am only five feet two inches tall, but I looked down into their tiny faces with a start, wondering at the deep, ugly scars slashed across their cheeks.

Puzzled, I thought, Why are they pushing their babies into my face, and why are they shrieking in those high-pitched voices? Instinctively, I tightened my grip on my handbag, which was stuffed with the wool I had purchased. Suddenly, they moved off and in a flash were gone. I was confused. I looked down at my woven bag and saw it was still closed, clasped against my abdomen between my arms. Somewhat dazed, I walked into the artisan section of the market to admire the colorful hand-woven goods. A child pointed to my purse and said, "Mira, señora," while others laughed and snickered. I looked down and, with a sinking feeling, realized that my purse had been slit open from underneath. I had felt nothing as someone, probably a child using the shrieking women as distraction, slit my bag and removed the wallet filled with my money and passport. I felt helpless and very foolish.

I was offered no sympathy by our group leader who just shrugged his shoulders, and I had to spend the rest of the day making a report in a run-down police station, a process that was excruciatingly slow and my first lesson in Peruvian bureaucracy. When I described the scars on the women's faces to an officer, he said that particular group of women were known for their involvement in the underworld. Whenever they were caught stealing, their cheeks were slashed to brand them as thieves.

I was frustrated by my poor Spanish, and vowed that when I returned to Peru—and there was no doubt in my mind that I would—I would speak fluently. My husband, fortunately, had enough money to pay my way for the rest of the trip, and he accompanied me to Lima to get another passport, a process that shortened our trip by two more days.

The market experience proved to be invaluable for me in the years to come. For some reason it did not engender fear in me, a life-limiting emotion, but it did teach me the value of wariness. I learned to be aware of my surroundings and always wore my money belt under my clothes around my waist. I discovered how altitude could affect and disorient people, and it motivated me to learn about being mindful at all times. I would consciously place a protective energy field around myself when walking into busy areas, and would arm myself by sending a warning glare toward anyone getting too close to me. Then I would watch them slink away.

A year later I returned to Peru. In the early 1980s, flights from California to Peru arrived around 2:00 A.M. Military presence was everywhere, and roadblocks manned by young, trigger-happy youths were positioned around the airport. They would stop the taxi and ask for my passport, then beckon the driver to move on. But I was unafraid.

Terrorist activities gave the foreign press much to write about, and Americans were advised strongly against travel to Peru. To me, the threat seemed as remote as faraway unrest in Soweto, South Africa, or East Los Angeles, and besides, there were no problems in the main tourist areas. Each time I returned to the United States, customs officers would regard me with suspicion, searching my bags for drugs. They could not comprehend why a middle-aged woman traveled alone, and often, to Peru.

On this second trip, before joining up with another shamanic group, I tested myself by spending three days wandering alone in the heart of crowded Lima. The streets were filled with vendors and pedestrians, but I had no fear and knew I would not tempt thieves. Again, I was thrilled with the medley of sights and sounds, all a refreshing contrast from orderly and upscale Santa Barbara.

Once again, I traveled to Trujillo to visit Don Eduardo. He was pleased with my eagerness to learn and invited me to be his assistant and hold the feminine energies at his mesa. That afternoon, our group went into a guinea pig healing ceremony, but I declined to participate. I had been present the year before, and still was haunted by the sounds of the little critters screaming as they were being skinned alive.

Since ancient times, healers have used the *kkowi*, guinea pigs, as a diagnostic tool. They pass it over the body of the patient, then immediately skin it alive to activate the technique. The kkowi is slit open down its middle for examination of the body's organs and bones and used like an x-ray machine. During this brief ceremony, the animal absorbs the illness of the patient into its organs, and by looking at the marks on the animal the healer can diagnose exactly the illness or injury of the sufferer.

I did not need to experience this ritual a second time, and went wandering outside of Eduardo's fish restaurant on the beach. His older son showed me an interesting stone with a serpent etched into it, declaring that it was very old. I believed him and bought it, but soon realized, after paying him a hundred dollars and taking it back to my hotel, that I had been duped. I became angry with him, and with myself. Before the ceremony that evening, I marched up to him and handed him the stone, sternly demanding my money back. Without saying a word, he took the stone and handed my hundred dollar note back to me.

The desert healing ceremony again began after ten that night when the energies were at their highest, and we were told it would continue until dawn. This time I did not throw up after drinking the boiled San Pedro cactus, and each ceremony moved me to a new place. I realized that during my first visit, keen as I was, I was more of a spectator than participant. When I returned, I had gained experience, and learned how to participate by immersing myself in the energies created by the shaman, and directing them to assist in healing myself on a physical and emotional level.

At night, local Peruvians, some with serious illnesses, would join our group rituals to receive healing from Eduardo. As honored assistant at the "main table," I was expected to follow his lead and pour liquid tobacco juice, which he passed to me in a flat shell, down my nose and into my throat, each time Eduardo doing the same.

The cold liquid was miserably unpleasant, burning the tender tissues of my nasal passages as it dribbled down to my throat. I forced myself not to block the nasal passages or gag, as that made it painfully worse. Each time a sick person came up to be healed Eduardo began again, ceremoniously ingesting the tobacco juice. Again and again, he passed the flat shell to me, and also to an American psychotherapist who apparently was holding the masculine energy for the rite. I knew I was sitting in a place of honor, and clearly understood that if I refused the ceremonial liquid I would be interfering with the healing process. I remember looking up at Haley's Comet, passing through the desert skies at that time, begging it to help me get the stuff down my nose.

The ceremony continued for hours, and I would surreptitiously spill some of the liquid onto the dark desert floor before formally pouring the rest down my nose. I asked the spirits to forgive me, believing they would understand my situation. I began to sway from the sickly effect of the medicine in my body, praying that no more people would ask for healing, but they kept on coming. Eduardo was a sought-after healer, and this was important work.

I saw Eduardo's son looking at me, surprised to see me placed by his father in an honored position. He must have been watching me closely, as he seemed to spring into action at the moment I plainly could not take anymore. I knew that if I poured any more tobacco juice down my nose, I would simply fall down in the sand and die in front of all these people. Eduardo's son took the shell with tobacco juice—just passed to me by his father—out of my hand and proceeded to pour it down his own nose on my behalf. I stayed in my position while he repeated the process until all the patients had been treated. It seemed acceptable to Don Eduardo, and I was grateful to the son for rescuing me. His silent endeavor to apologize and make up for what he had done earlier that day was deeply appreciated.

Alberto then invited our group to join him on what was his first visit to the jungle site near Iquitos that belonged to the master of *ayawaska* ceremonies, Agustin Rivas. Alberto had given money to an Indian woman to buy food for the group, and she spent it all on salt and soap, staples not found in the jungle, and some pasta. Agustin effusively welcomed us to his power place, but he was not prepared for this assemblage of foreign guests. There was no food and just a couple of empty grass shelters awaited us in the heart of the Amazon. Agustin proudly took his rifle and shot a monkey for our dinner, and the creature was served with sticky pasta smothered in salt. I was not into eating monkey and so went hungry. We were told that fasting was very appropriate prior to the forthcoming ceremony.

Agustin set about chopping down small trees to construct some makeshift benches for the evening's ritual. There was an air of expectation and excitement as we gathered around the open hut late that steamy night in the deep Amazon jungle, anticipating our part in the ayawaska—vision vine, or vine of death—ceremony soon to begin.

I was given a small amount of the specially prepared liquid, and within minutes my body rebelled. I could not stop everything inside myself from coming out, and I continued to vomit uncontrollably for what seemed like forever, even though there was nothing left within.

I felt miserable, weak, cold, and alone. Alberto would come by and tell me to sit up straight, open my energy centers, and get beyond it. Periodically, Agustin would stand behind me and blow tobacco smoke from his pipe into my body through my crown chakra, which completed the healing. I could feel the smoke whooshing down my spine, but the strong smell of tobacco only made me feel worse and I wished he would leave me alone.

The majority of the group clearly were having a much better time than I. Some of the men were going up to Agustin for refills of the ayawaska, and others were gliding up and down like Inkan lords with big grins on their faces. Finally, I settled down and, although exhausted, I relaxed and enjoyed a peaceful kaleidoscope of colors and snake-type visions before being allowed to return to my mat on the floor of the hut to sleep.

Leaving the jungle the next day, I was so weak from lack of food, liquid, and sleep that I could hardly walk. My European friends were carrying Swiss energy tablets, which revived me somewhat. I felt disappointed that I had not achieved much in that ceremony, but a supportive friend assured me that I had had a wondrous cleansing.

Months later it became clear that I had left that jungle ceremony with more than a cleansing, for the ayawaska had shifted me completely. I had walked out of that jungle with the gift of a new beginning to life and a sense of gaining back my personal power. From then on, I was able to make decisions more clearly and precisely, and was left with a sense of knowing what it was I had to do. That feeling has never left me.

In 1986, I started bringing groups from the United States and South Africa to visit the Amazon and sacred sites in the Andes, and participate in rituals of authentic jungle shamans and Andean pakkokuna. In spite of American travel advisories not to come to Peru in the 1980s, I never felt unsafe, and encouraged my visitors to come. Our Magical Journey groups often had the privilege of being the only tourists in the city of Machu Picchu.

Although my initial ayawaska experience had been overly dramatic, I came to accept its potentially powerful benefits when I witnessed the wonderful healings taking place within groups I was bringing to the jungle. Today I work with an Amazon healer who uses the ayawaska vine as well as a variety of other medicinal plants for healing purposes. I remind everyone to use the ceremony as an opportunity to ask the spirits, the divinity, whomever, for something they think they need: to be healed; to learn something about their lives; their meaning and purpose. Our groups gather inside a hut where the only light comes from moonbeams filtering through the wooden walls. The night air fills with the music of birds, insects, and small jungle creatures while the mighty Madre de Dios river booms softly outside. Healing energies fill the room and the atmosphere is peaceful and relaxed. I no longer drink the brew. I prefer to be supportive to those being healed, and if necessary, translate the shaman's questions to his patients. Some guests choose to drink the carefully prepared ayawaska medicine while others silently sit and listen to the shaman singing his beautiful medicine songs while working on individual patients throughout the night. At dawn, he concludes the ceremony by offering a grateful prayer of thanks to Pachamama and the spirits of the plant medicines.

In 1988, I hiked the Inka trail to Machu Picchu for the second time, bringing a group from the United States and South Africa. After four splendid days of hiking and camping, we arrived at the Inti Punku, gateway to the sun, the original entrance to Machu Picchu, ancient city of light. We paused to rest, and as I sat on a ledge overlooking the city below, I glanced down at my swinging leg, suddenly realizing that I was wearing white sneakers.

"White shoes," I said to myself. "High mountains," I mumbled, as I looked up at the spectacular snow-covered peaks surrounding me. I glanced over my shoulder and looked back at the group of seventeen people I had just led through the mountains to Machu Picchu, and smiled. Years back, in my first trance channeling session in Santa Barbara, I had been given this information, long before I ever thought of Peru.

Having beheld the healing ceremonies of Northern Peru and the Amazon, my focus turned to the spiritual wisdom of the Andes, in the areas where I felt most drawn: Machu Picchu, the Sacred Valley, and the surrounding Andean mountains.

In 1992, Romulo came to guide one of my groups on the Inka Trail, and soon after introduced me to his mother, Señora Fortunata Lizárraga. She welcomed me to her family farm at the base of Machu Picchu peak, and over the next few years taught me the simple truths of their ancient cosmology. She and many of her Kkechuwa-speaking friends, all elders of the Machu Picchu district, shared their stories of the true discoverers of Machu Picchu, their deep respect for the apukuna, and their profound connection to Pachamama, Mother Earth.

Accompanied by Rómulo, who translated the Kkechuwa language into Spanish for me, I spent weeks visiting isolated communities around Salkkantay mountain and the valleys behind Patakancha. We would arrive in these remote villages by horseback, always welcomed by children offering us a bowl of steaming potatoes.

I was drawn to the simplistic lifestyle of working closely connected to Pachamama. Many of these isolated Andean communities, untouched by modern civilization, continue to observe the ancient spirituality as practiced thousands of years ago. Wherever I traveled, the system of ayni, their ethic of reciprocity of work and energy, was in evidence.

I met dedicated Kkechuwa-speaking pakkos, healers who had never worked with foreigners before, and watched them prepare their *haywarikuykuna*, the offerings to Pachamama and the apukuna. I learned the great ceremonial importance of coca leaves, the only plant medicine used in Andean rituals. Blowing one's essence into a *k'intu* of coca, three coca leaves, connected one to the spiritual world of the Andes, and I learned to chew the coca leaves with *llipta*, lime ash, used to activate the leaves. (Read Chapter 5 for more on coca leaves.)

True healers of the Andes—whether called *pakkokuna* for the men, *laykkakuna* for females, a *pampamisayok* or *altomisayok*—are those who live and work their entire lives in *ayllukuna*, communities where they tend to the physical and spiritual needs of the campesinos. All are born with a gift to serve and act as intermediaries between members of the ayllukuna and their Gods, the spiritual forces of nature. They keep the lives of the campesinos in balance and harmony with Mother Earth and the mountain spirits. Sending special offerings to Pachamama, reading coca leaves, and healing with medicinal plants grown in the Andes is the main focus of their work. Healers who work exclusively with the local campesinos do not charge for their services, but exchange healings for gifts of food from Pachamama.

▼▼▼

During my early visits to Peru, the shifts taking place within my being were unexplainable and very confusing. By comparison, life in Santa Barbara seemed empty and meaningless, and I became dissatisfied with my marriage. I did the best I could as wife and mother as my children completed their high school years, but it seemed that whenever I had a spare moment I would read, write, or talk about my journeys, a process that constantly fed me with Her energy.

Each time I visited the Andes, I entered into a magical realm. I found myself communing with nature and connecting to all Her forces. I could move clouds and bring out the sun if it was really important to do so. If I needed to summon someone, I would focus on that person, and at what always seemed the appropriate time, they would appear. I felt like a child playing joyfully in a faraway magical land, where everything I needed would appear at the right time.

With each meditation at the sacred sites, I could feel pure Andean energies flow through my being to nourish me. So much incoming energy at times left me feeling sick, emotionally worn, or deeply introspective, but the process forced me to get in touch with my physical self. I became more aware of my connection to Mother Earth: how my body was made from the same material as She and how I sustained myself off what She produces. I would feel this energy penetrate deeply, creating changes in my consciousness. When I returned home after these meditations I would feel disoriented, with at least four weeks passing before I felt realigned with the world. Once my body began to shift, I knew the conversions were irrevocable, and I could no longer back away from the process.

By the time my youngest daughter, Romi, entered into her last semester of high school in 1995, I was feeling freer of my role as mother to my now adult children. I knew that I had to commit myself more deeply to the path on which my journeys to Peru had placed me. Unfortunately my need to be free to follow the call of my soul, with integrity, led to a divorce. I was now free and challenged to move to Peru and allow whatever it was to evolve. I made the decision to let go of my comfortable life in Santa Barbara, and trust that everything else would fall into place. It did.

For a few months I felt as if I was flying in a void with nowhere to land. I had severed all my security ties and did not allow myself to think of what it would be like, after twenty-eight years of marriage, to have a family structure no longer. All four of my children had been on journeys to Peru and were familiar with the country and language. Although already in college, the two younger ones were upset with my leaving, and the older two expressed their concern for my well-being. But the force pulling me was getting stronger so I moved toward it.

Always, I had paid respect to nature, the Quechua people, and their Andean cosmology. I had no doubt that I would be protected and welcomed by the spirits of the land I had just bought in the Sacred Valley a year before.

At that time, I saw a 500-year-old Lucma tree standing amidst overgrown brush on a stone-filled, overworked piece of land. I could picture some long-ago Inka children cavorting around the young fruit tree at a time before the Spanish invaders decimated their empire, and I chose that site. The tree embodied an exceptional energy, and I determined the Lucma would become my personal teacher. I intended to build myself a small adobe brick house on this land I had bought in the Sacred Valley, create a beautiful garden of medicinal plants, and work on my spiritual evolution. The spirits of Willka T'ika, it seemed, had other plans for me.

Salkkantay was known as the "wild" mountain and, after writing about healers going on pilgrimages and undergoing initiation ceremonies in its glaciers, I desired to experience the energy firsthand. I was so in awe of the mountain and the scenery that each year I invited groups to accompany me. In 1995, I led a group on a wilderness expedition to Salkkantay, my fourth journey to the majestic peak.

The weather that June was spectacular. Traveling on horseback, we climbed over two treacherous passes at 16,000 feet. After meditating at the base of the glacier and making an offering of coca leaves to the apu, we walked a while down the valley and then set up camp. That night we huddled close together on the floor of a cold tent, trying to keep warm while the Quechua cooks prepared our hot dinner. Bone-chilled members of our group reminisced wistfully about exotic resorts and sunny tropical beaches they had visited around the world.

Longingly, they recollected more luxurious accommodations, with hot towels coming out of the walls of hotels they had visited in the South Pacific, Caribbean, and Indian Ocean islands. Since I had chosen just recently to move permanently to the Andes, with no specific job and a very short-term income, I sighed, "I guess I will never get to the Seychelle Islands." Mark Hennessy, a South African in the group, responded, "Oh, I'll take you to the Seychelles," to which I smiled and thought, Yeah, yeah.

Four months after the Salkkantay journey, I received an invitation from Mark to go to the Seychelles, along with an offer to revisit my home country, the new South Africa. My house in Peru was not going to be ready before the beginning of 1996, so I accepted. Mark suggested that he return to Peru with me to help me move into my new home.

I mention Mark because I appreciate now that the Andean gods sent him to me. They must have looked down at me and seen this determined, headstrong lady uprooting her life to move to the Sacred Valley. In their wisdom, they knew I needed help. They saw that Mark was available to assume the role of partner and companion, and he simply arrived to support me. His presence, along with our similarities in background, culture, and spiritual beliefs, helped me maintain a balance between my old life and this very different new world. He gave me the freedom and support I needed to put all my attention and energy into a new project about to unfold.

When I bought the land in Sacred Valley, I had envisioned our Magical Journey groups visiting and simply enjoying a day in the country. Once I moved there, I was filled with a greater vision, that of creating a spiritual retreat center for nature lovers and special interest groups. I knew groups would relish staying at a beautiful, secluded Sacred Valley retreat, where they could relax and absorb the special energy while feasting on organically grown salads and Andean vegetarian food, rarities in Peru.

The Sacred Valley project took on a life of its own. With the help of a few Quechua neighbors, I decided to take charge of the building operation, while Mark helped manage the finances. I loved the idea that everything that was needed for building was made on site. We had no American-style hardware stores to run to, and this enabled us to think and work creatively. I loved not being burdened by building inspectors and house plans. I especially loved the earthiness and texture of bricks made out of oozing mud from our land and mixing it with ichu grass from the hills above. I decided to build a large yoga and meditation room, along with a few more guest houses with top-quality bathrooms. I employed seven carpenters to live on site and cut and hand-carve local wood for doors, floors, and window frames, and make all the furniture.

I was happy out there, supervising the workers, and each day ended with a great sense of achievement for us all. The Quechua men were hardworking and pleasant. Women would arrive with plates of hot food to sell for one *sole*, thirty American cents, and I would donate money for their daily *chicha*, a homemade beer brewed from fermented corn. This kept them happy and never slowed the pace of their work. I wrote to my friend Linda Egan and told her how much fun I was having, but mentioned I was not sure who would come to enjoy all those buildings. She wrote back with a saying from an American movie: "If you build it, they will come." And she was right.

When the workers went home for lunch at noon each day, I would sit quietly under the 500-year-old Lucma tree, meditate or converse with nature, and visualize how I wanted the barren garden to unfold. I believed that nature was guiding me and, after all the stones were cleared and built into a wall, I knew I was to build a huge spiral, creating a special garden within it that would allow nature to work with the concentration of special energies. Using my pendulum, I consulted nature as to whether the paths within the spiral should be three, four, or five feet wide. I was told, "No." Puzzled, I asked about a six-foot width and got a resounding "Yes." That seemed rather large to me, but I accepted the guidance.

The pendulum directed me to what was to be the center of the land, and at this point I brought in Mark, who spent ten years navigating ships in the South African Navy. Since Mark had a degree in mathematics, I asked him to determine precisely the four cardinal directions and calculate where the paths should go. I was delighted to see that the huge spiral, with six-foot wide paths, fitted beautifully into the parcel of land we had, within twelve inches of the property on either side. I realized that the six-foot width would allow me four feet to grow medicinal herbs and leave a path one foot wide on each side of the stones. Visitors would be able to walk the entire spiral as a meditation or energy-balancing exercise. I thanked nature.

Quechua campesinos grow vegetables in rows and restrict their farming to crops they eat, so at first they were puzzled by what I was doing with this valuable piece of flat land. We devised ways to water the gardens, brought in cattle and sheep manure and started a large compost heap to which we added *lombrisas*, a type of earthworm. The workers brought cuttings and seeds of various medicinal plants native to the area. The seeds I had brought from the U.S. and South Africa sprouted quickly, and it became clear that the energy created in the spiral helped these plants grow faster and healthier than other cuttings we had planted closer to the house. I referred to the spiral as "the hospital," and my young gardeners became believers in no time.

The guest houses and gardens of Willka T'ika, which means "sacred flower" in the Quechua language, were completed in under two years. There are hundreds of varieties of medicinal plants, herbs, and flowers growing. My full-time gardeners are familiar with the medicinal properties of the plants, because they have used these herbs for healing at home. My Quechua assistant, Antonia, uses a variety of herbs from the gardens to treat visitors with bodily aches, pains, bruises, fractures, altitude-related sicknesses, and stomach problems, which are widespread in Peru. A local herbalist comes often to teach our groups about the medicinal uses of native herbs and prepare special remedies for their ailments. I have observed and aided Antonia and the healer in giving patients steaming hot herbal baths, followed by wrapping them warmly and putting them to bed. Always, there is a positive outcome.

In time, I plan to develop my ability to commune directly with nature and learn more about the unique energies of the spiral for use in healing. I was trained by the Flower Essence Society in California and have worked with various flower essences for the past sixteen years. At Willka T'ika, I hope to research spiral flower essences, which I will be creating over the next few years.

I invited Andean healers to come and send special offerings of thanks to Pachamama and the apukuna, the mountain spirits that guard Rumichaka, our area. They suggested I close the gates and become discerning about those I allow within, and this seemed wise advice. The healers cleared out residual negative energies and left Willka T'ika with an aura of peace and tranquility that is sensed by all our guests.

A walk through our neighborhood in the Sacred Valley is unlike anything in the United States. Foot paths lead past irregular, unpainted adobe houses, their outdoor patios filled with small children, dogs, and chickens. White, purple, and golden corn cobs are set out to dry in the sun, along with clotheslines filled with colorful wash. Paths wind their way through farmlands of sacred corn, *sara*, and scruffy-looking children play safely in the dirt while their parents work the fields. Campesinos, strangers to me, always take a moment to acknowledge my presence and greet me politely. Often, I am invited to sip chicha from a nearby jug, which I have respectfully learned to decline. I don't care for the taste, and recommend that visitors only drink chicha brewed with boiled water.

It is understandable how this valley became sacred to the Inkakuna. Inti, the Father Sun, shines all year round, with his giant rays illuminating the Sacred Valley. Clouds may suddenly burst from the heavens, shrouding the 20,000-foot peaks in stormy blackness. To command respect and remind farmers of their awesome power, Andean gods may roar with thunder and fill the skies with electrifying flashes of lightning. Living in the Andes, I am surrounded continuously by the power of nature and swept into Her rhythms.

Sacred waters still flow from mighty glaciers above to the farmlands below. Dazzling flowers bloom throughout the year, and Pachamama always provides an abundance of delicious organic vegetables ready to harvest and eat. Every medicinal herb needed to keep my body in balance with nature grows wild in the valley where I live, and birds and insects fill the gardens with their songs and life-giving energies; there are none of the irritations and noisy distractions of the big cities.

What was it that drew me to Peru all those years ago and kept me returning? What is here that continues to draw like a magnet thousands upon thousands of people from all over the planet to the Andes, the ancient cities, and the Sacred Valley? Snow-capped Andean peaks, mysterious ancient cities, cobblestone streets, gentle Quechua campesinos dressed in vibrant traditional clothing, artisan markets filled with hand-woven goods, cereals of the Gods, and haunting, lively Andean music are just some of the attractions of Peru.

But to those on a spiritual path, there is clearly something more. Without knowing anything about Peru, there are many who feel a tug at the soul level to come here. And they do.

I thank Peru for reconnecting me so deeply to the feminine energy of Pachamama. She has reminded me that, like Her, my body is sacred and must be cared for and respected. I still feel Her energy flow through me, stirring and healing my feminine spirit. She has helped me begin to understand my needs, to learn to trust and embrace them.

My journey to Machu Picchu fifteen years ago triggered a process in me to grow into who I really am. It has allowed me to feel part of the birthing of a new feminine consciousness on this planet, and has gifted me with awareness and profound inner healing.

2

Pachamama: Mother Earth

To the Quechua,
The Pachamama, the earth, is the Mother,
the Mother that gives us food.
From her comes water and life.
Our past comes from the Pachamama.
We are living our present on Pachamama
and our future will always depend on her.
Pachamama is used by man and by animals.
Plants grow within her.
If there is no Pachamama there cannot be
a humanity nor a plant or animal kingdom.
—Rómulo Lizárraga

As this millennium comes to a close, humankind is beginning to understand the importance of treating our planet with care and understanding.
Pachamama is a living planet, and without our care and love there will be
no future for us. Westerners refer to Mother Earth as Gaia, the earth as a
living organism.

Since the days of their pre-Colombian ancestors, the Andean people
have known that the Mother Earth is of great importance. The Quechua
word *pacha* means "planet earth, world, universe that we inhabit."

As the name Pachamama suggests, the Quechua respect and honor Mother Earth. It is from her, the female Goddess, that they get life. It is with Her that they share life and, just as giving and taking is a basis of existence among people, so the Quechua believe they must give as well as take from Pachamama. So dependent are they on Her, so involved is their relationship, that they regard Pachamama as an extension of themselves— a being that needs taking care of—a force that must be nourished and protected lest it die.

Because of Her importance to a community that is primarily agricultural, the Quechua share the food and drink they love with Pachamama. Before drinking akkha or any alcohol, a few drops are spilled on the earth as an offering to the Mother Earth. She is also offered small portions of food before it is eaten. Pachamama loves to receive offerings of flowers, food, and coca leaves from Her children.

The Pachamama is summoned on all special occasions and permission is asked of Her before any activities take place in the community. Before building a house, for example, a special ritual is followed so that the Pachamama will not be angry with the new residents and she will protect them from danger, sickness, and even death.

Pachamama is kind and tolerant, but she may also turn vengeful to those who forget Her. She may appear as aggressor if the rituals are not performed with integrity, and with issues of importance She expects offerings, known as *haywarikuy*.

The offerings protect specific occasions. August, September, and October, the time for sowing, are significant months for the goddess Pachamama. On these occasions a ritual specialist becomes the intermediary between man and Pachamama so that She may effectively receive Her offering, assuring that seeds will germinate and grow with abundance. Every communal action, ritual, and request is accompanied by a simple prayer:

> *Pachamama, receive this offering I send to you with all my love.*
> *As good provider of my family and my people,*
> *receive this manifestation of my love.*
> *Receive your children's offering that honors all humanity.*
> *Don't forget to recommend me to the Sun*
> *that he give me his light and healing.*

Since ancient times the Quechua have believed Pachamama is the biological mother of children. She is connected to everything, and all things are a part of Her.

Some Quechua presume that dieties leave pre-human children in places such as caves, rocks, and rivers before the elements assist them to be placed in the womb of a woman. The sexual coupling between man and woman gives life and form to the fetus, but spiritual values, intelligence, and love are transmitted by spiritual entities who perform this miracle. They believe this miracle to be natural, and that procreation of man and woman is by means of the mother's union with Pachamama. The spirit comes from the Creator Uywakke.

This is a unique pre-Inkan stone of the female goddess, Pachamama. It is the only one the authors have ever seen.

The father provides the human-forming of the fetus, endowing the baby with his wisdom, maturity, and authority. Ayar Mánkko, through intervention of nature, came through a window of stone at Pakkarikk-támpu. He did not know his mother or father. Many stories in history, such as Romulus and Remus, depict births whereby the child was born through intervention of nature, without knowing a mother or father. To the campesinos the story of Jesus fits in perfectly with this concept. Maria, the loving mother, gave birth in a cave, while San Jose, or Joseph, was the adopted father. The mother displaces the father in importance.

The Pachamama affirms her maternity by assuming the role of protector of the children, the weak and the sick.

She may be seen as old and wrinkled, like the mother that has given birth so many times. We are tied to Mother Earth by an umbilicus or life cord that connects us to her womb of creation. If part of Mother Earth is suffering, then the world suffers too.

Traditionally, people placed their *wawakuna* (babies) in a hole in the earth and today some Andeans still observe similar practices. The mother places the baptized child in the ground from where the father takes it. Sick children are covered in earth, leaving a place for them to breathe. Covering injuries with earth casts and the act of chewing clean earth together with coca leaves still are well-known medicinal practices.

Despite 460 years of Christian indoctrination, the Goddess Mother Earth, Pachamama, continues to be adored by all Quechua men and women. The Quechua see Pachamama outside of themselves and inside of themselves as well. They see Her everywhere, in the wind that carries the clouds, in the clouds that bring the needed rains and in the sacred rivers that flow through the land. They see Her in the faces of their children and in the eyes of the puma, the condor, and the serpent.

The Quechua understand that earth is suffering, and suffer with Her. They love Pachamama in every moment and know that only She can take away their pain. Pachamama brought them to life from Her womb and She will take them back again. They accept that birth and death are present in every moment.

3

Mountain Deities; Pilgrimage

The apus are with us through the night and day.
—Line from group song composed
by English-speaking travelers

Apukuna are the divine lords of the sacred mountains. They have been worshipped since pre-Inkan times and are considered to be the most powerful of all traditional deities. They play a vital role in the daily lives of Andean people. The Quechua show the utmost respect toward the apukuna and acknowledge their importance in ritual and ceremony.

Awsankate (20,900 feet) and Salkkantay (20,574 feet) are two of the highest and most revered mountains in the Qosqo and Machu Picchu areas. Both are believed to be fierce deities who take revenge on those who make them angry, yet they are also the protectors of the people. It is believed the mountains communicate with each other, and the stars and the sun acquire great powers when they are associated with the mountains.

Ritual specialists from the greater areas of Qosqo and as far away as Killapampa, known as Quillabamba, K'osñipata and Shintuya in the jungle, have always come to these mountain peaks for their empowering initiation ceremonies. The mountains are regarded as so powerful that only the most experienced healers and ritual specialists can deal with them directly.

One of the highest mountains, Apu Salkkantay is also one of the most revered mountain deities by Andean people living in the countryside today.

Worship is not confined to the great mountains. There are local apukuna, regional apukuna, and national apukuna whose powers are judged on a hierarchical scale. This hierarchy appears related to the source of natural assets.

Most apukuna are referred to as lords who are masculine, but some are said to be female. Two mountain peaks together, such as Sawasiray and Pitusiray, are regarded as a couple, male and female.

From the highest mountains comes the snow that feeds the rivers, which in turn carry water to the valleys below and into the lowlands of the jungle. The Quechua believe the high mountains control the weather. Hail, snow, rain, and thunder originate there, and therefore have an effect on the success or failure of their crops. Thus, the highest mountains deserve the greatest respect and honor.

The apukuna are also believed to be the owners and controllers of the wild animals such as pumas, bears, and poisonous snakes. Llamas, alpakas, vicuñas, and guanacos live on mountain slopes and are important for the economy of the people. The apukuna are responsible for their fertility.

The Quechua make offerings of coca leaves to the spirits of the mountains for protection of their homes, families, and livestock. They ask for healing and for personal and business advice. They also ask about their future and for help in finding lost objects.

The Andean Quechua can establish a direct contact with the apukuna through the intermediary of an alto misayoq (healer or ritual specialist). If they forget to make an offering before making a request, they may cause harm to themselves. Without the protection of an offering, evil spirits and negative energies may become active and cause illness and disaster.

Small stones shaped like animals, called *illakuna*, sometimes are found on the mountain slopes. They are believed to be gifts from the mountain deities and taken as a good sign that the size of the herds of llama, alpaka, *wik'uña* (vicuña) and *wanakokuna* (guanacos) will be increased.

Apukuna in Qosqo

Awsangate and Sallkantay are the most respected Apukuna, however, in the Qosqo area, there are many major apukuna of importance.

Apu Wanakauri

This apu, situated southeast of the city of Qosqo, is concerned with the well-being of man. Apu Wanakauri supervises individual behavior and makes sure each person interacts well with others, developing into a decent member of society. He is known as the apu of well-being, in both the material and interpersonal sense.

Apu Kkañaqway

Located east of the province of Paukartampu, this apu oversees rain and the care of cattle. On his mountain slopes live herds of cattle, along with a special breed of a supernatural species called *iwayllu*, believed to fertilize the females of the herd.

If an individual is on bad terms with the iwayllu, the apu may cause the farmer to lose his cattle or have them stolen. To ensure that this does not happen, the farmer makes a special offering of coca leaves to the apu.

Apu Kkolkkepunku

In the valley of Qollpa, area of Qeros, is the apu which keeps watch over the health of the people. Apu Kkolkkepunku knows the etiology of all diseases, and the Andeans appeal to her for good health or go to her on pilgrimage to be cured.

Apu Yaya Jesucristo

As many of the Andean traditions became mixed with the Catholic belief systems, Jesus Christ became an apu. He is treated as a son of God who was persecuted by his enemies in ancient times. His specialty is justice and he is the balance between good and evil.

Pilgrimage to Qoyllur Rit'i

Qoyllur Rit'i is one of the true Andean expressions which clearly shows us that the ancient Andean traditions and concepts are still alive and vivid. Despite an invasion of citizens from Qosqo and Arequipa joining the pilgrimage in the past few years, Qoyllur Rit'i is still the best document on the Andean way of thinking concerning religion and cosmology. It is difficult to explain and still is being studied by anthropologists, but it is the best tool we have.

—Aurelio Aguirre
Professional Quechua Guide in Qosqo

Qoyllur Rit'i has called pilgrims to her for thousands of years. Since ancient times inhabitants of the Andes have traveled to the mountain Sinakara and climbed to a sacred site below the snow peaks, to make offerings to their gods and apukuna. This sanctuary, called Qoyllur Rit'i, was revered by the Inkakuna, priests from temples throughout the empire, as well as the Andean Masters who possessed great spiritual wisdom. They ascended the mountain together with their initiates, accompanied by their families and members of the *ayllu* (community).

During the centuries after the arrival of the Spanish in the Andes, the Quechua and Andeans of mixed blood continued with the pilgrimage. The Catholic Church, aware of Qoyllur Riti's great spiritual importance to the Andean people, could not succeed in breaking the ancient tradition.

In 1720, the Church constructed a small chapel at the holy site. Soon after, an image of Christ, crucified, appeared painted over a rock where offerings had been made for centuries. Thus began the commencement of the Christian pilgrimage to what became known as Lord of Qoyllur Rit'i.

Each year, a few days before the winter solstice, thousands of Quechua and mestizo pilgrims in the Andes and Amazon

Mountain travelers place stones on an apachita (mound) as an offering to Apu Machu Picchu to provide safe travel.

jungle make their way to this sacred place.

The great festival takes place in June during the eight-day period when the rains have ceased, the days are hot, and the nights are icy cold. The Andean year begins when the Pleiades, called *kollka*, and translated as "storage house" or "seeds of the nursery," become visible for the first time, and remain so for the next eleven months.

The preceding month is considered a period of chaos, a period when time is not recorded. During this month one can go back into the past and talk with the *mallkikuna* (ancestors) and, through rituals using the San Pedro cactus, foresee the future. Once the Pleiades become visible, order returns and humanity returns to the concept of linear time, whereby one lives in the present and cannot go back to the past nor to the future.

In attendance on the mountain are every element of the Andean world: dieties, celestial skies, thunder, clouds, snow, stones, minerals, plants, animals, birds, and humans.

Pilgrims from everywhere, wearing traditional dress and special costumes, go to renew their connection to ancestors and dieties that have been there forever.

After traveling for days, they pour into the province of Quispicanchis. There is a grand reunion, with some bringing babies to be carried to the peaks and others are elders determined to make this journey before they die.

Farmers, learned masters, teachers, traditional healers, scholars, musicians, dancers, the healthy, and the sick brave the freezing, erratic weather conditions. Andean healers prepare for their initiations in the glacier peaks, and all climb to the painted rock that sits below the snow levels at 15,650 feet. Here, together, they offer homage to Qoyllur Rit'i.

Most numerous of the pilgrims are the Wayri Ch'unchu, the "wild ones" from the jungles of Paukartampu (Paucartambu). They wear spectacular headdresses adorned with feathers of colorful parrots.

The K'achampa and Machula regard this as an opportunity to acquire new clothes and go to the festival for the purpose of rejuvenating themselves, their land, and crops. The boys' costumes represent the *machukuna* (ancient beings) who populated remote areas of the high Andes.

The Kollakuna travel from the altiplano (high plains) of Lake Titicaca. They dedicate themselves to commercial ventures by collecting pebbles from the sacred peaks and selling them back home.

The Pabluchakuna, or Ukukukuna, are young men dressed in multicolored garb representing the bear, an animal who is greatly respected. They carry whips which they use to control the behavior of the pilgrims. The Andean spectacle bear is considered a human who converted into an animal because he fell into disgrace with God.

Mythology tells the story of a beautiful girl who fell in love with a semi-god, Kukuli, who looked like a bear. Although everyone was against her marrying him, Kukuli took her to live in the mountains and their offspring were called Ukukukuna—half-human, half-god. The Ukukukuna are said to have the awareness of both animal and human life.

On pilgrimage, the Ukukukuna dress incognito as bears walking in silent reflection. They meet up with other Ukukukuna who have come to ask for pardon, a miracle, or to give thanks.

Recent studies on the Ukukukuna offer a different concept. They say the people are not playing the role of the bear, but rather that of the alpaka, wearing alpaka garments and masks made from alpaka wool. They even make the sounds of the alpaka and play with the people. In those mountains there are no bears, only alpaka who depend on the mountain and are the link between mountains and humans.

The festival is important to the Andean campesinos to preserve their agricultural crops and livestock production. Andean healers accompany the pilgrims to make haywarikuykuna (offerings) to the dieties and apukuna, renowned for the protection of man and animals.

Before setting up camp in the large outdoor sanctuary, pilgrims wash and purify themselves in a natural spring. The atmosphere is festive; musicians play, dancers perform traditional dances, and enterprising people sell hot food and drink.

Paper money is offered in exchange for specially shaped pebbles that symbolically bring the buyer what he desires in the coming new year. Masses are held in the chapel.

Stars are at their most brilliant during the days of the festival, and the night skies offer spectacular shows of stars taking their positions in the constellations.

The Ukukukuna mentally prepare to journey at night to the glacier ridge above the holy site. They understand that, should they fall into a snow crevice, no one will be allowed to assist them. Dying there means they were meant to be sacrificed and become the seed for the next year. During the night, groups compete to carve out huge blocks of ice they will carry on their backs to the sanctuary.

The Ukukukuna are on the icy ridge to witness the precise moment when the Pleiades appear, and the rising sun reflects on the ice of the glaciers. They are willing to risk their lives to be present when order and the will of God comes into the world. The Ukukukuna place candles and a cross in the snow and carry out their rituals throughout the night.

At the first light of morning, Kkoyllor (Venus), the major star, appears over the snow peaks behind the sanctuary. From this splendid sight comes the name Qoyllur Rit'i, "Star of the Snows."

The pilgrims look to the stars in the celestial skies. As the sunlight hits the snow, a wave of silence sweeps through the crowded sanctuary. Moments later, musicians everywhere simultaneously play an ancient pentaphonic melody on their drums and flutes, announcing to the world that order has returned.

*Upper section of this carved stone at Machu Picchu appears to be
a miniature of the mountains in background.*

The Ukukukuna return at dawn, triumphant and exhausted. The
water, frozen into a block of ice, has witnessed the light beaming from the
sun and stars at the same time, signifying the beginning. Within this
potentized frozen liquid is captured the essence of order. The ice contains
the properties of the celestial skies along with the vibrations of the flowers, plants, and stones.

With this new order, rain will come when it is supposed to,
Pachamama will produce abundantly and the people and their animals will
be blessed with health, prosperity, productivity, and fertility.

Blocks of ice are packed with ichu grass and carried on the backs of
the Ukukukuna to their respective villages and towns. The melted holy
water is used to heal the young and old.

The festival concludes in the plaza of the town of Ocongate where
there is more music, dancing, and feasting. A ritual battle takes place
between the Wayri Ch'unchu of Paukartampu and the Kollas. The Wayri
Ch'unchu set out to capture the *imillakuna* (meaning "ladies" in the Aymara
language of the Kollakuna) by overcoming their protectors. The "wild
ones" from the jungle regions are said to always win.

Pilgrims return home rejuvenated, humbled by the mountain, and
strengthened by their journey to the Star of the Snows.

Victor Estrada's Story

 "A pilgrimage to Qoyllur R'iti in the Peruvian Andes changed my life. During my university years, I was an atheist and did not believe in anything that didn't come through my five senses. The Catholic religion had no meaning to me; I was into materialism, militant and expounded communist ideas that were in vogue among students twenty years ago."

[It is of interest to note that such ideals were cultivated twenty-five years ago by intellectuals such as Abimael Guzman, a professor at the San Cristobal de Huamanga in Ayachuco. Guzman became the leader of the infamous Sendero Luminoso (The Shining Path), a communist-backed terrorist group. Sendero Luminoso became involved in the narcotics trade and was responsible for the massacre of thousands of Quechua campesinos, as well as a multitude of urban deaths caused by their terrorist acts. In 1993, Guzman and many of his cohorts were captured. By the end of 1994, acts of violence diminished in the country and there are signs of movement toward peace.]

"Each year in June, thousands of people go to Qoyllur R'iti, Star of the Snow. I went to see the folkloric dancers. There was a group in particular from Lima that interested me. I had watched them practice their dance for two years, and they never tired of perfecting it.

"On the mountain I spent time speaking to the dancers, and I began to feel there was something present that was greater than the dance. I asked a dancer, 'Why do you dance here? You are twenty-five years old. Every year, you come from Lima for a month. How long will you continue to dance here?' He replied, 'Until the Señor takes me.' I understood it had something to do with the Catholic Church, but also felt there was something more.

"I continued to observe this same group of thirty dancers. They were joined by dancers from all over, a fraternity of dancers. They all had this intensity and fervor, which began to move me.

"People of all ages, healthy and sick, braved the icy weather and participated in the pilgrimage to the mountain. They made offerings to Pachamama and the apukuna, the mountain deities. They shared their food, played their music, sang, and danced.

"I turned my attention to the Quechua campesinos and noted their expressions, their attitudes and treatment toward each other, their llamas and alpakakuna. They moved with a sense of great purpose.

"I observed how the *pabluchakuna* (the wild men of the jungle) braved the icy glaciers at night and returned to the crowds with blocks of ice tied to their backs. Some of the men fainted from fatigue, but never gave up. A man collapsed and died.

"It all surprised me. There was no explanation for this. I had never seen anything like it before and wondered what was behind this, I felt there was a strong force. I felt the passion of these people.

"I returned home and was unwell for months. For the first time I remembered how, as a young child, I would disappear in the countryside and observe the mountains. I had felt great peace and joy before my family moved to the department of Puno, where I was separated from nature.

"I began to have vivid dreams about the snow, the mountains, and this huge area being part of the whole. I saw it all as manifestations of the Father Creator. I felt my emptiness, the senseless beliefs I'd had as a student.

"One night I was walking in the full moon. It was the first time I got to feel the spirit of the mother moon. I was overcome with emotion, and it made me cry. What was happening to me? Where was I? What had I lost over all those years?

"This was a new beginning. I consciously let go of my past. I studied with pakkokuna, curanderos, and began to understand many things. I learned from oral information passed down from our ancestors and studied the esoteric world with special teachers."

4

Community and the Gift of Sharing

Observe any group of campesinos working in the land. Watch the way they go to work, early in the morning, and you will see happiness. You will hear them singing, whistling, and telling jokes. They are transmitting the love they feel for Pachamama.

The Quechua campesinos are the remnants of a highly developed civilization. They went back to their roots, to normal practices they were used to. They are intelligent people who are dedicated to preserving this planet because they revere Pachamama and because they love having contact with the earth in their daily life.

Many have chosen to live far away in isolated places where they are happiest and without the influence of this modern lifestyle that has eroded their traditions.

The Quechua are simple people who want happiness and freedom. For them, life is simply like it is. They have some needs and we can help them, but let's not spoil their way of life. Let's not change them. Let them live as they are, let's learn from them; we always do it the other way around and force them to learn from us.

—Aurelio Aguirre

The Ayllu

Scattered throughout the Andean regions of Qosqo and Machu Picchu are hundreds of indigenous communities called *ayllukuna*. Since ancient times, the Andean people have established a strong connection to the land they live on. Originally all members living in an ayllu (community) were considered to be distant relatives, their land inherited from the previous generation.

Many of these agricultural communities were formed during the period of unrest that preceded the Land Reform Acts of 1969. Land was distributed to farmers according to their needs, and the community was given communal titles to the property.

Today, if members of an ayllu are not related by blood or marriage, they can still live there as *ayllumasis* (companions of the ayllu). All members are referred to as uncle and aunt, and the elderly are called by the Spanish titles *abuelo* or *abuela* (grandfather or grandmother). The children are regarded as cousins.

In the river valleys where there is fertile flat land, *aylluruna* (people from the community) cultivate maize, vegetables, and fruit. Those in higher altitudes farm a variety of potatoes, grains, and broad beans. Land

Andean homes in the community of Soraypampa, on the route to Salkkantay.

at the highest altitudes is used for communal pastures for herds that provide the community with a source of meat and wool.

A sense of unity is vital to members of the ayllu, and sharing is their most important concept. Active participation in the communal life is an essential condition to living in the ayllu. This involves religious celebrations, agricultural rituals, working the land, and honoring their duties and obligations to all the members of the community.

All members of the ayllu take turns in leadership. Age grants respect and authority and through their experience with community affairs, people become eligible for leadership. However, in order to participate fully in today's external commercial world, traditional criteria for leadership are being passed over in favor of those who have literacy and knowledge of the Spanish language.

Ayllukuna situated in areas not too far apart may differ greatly in their social structure, administration, religious practices, cosmology, ecology, and economic structure.

The Role of Women

The most important work of women in the community is to manage the household resources and maintain the prestige of the family. Women cook meals for the men working in the fields and take care of their many children until they are weaned, when siblings take over. They are kept busy with a multitude of agricultural and livestock tasks and supervise household animals, such as chickens and guinea pigs.

Women are responsible for storing and maintaining sufficient seed for the following agricultural year; they exchange goods and go to the markets to buy and sell. Their days are long and the work is never done.

The Quechua build their own homes out of adobe bricks, and include areas for cooking and sleeping. Each family works its own plot of land in a reciprocal labor arrangement called ayni.

Ayni

The word "ayni" does not have an equivalent in other languages. It means "today for you, tomorrow for me," the idea being that all work is shared and that each man benefits from helping others. Ayni is a reciprocal form of labor. It was practiced in ancient times, and the Inkakuna used it in their agricultural program.

*Quechua women spin yarn from llama wool as part of
their role in maintaining the family.*

In the sixteenth and seventeenth centuries, the Spanish attempted to
do away with ayni. The Andeans were resettled in towns where they had
to pay taxes and work for the benefit of the Spanish landowners. The
Spanish confiscated ancestral lands of the campesinos and forced them by
law and torture to give up their pagan agricultural rituals. The Andeans
converted to Catholicism and churches were placed on their sacred sites.
Despite 500 years of suppression, ayni has survived, and land was returned
to the Andean people through the Reformation Land Act of 1975.

The Quechua, whether living in an ayllu or on an isolated farm,
maintain relations of reciprocity with other Quechua. They live, work,
drink, pray, and play in a universe governed by reciprocity. Ayni tells them
how to live and what to expect from others; it permeates all aspects of
their daily lives. Every action in the Quechua world gives rise to ayni.
Services are performed and it is expected that at some time the favor
will be returned.

Each family member maintains a separate network of ayni companions. Men recruit help for agricultural labor. In the Andes the campesinos
work under difficult conditions, farming in harsh climates on steep slopes
at high altitudes. The load is eased when groups of neighbors take turns
working together at each *chabra* (farm).

Group energy helps the campesinos get through an arduous day. They banter with each other and are supplied with ample akkha and food by the host's wife. It is important that the Quechua host shows that he is generous and a good provider. The day ends by relaxing at the host's home with songs called *harawikuna* accompanied by musical instruments. *Kkenakuna* (flutes) and drums are played in the rainy season to help grow the maize.

Through their own ayni network, women will seek help in preparing large quantities of food for the working men. Children help each other with different community tasks. The ayllu expects its members to maintain ayni and live by its premise, and those who do not may be banished from the community.

Reciprocal relationships extend beyond the human being to include the Pachamama, the sacred mountains, apukuna, and the rocks and springs that have given birth to the ancestors. Community for the Quechua includes animals, plants, and also ancestors and invisible beings. Communities can be lived in and experienced as a whole system of interrelated forms and species engaged in common activity. Pachamama is a being of many families interacting and exchanging energy by way of everyday ritual practices and seasonal agricultural ceremonies.

Ayni means being able to live with the world in a very special way. It

This woman known as the angel of P'isaq, contributes to ayni in her own special way, helping visitors climb to the ruins by "sending energy from behind them."

means people sharing the land with the animals as if they were their brothers and sisters. It means a Quechua neighbor is a friend you have always known. No one lives in isolation; human beings and nature are inseparable. The system of ayni implies interconnectedness and interdependence.

For the Quechua there is no separate individual self. They speak in the third person ("we") instead of first person ("I"), illustrating the sense of unity in their lives. Words that mean sharing are woven into their language. When something is accomplished in the community, they all enjoy the fruits. When someone steps out of line, they all accept the blame.

A few years back, Rómulo, who works as a professional guide in Qosqo, was leading a group of Magical Journey hikers on the Inka Trail to

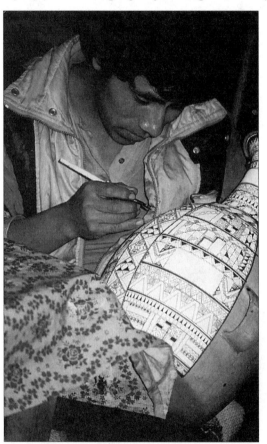

This Andean man shares the craft of ceramic painting with his community by displaying this vessel.

Machu Picchu. Quechua men from a nearby community served as porters for the hikers, and on that day a younger member of their ayllu had joined his companions for the first time.

As is customary, the bags and equipment to be carried were evenly distributed among the porters. Rómulo noticed that from the start the fledgling porter was finding it difficult to carry his pack, but since this was his first trip Rómulo surmised that he would soon get the hang of it.

After lunch they began to ascend the steep paths. Rómulo saw the young porter sweating and struggling under what looked like an average-sized load. He called to the porters to stop, and in

Kkechuwa told the young porter to bring him his pack. He opened it up and under a sleeping bag he found some heavy rocks which he spilled onto the ground. The other porters stood around with expressions of great amusement on their faces. The young porter was flabbergasted when he saw the heavy rocks and realized that he had dragged them up to a height of 12,000 feet.

Sternly, Rómulo asked in Kkechuwa, "Who put these rocks in his pack?" In unison the porters answered, "We did." By their ayllu rules, no one person would get into trouble for the mischievous deed. The young porter was now initiated by his peers and would be accepted as a fully fledged porter.

When Quechua people meet strangers in isolated areas of the Andes, they offer some form of hospitality. No matter how little they have, the campesinos share their food or drink. When necessary, they offer their help and tools. When a place to sleep is required, they offer their blankets. They are generous and hospitable and they treasure these qualities and the qualities of ayni above all.

The Gift of Ayni: A Story

 In the beginning, our Father Taytanchis, Padre Teksi-wirakkocha, created the world. He had a son, Munayniyukk, and ordered him to go and populate the world. As his inheritance, Taytanchis gave him a special gift and proclaimed him *munay phiwiwawa* ("the first-born son who had the gift of love"). Taytanchis hid another gift called ayni inside his son's heart. A population was created in the Andes. Using the gift of love, the Andeans cultivated the earth, domesticated the animals, and lived in complete harmony with the Pachamama. Everything flourished during those times. These people were called Kkeswarunakuna.

Time passed and Taytanchis had a second son. He too was sent to populate the world and his inheritance was *llank'ay* (the gift of work). He became the father of the second humanity. Sacred cities were built. Munayniyukk was instructed to guide his younger brother, Llank'ayniyukk, and they both populated the same world. They constructed the city of Qosqo in the form of the puma as a symbol of power and strength. Qosqo was the center of the world known as Tawatinsuyo. The people of Qosqo were called Inkakuna, children of the Sun.

*P'isaq marketplace, where Quechua people
regularly gather to exchange and sell their handcrafted goods.*

With the gift of love and the power of work, these humanities discovered the gift of ayni that was hidden in the older brother's heart. This gift was the ability to share, to work for the mutual benefit of one another.

In the practice of ayni, everything became more prosperous. Farmlands were fertile and fruitful and canals carried water. Roads went to the four corners of the world and there were inns with food and drink.

A long time after, the prosperous territories expanded and the Inkakuna began to misuse their power. Instead of using the gift of ayni, they became the owners of the kkeswakuna, the people born to the first son with the gift of love.

Taytanchis had a third son, Yachayniyukk. He was given the gift of *yachay* (knowledge) and he was called *chana wawa yachayniyukk* ("the last son with the gift of knowledge"). He was to populate the part of the world on the other side of the sea. This son was very adventurous and he loved to invent machines and travel. He could do things differently and he was known as the father of the third humanity, the humanity of the white man who had knowledge.

Some time later, Yachayniyukk traveled back from across the sea to his brothers in the Andes. They began to fight and this caused great unhappiness. The youngest brother abused his power of knowledge, and because he knew how to make machines, he created them in order to kill. When he saw how prosperous the older brothers were in the Andes, he used his machines against his brothers and they were forced to work for him. The brothers could no longer work in the *mink'a*, which was the work of the community, for the community. All work now was carried out for the benefit of the younger brother only. The first two humanities were converted into slaves.

The fields and farms no longer flourished. The towns were neglected and fell into disuse. The happiness of Tawantisuyo had ended. The sons of the first humanity could do nothing, so they escaped to the mountains where they worked and guarded their secrets, waiting for the bad times to pass.

The bad times are now coming to an end. Soon it will be the time of Pacha-kútekk, the time when the world will turn over, when it will turn back to what it once was. Our Father Tay-tanchis does not want more sons, he wants the brothers to get together in Qosqo and talk.

Taytanchis has said, "*Ayninakusunchis:* 'we must remember how to help each other.' Let us go and communicate with all the brothers of all the humanities that popu-late the world. Those that have the gift of

Ayni, encompasses bartering, a concept upon which the Quechua base their lives. This is exemplified in their community marketplaces.

love, the gift of work and the gift of knowledge: *munayniyukk, llank'ayniyukk,* and *yachayniyukk.*

"The oldest brother will teach everyone the ayni, because he is the only one who remembers it. The second brother will work together with ayni, and they will remember that to work gives life a great purpose. Once again the earth will become fruitful and plentiful. The third brother will teach them all the knowledge, and when he learns to love, share, and practice ayni, his knowledge will convert into wisdom. Wisdom will begin a new era for the three humanities, the era of Pachakútekk.

"*Ayninayukusun:* may we share all the gifts of munay, llank'ay, and yachay, and become one Earth, one Humanity, and one Spirit. That is how the era of Pachakútekk will be."

—Adapted from a story in Spanish
Gnossis Revista, Juan Nuñez Prado

5

Coca Leaves:
Connection to the Divine

How does the West perceive the words "coca leaves?" During the Bush administration, Westerners read that the United States of America, in order to combat the war on drugs, used military helicopters to spray poison on the coca fields in the Peruvian jungle and the Andes.

To the majority of Westerners the coca leaves are synonymous with cocaine, drug trade, and drug trafficking. This is an unfortunate, limited view of a natural substance that has from time immemorial been an integral part of Andean cosmology.

In the subtropical valleys of the Peruvian Andes, fields of coca leaves, called *kuka* or *hojas de coca,* have been harvested by the Andean campesinos for millenia. Visitors arriving in Qosqo are offered hot cups of *mate de coca* (coca leaf tea) to help them acclimate to the 11,000-foot altitude. However, the coca leaf has still greater symbolic power.

According to mythology, the coca leaf plant, erithoxylon coca, before becoming a plant, was a beautiful woman with a gorgeous figure. The woman used her body "in a bad way" and she was killed and cut in half. From her was born a tree which was called *mamakuka* or *kukamama.* She became known as the kukamama diety. People began to eat from her and it was said that they carried the leaves in a bag that could not be opened until a man copulated with a woman. In ancient times a goddess could be a tree, stone, or human being. Humans were not separate from nature.

Importance of Coca Leaves

Coca leaves are one of the most important plants used in the Andes of Peru. Excavations of ancient burial sites have shown that coca leaves were used ceremonially thousands of years ago. They were important to the Inkakuna, and the Quechua continue to use coca leaves in their daily lives as well as in ceremonies and rituals.

Coca leaves connect man to the sacred and divine energies of the Andean cosmology. They act as a channel for communication between the two.

Picchar kuka is the act of chewing coca leaves. Coca leaves are chewed together with *llipt'a* (a small piece of lime ash), which releases the alkaloids from the leaf and acts as a soft stimulant. (There are more than fourteen alkaloids in the coca leaf, only one of which is cocaine. The others are important in regulating the cardio-respiratory system and helping altitude sickness. The Western world only has learned to distill the cocaine alkaloid. Cocaine is still useful in medicine as a topical anesthetic but its other uses have lead to disastrous consequences.)

The coca leaf as used by the Andean people has beneficial effects. The chewing of leaves helps the Quechua work at a high altitude, and endure long periods without food or sleep. It diminishes the effects of hunger, thirst, and fatigue. While chewing the leaves with llipt'a, the saliva activates the leaves and extracts a source of Vitamins C and B.

Common Rituals Using Coca Leaves

Hoy por ti, mañana por mí: "Today for you, tomorrow for me."

Mink'a and Ayni

In the previous chapter, we explained ayni and how all social interaction in the Andes is based around the concept of giving and receiving. Coca leaves play an important part in this interchange and serve as a symbolic contract for this reciprocal help.

In a ritual called *mink'a*, the Quechua campesinos may ask their family or friends for help in their cultivation of crops. The person requesting help offers them coca leaves. By accepting the coca leaves, the people show their commitment and become obligated. The leaves serve as a symbolic contract for this reciprocal help.

Kuka K'intu

A *kuka k'intu* is a brief ritual offering of coca leaves to the Andean deities, Pachamama or the apukuna. The campesinos offer a kuka k'intu before beginning the work of the day. It also is offered at all Quechua ceremonies, at the commencement of a special

A coca leaf reader throws the coca leaves.

journey, before visiting a sacred site, and on many other occasions.

Leaves of the best quality of coca are usually arranged in threes, with the upper, dark green side facing the top. The Quechua lift the k'intu in front of the mouth and, without letting them go, blow them three times. The blowing is called *phukuy*. The Quechua respectfully call upon the local apukuna and the Pachamama, and may offer a silent prayer or make a request before beginning to chew the coca leaves. The leaves are a form of payment or offering to the Pachamama, apukuna, and divine energies in the Andean cosmology.

A Quechua healer from Patakancha
blesses the coca leaves in a kuka k'intu and
then offers them to the apukuna.

Hallpay

Hallpay is the act of chewing coca leaves, which may be a routine daily act or performed as a ritual. Hallpay may be done up to six times a day. Leaves are chewed by farmers before beginning the work of the day and then after breakfast, mid-morning, after lunch, mid-afternoon, and after work. Before beginning to chew the leaves, the Quechua make the k'intu offering.

When two or more Quechua exchange and chew coca leaves they follow a traditional format of inviting the others, accepting the offer, thanking the other, exchanging the leaves, and honoring the apukuna, Pachamama, and the place itself.

In silence, focusing their attention completely on the act, they then chew the leaves and carefully return them to the earth. The Andean dieties receive the essence of the coca leaf. This beautiful exchange establishes a closeness in their relationships and reaffirms their sacred alliance to the Pachamama and all the interconnected elements of nature. Coca leaf chewing is an especially resonant expression of reciprocity. It is high on the list of cultural characteristics.

Coca Leaves and Altitude: A Story

Recently, Rómulo escorted a group of seven hikers on the Inka Trail and I met them with the rest of the group at Machu Picchu.

One of the hikers was Virginia, a tall blonde business executive from California. She had a wonderful laugh. She stopped laughing on the first day of the trail when she became ill with severe stomach cramps. The group among them had a pharmacy of the latest medicines from all over the world, none of which were of any use. Even the nurse in the group could do nothing to help Virginia. Her condition deteriorated and a horse was brought in to carry her to the top of the highest pass, aptly named Warmiwañuskka (Dead Woman's Pass). The horse could go no farther and Virginia had to walk down the steep, rocky pass on the other side. She fell into a heap and told the others to leave her there to die.

Rómulo, who has spent his life in the Andes, knew that she was suffering from *sorokkch'e* (altitude sickness). Politely he said to her, "Now, Madam Virginia, we cannot leave you here to die. You are going to walk with us to Machu Picchu." Now that the group had tried all the Western medicines ever made, he suggested that she allow him to heal her, the Quechua way. He prepared the medicine and rubbed it over Virginia's chest and stomach. They then wrapped her up warmly and porters took turns in carrying Virginia to that night's campsite at Runkurakkay, where once again Rómulo prepared and applied the Quechua *hampi* (medicine).

Virginia woke up a new person. She and the group hiked and sang their way through the magical Inka roadways high in the Andes. I watched a triumphant Virginia proudly march into the ruins at Machu Picchu. She called out that she smelled like a dead body, yet was alive with the joy of hiking the Inka Trail.

After the group left, Rómulo and I visited the cook Zoila and a porter, Palermo, in their home in the ancient city of Ollantaytampu. I asked my three Quechua friends to give me their version of the episode with Virginia. Palermo, short and stocky, mused that despite her vomiting on him, carrying a six-foot-tall, 135-pound blonde woman was a nice change from carrying tents and equipment.

Zoila smiled and said that foreigners never seemed to know how important it was to keep themselves covered and warm. If they would listen to the Quechua instructions they would recover sooner.

I then asked the merry threesome to tell me exactly what was in the medicine. "Oh," said Rómulo, "Coca leaves boiled in water, with cane spirits and urine added."

I said, "What?"

"*Orino* (urine)," said Zoila. "The first time, Palermo donated some, and the second time Rómulo helped out."

I now understand why Virginia kept saying that her body smelled like a dead person while on the trail. Since she did not ask me I decided not to tell her about the contents of the medicine.

Life in the Andes: A Train Ride and Working Women

If you take the train from Machu Picchu to Quillabamba and back, you see another side of life in the Andes. Twice daily a train runs from Qosqo to Quillabamba, the last stop in the jungle.

On your journey back from Quillabamba to Machu Picchu you can become part of a vibrant experience. To the Andean people, this train ride is their only lifeline to the outside world. At each stop, Quechua women pile up their sacks and bundles of jungle produce that they sell to the markets that supply Qosqo. They hide numerous bundles under the passenger seats to keep an eye on them and avoid paying freight charges. Almost every woman is selling something. In between stations some women serve up their delicious hot cooked foods to passengers while others walk up and down selling *chicha morada*, a refreshing non-alcoholic drink made from blue corn, and other cold drinks. There is a constant parade of sellers offering tropical fruits and exotic flowers while children sell candies and small bags of coca leaves.

For Rómulo, this train ride is no novelty. He tries to sleep while the women are bumped from side to side as they make their way down the crowded aisles of the rickety, wobbling old train. I admire the way they can balance their goods, serve the passengers with a smile, and sell and change money all at the same time. I also feel great empathy for these women who work so hard trying to earn a few pennies to take home to their families.

The train stops at all the little jungle stations along the way. In those few moments, more hurried bartering takes place through the windows. New goods are sold to the sellers inside and they in turn will travel out of the jungle and sell them to the markets in the Sacred Valley. People are courteous and understanding. No one shouts at the women and children doing their daily work.

It is only when the tourists get on at Machu Picchu that the atmosphere changes. The visitors push and shove, trying to get a seat so that they don't have to stand all the way back to Qosqo. They yell at their buddies and fill the crowded aisles with cigarette smoke. The non-paying Quechua children and the working mothers must give up their spaces to the visitors.

This is the local train, which is cheap. There is a special tourist train that goes directly to Qosqo with barely a stop. It has luxury seats and not a vendor in sight. It is expensive. The tourist who prefers quiet and comfort can pay $75 for a return ticket, while the local train costs $7.

But in February 1998, the train line between Machu Picchu and Quillabamba was washed away by landslides and torrential rains. This lifeline was severed, leaving hundreds of farmers without any means to transport their fruit and crops to the markets in Qosqo.

The Coca Leaf Girl

 Miriam, a little, wide-eyed girl with typically Andean features, matted hair and skin covered with unhealthy looking sores, came to share my seat. I offered her soda crackers and she immediately called her five-year-old brother, Moisés, to come and share them. She muttered something in Kkechuwa to Rómulo, apparently telling him to say that the bundles at his feet were his. Rómulo nodded his head and continued to doze. Miriam busied herself under the seats, closing and opening bundles. She then took off to do her selling.

Suddenly she came charging through the crowded aisles, white as a sheet. She quickly said to Rómulo in Kkechuwa, "Say they're yours, say they're yours." Within moments two uniformed policemen with spear-like bayonets walked up the aisle poking at bundles. They stabbed the two bundles under Rómulo's feet and immediately yanked them out. The policemen ignored us and glared at the little girl. The train stopped and we watched them load piles of bundles onto the station platform at Santa Teresa. This area is known as the *ceja de selva* (the brow of the jungle).

Miriam sobbed and sobbed. Her mother had sent her off to sell two large bundles, each one filled with twelve kilos of coca leaves. She would sell little packets of the leaves in legal amounts to passengers. She probably would have sold the rest to market vendors. She told us that her family was very poor and that coca leaves were their only source of income.

Poor Miriam. She was petrified when the police came. Her little brother just sat silently. I sat there mumbling at how unfair it was of the mother to give a young child such a job. Her mother probably knew the authorities would do nothing to the little girl. Miriam cheered up considerably when I discreetly made a donation to offset her loss. Rómulo muttered that the mother would have her child back on the train the next day. Some days they were luckier than others. He also commented that as a *gringa* (foreigner), had I tried to interfere with their work, the police would have had me in jail in minutes.

How to Cure with Coca Leaves

To cure Virginia of sorokkch'e, the guides boiled some coca leaves. They then added *cañazo* (malt from sugar cane, usually carried by Quechua staff and mountain people), some urine, and salt. The Quechua usually drink half a *tot* (measurement) of this, one time, then rub the rest over the chest, stomach, and abdomen area. The patient is wrapped warmly. In the instances where simple Quechua remedies, hydration, and rest do not help, the patient must be evacuated to a lower altitude.

The Quechua believe that urine is important because it contains acids, creates heat, and removes toxins from the body. Hikers may develop altitude sickness which can present in many different forms, the most lethal of which are cerebral edema and pulmonary edema (swelling in the brain and in the lungs from excess fluid). In the instances where simple Quechua remedies, hydration, and rest do not help, the patient must be evacuated to a lower altitude.

Señora Fortunata de Lizárraga, Rómulo's mother, gave birth to ten children and brought them up in the Andes, on a chahra near the slopes of Machu Picchu. At eighty-six years of age, she is still strong and fit. At six o'clock each morning she crosses the roaring Urubamba River on an *oroya*, a small platform that swings her across the river when she pulls a chain attached to steel cables. She waits for the train from Quillabamba and quickly sells her surplus fruit to sellers heading for the Qosqo markets.

We asked Señora de Lizárraga for her proven recipe to cure sorokkch'e. She told us that walking in the high altitude may throw a body out of balance, causing nausea and headaches. The remedy for this is to chew coca leaves with a bit of sugar and earth extracted from the underside of a stone. It must be clean earth. The tiny bit of earth is mixed with sugar, wrapped in the coca leaf, and placed at the side of the jaw in the mouth. This form of chewing gives you strength and helps you feel better.

To cure stomach pains and cramps at a high altitude, first boil the leaves of the coca. Place this water in a glass and mix it with a tot of cañazo,

Señora de Lizárraga is a Quechua elder known for her effective cures with coca leaves.

and let it ferment. The liquid will turn yellow. Take a piece of cotton soaked in the liquid, and rub it over the stomach area. A little while later, the stomach pains disappear.

Before the 1998 landslide, Señora de Lizárraga left her farm each day and crossed the sacred Urubamba River on an oroya, to sell her fruit. The oroya has now disappeared.

In our years of traveling with groups in the Andes, I have observed Rómulo use this mixture to heal visitors suffering from severe stomach cramps caused by the altitude. Both adults and small children have responded favorably to the medicine.

The Quechua refer to the sickness as a cold wind entering the body. After applying the medicine to the stomach and chest areas, the patient must be wrapped warmly. Usually within ten minutes the patient is calmed and the spasms cease.

Offerings to Reach the Earth

The sending of an haywarikuy, or offering "to reach the earth," and commonly known in Spanish as a *despacho,* is a common practice among the Quechua today. Haywarikuykuna are used for all matters that are considered important and are sent throughout the year. They are dedicated to the apukuna, Pachamama, and the invisible forces, and are used for healing grave illnesses and warding off witchcraft and sorcery.

An offering also may be sent when a person feels that someone envies him, that there is negative energy in his house, his cattle are dying, production is low, he loses his job, or his family and children become sick for no apparent reason. Offerings may be sent to cause harm to another person.

Eliseo: A Farmer's Story

"About ten years ago, my wife suddenly became very ill on our farm. We took her to Qosqo where she saw the doctors and was tested by specialists in the hospital. They could not find the cause of her illness. Over time she saw different traditional healers and they too could not help her. She became worse and behaved strangely. She was always angry and acted in a crazy and hateful manner toward me. Our marriage suffered greatly and life was very difficult.

"Three years later we met a certain pakko (healer) who said that he could help her. He read the coca leaves, and said that a haywarikuy had been placed in our house years ago. He diagnosed her case as one of *embru-jería*, an act of sorcery or witchcraft done with evil intent."

[Unlike positive offerings, harmful offerings use special items for negative outcomes. The offering is not burned, but rather placed in the home of the recipient without his or her knowledge.]

"At that time I was skeptical and did not really believe in those healers. But I watched my wife get worse and I was desperate and willing to try anything. So this elderly pakko with an excellent reputation was brought to the farm. Once again, he read the coca leaves and was able to identify a 55-year-old neighbor who had wanted to harm us. The man had borrowed money from my wife and there was ill feeling between them when she asked for it back. He also was envious of our success and prosperity on the farm.

"The pakko asked my wife to show him all the areas she would like to sit in around the house. Soon after, and still working with coca leaves, the pakko was able to pinpoint the exact location where the malicious haywarikuy had been placed. Buried there they found the remains of the contents of the offering. There was a dog's and cat's tooth to instigate fighting between my wife and myself and some woman's underwear to represent my wife. There were two effigies of a man and woman made out of twisted iron with rope tied around their bodies to strangle them. There also was a coin of low monetary value so we would fail in our farm work.

"A decision was made to have the pakko immediately return the haywarikuy to the sender. He would add his own prayers. I did not regard this as a bad thing to do. I simply wanted to send back what he'd sent me. My wife became well, completely well, and our marriage has been good to this day.

"Soon after, my neighbor's wife got sick and died. Then he himself became ill and lost his vision. Not long after he died it became clear that the power of an offering has an even greater force when it is returned to the sender."

Campesinos send offerings to the apukuna.
Below Apu Machu Picchu, a treacherous pathway runs from the
ancient city of light to Willkapampa.

Quechua campesinos send offerings for the benefit of their families, land, livestock, and crops. On the first of January each year an offering is sent to ensure a good and healthy year for the family and home. The Spanish introduced the festival of Carnaval to the Quechua. In February, elders give away inheritances of cattle to their family members. Offerings are made to ensure that their animal gifts stay healthy and reproduce abundantly.

During Easter week, Pachamama takes a rest and no offerings are received by Her. (Indeed, Christ's Passion and Resurrection at Easter is a holdover from pagan fertility rituals in which "the young god king" used only to impregnate the Goddess Queen was ritually sacrificed to ensure renewal of nature.)

The colorful ceremony of Khawa which takes place in June is highlighted by special offerings to the apukuna to take care of the animals on the mountain slopes and ensure that they reproduce. The animals are marked and identified by strands of colored yarns threaded through their pierced ears.

In Inka times, offerings were made during the winter solstice for the benefit of the llama and alpaka. Today, each June 24 is celebrated by the Festival of San Juan, named for the patron saint of the sheep. This is an important time for the farmers, and offerings are needed to ensure good health and reproduction for the wool-producing sheep as well as the llama and alpaka.

From the first of August to September, campesinos send offerings in the most important ritual period. During July and part of August, the Pachamama has been at rest. No work is done on the land. The Quechua make special offerings to Her in gratitude for what they have received during the past year. Pachamama begins to stir with the first rains in August. After the dry season, the rains quench Her thirst and She awakens. She is now hungry to receive the seeds, and offerings are made to Pachamama with the new hope and promise that She will have a bountiful year.

Before undergoing a special journey, an individual, family, or a large group makes a special offering to the apukuna asking for permission to pass through the mountains and for protection.

Offerings consist of a variety of important items of animal, mineral, and vegetable origins. Pre-packaged offerings for specific purposes can be bought in the central market of Qosqo, in the section of *hampi kkatu* (traditional medicines). The sellers are usually specialists who put together the haywarikuy according to what one needs.

The following is a detailed list of the items that you may find in a complete offering. The contents differ depending on the practices of the specialist. Some specialists use many items with Christian symbols; others, especially those from the jungle areas, may not use any at all.

Offerings of Animal Origin

concha—Since early times the sea conch was used at ceremonies as a cup to serve holy liquid and foods to the gods.

ch'aska kuti—Sea star may be used by some practitioners to carry out witchcraft or counteract its effects. It also may be used for luck and to indicate a certain direction a person needs to take.

kkawa—Seven strands of wool of a *pakocha* (hybrid of the vicuña), each representing a color of the rainbow. The Quechua do not necessarily use seven colors of the rainbow. Their preferred colors are blue, red, green, yellow, and white. These wool strands must be used for offerings to stop the effect of *pujyu*, the ill wind, or the malevolent acts of k'uychi, the rainbow.

sullu—Fetus of vicuña, alpaka, or other animal, depending on the purpose of the offering. The fetus represents a reproducing animal and will symbolically assist the earth to produce a bountiful harvest.

Offerings at the Festival of San Juan ensure good health and reproduction of wool-producing animals such as the llama.

untu—Fat of the llama and alpaka is appreciated by the supernatural beings.

Offerings of Plant Origin

hanku kk'añiwa—Cereal and grain is well received by the gods.

kuka mukkllu—Seed of the coca plant. Twelve pairs are used. Each seed represents twelve kilos of coca leaves and is welcomed by the gods.

machu incienso—Incense, when burned, gives off an agreeable aroma for the spirits.

wira q'oya—The supernatural beings enjoy receiving this plant together with the food that is offered.

wayruru—Seed from the jungle, small red and black fruit. Red is used for benign offerings, positive energy. Red with black stain is used for malicious offerings.

sakksa kuti—Piece of curly nut, also used to carry out or counteract the negative effects of witchcraft.

Offerings of Mineral Origin

chiuchi piñi—Various colored glass beads with holes.

cross—Cast in lead, three centimeters long, the cross symbolizes the Catholic ritual, and today it is incorporated into the traditional Quechua offerings in the ceremony.

kkhaya chonta—A strip of pure white quartz to counteract negative deeds.

kkolkke recado and *kkori recado*—Little silver figures cast in lead represent gold and silver statues used in Inka times.

kkori botija, kkolkke botija—Jug of gold and silver to bring the receiver gold and silver.

paña taku, llo'ke taku—Red and blue vermilion stone placed on the left and right side of the offering to counteract negative energy that evil spirits send or plan to send.

oro pimienta—Stone of raw material of iron. Yellow color represents the gold. Form of payment to benefit recipients.

Other Elements in Offerings

akkha or *chicha*—Andeans use akkha, an alcoholic beverage, which is made from maize. Wine has been incorporated into some rituals through the Catholic influence.

Clavel t'ika—Carnation flower, generally red or white, for offerings to keep the sender healthy.

Haywarikuy paper—Size 34x33 centimeters. White paper to wrap offerings. Black paper for malicious offerings.

kkori libro, kkolkke libro—Pairs of gold- and silver-dipped leaves representing payments in lieu of money.

kkori pinkuyllu, kkolkke pinkuyllu—Paper dipped in gold or silver and flute-shaped as an offering for the sender to get rich.

kkhaskka sara—White maize was regarded as sacred in ceremonies during Inka times. It was regarded as a gift from God, and signified wealth and an abundance of food.

Women of the community get together to share akkha,
an item always included in their offerings.

kuka k'intukuna—Leaves of coca arranged in threes. To some this represents three important apukuna. To others this may have a Catholic interpretation of the symbol three. Specialists may choose up to twelve to fifteen groups of three depending on their needs.

llo'ke seda, paña seda, panti seda—Left silk, right silk, pink silk. On the right the specialist places silk threads of clear colors, such as white, yellow, and orange for good offerings. On the left there are silk threads of dark colors such as black, indigo, and violet for malicious offerings. Panti, the pink silk and red silk, is needed in all offerings.

San Nicolas t'anta—Bread of Saint Nicholas. These are two miniature wheat breads with the imprint of the effigy of Saint Nicholas. It is used by specialists who incorporate Catholic elements.

A Sacred Ceremony

Haywarikuy Akllay (the ceremony of the selection and setting out of items to be used in the offering) is most sacred. The ceremony is performed by a qualified specialist called a pakko. He or she also is referred to as the alto misayoq, maestro, or curandero.

Methods of each specialist and the contents of the offerings may differ slightly. The appointed place is decided upon after the initial consultation as to the type of offering to be sent. A date is set usually for a Tuesday or Friday night when the energy is regarded as high.

A *haywaskka* (blessing/prayer) is made to the apu of the community, and colorful woven cloth is stretched out and pointed toward the setting sun. A small cloth containing leaves of coca is set out, and the pakko "reads" them to determine whether the offering is sufficient and the time appropriate to send to the supernatural beings for whom it is destined.

If there is negative energy present they must wait. If circumstances are favorable, the pakko begins with the haywarikuy akllay, the setting out of the elements prior to the burning of the offering.

The complete offering that was prepared by the pakko or purchased in the market is unwrapped, the paper carefully removed, opened, and placed on the cloth. Each item comes wrapped separately and must be exposed.

A typical baywarikuy. This offering was made by Professor Espinoza to wish the authors a safe journey to Salkkantay.

If there is a cross, it is placed toward the sunrise in the east and petals of a carnation are scattered over the center.

Kuka k'intukuna (twelve groups of three coca leaves) are chosen and placed in a semicircle face up with the stems toward the west. (The number of groups of three will differ with each specialist).

Three pairs of the k'intukuna are a form of payment given to the supernatural beings, the Ruak or Uywakke who takes care of everything, and their servants attending them.

The kkhasqa sara (white corn) is removed from the husk and the teeth are placed in pairs, between which are placed almonds and a piece of fat of the pakocha, in a semi-circle facing east. More pairs are added depending on the required service.

Scattered around are varieties of candies, crackers, wira q'oya (a plant), hanku kkañiwa (raw cereal), garbanzo beans, *pallares* (large white beans), *inchiskuna* (peanuts), and kuka mukkllu (coca seeds). The *paña taku* (bread) is crumbled and added.

Kkori pinkuylla, kkolkke pinkuylla, (gold and silver paper flutes) and kkori botija and kkolkke botija (a thin, small sheet of gold and silver paper) are each placed facing one of the four directions.

At the center of this cloth is an animal fetus with the head toward the setting of the sun. At each side of the head a kkori libro and kkolke libro (gold and silver leaf) is stuck with akkha.

The kkolkke recado, kkori recado and chiuchi piñi (silver figurines and colored beads) are placed between the feet on the sides of the fetus.

The bread of San Nicholas is placed a few centimeters above the head of the sillu (fetus) and the other below the feet.

A wayruru (seed) is placed near each ear of the fetus as if they were earrings. Paña seda (the right silk) is stretched across to the opposite corners of the paper. The same is done with the kkori lazo and kkolke lazo (gold and silver string). The sea conch filled with akkha is placed on the belly of the fetus. The whole area is sprayed with incense and machu incienso, and three drops of wine or akkha are sprinkled on the offering.

The offering is wrapped; first the side where the feet of the fetus are, then the left side followed by the right. Some specialists unveil the head and others cover it lightly, indicating its presence with the carnation. To complete the haywarikuy layout, panti seda (pink silk) is wrapped around it.

The specialist concludes the akllay. He or she has done this very carefully without error, placing each item in strict order. The pakko now asks the coca leaves if he or she has made any error and whether the offering will meet the demands of the supernatural beings.

To remedy any deficiency or mistake by accident, he or she may place a *doncella wallpakk runtun* (the first egg ever laid by a hen) over the offering. He or she returns to analyze the leaves of coca to see if it is the correct hour to burn the offering.

Sending the Offering

The actual steps of the sending of the haywarikuy may differ slightly depending on the specialist's methods, but they are always done in a respectful and sacred manner. Usually, assistants take the offering, fuel, paper and wood to the ideal place where it will be burned. This may be a cave, special rock, or ravine in a mountain where the apu lives.

The haywarikuy must be burned before the first crow of the rooster; if not, the offering will not be successful. Some specialists believe the offering will not succeed if a dog barks at them while they carry the haywarikuy to be sent.

From the moment the assistants leave the house with the offering, the pakko follows their actions step by step, by divining or reading the coca leaves. He or she tells those present exactly what is happening as if he or she were there. If the assistants make any errors, the specialist offers k'intukuna of coca and prayers so that the gods will pardon them.

At the specified place the assistants with the haywarikuy kneel down, and the designated male leader greets the Pachamama and hugs and kisses the earth. He calls upon the apukuna and asks them to please receive this offering. He then spills the akkha in all directions to cleanse away the evil spirits.

When this is done, he lights the fire. When the flames die down and the red hot charcoal remains, he places the package inside, facing east. He then returns as quickly as possible without turning his head back for any reason lest he should be punished by the supernatural beings.

It is said that at the precise moment that the offering is being burned, the uywakkekuna (supernatural beings) accompanied by their guests dance around the fire and are attended by their servants. The beings partake of the abundant food and gifts they have received and they are pleased.

The assistants return to the house, the specialist shares the coca leaves that he or she has used, and they are chewed by all present. The head of the household invites the pakko and assistants to dine at the house in appreciation of the work done.

Some ritual specialists prefer to wrap the items used in the offering at the site where they are ceremonially burned. When the offering is placed in the fire, those present recite prayers and chants, continuing until the offering is completely burned and received by Pachamama, the apukuna, and all the Andean Gods.

The following is an invocation to Pachamama that Faustino Espinoza Navarro learned from a healer in the Andes, eighty years ago. He incorporates it in all rituals and offerings.

Pachamama wiñay samiyokk allpa, mañakuykikun allin kausayta;
Llank'askkaykupi allin ruruta, samit'ay,
Pusariwayku sapankaykuta, chay ununchaypitaq chaskiykuwayku kay haywakuyniykuta
Aylly Pachamama! Aylly Pachamama!

Pachamama, Mother Earth, our eternal happiness and bed of satisfaction:
We ask that we may be healthy and abiding, faithful and true in our work;
That we may be fruitful and abundant, that success steer us on the right path.
On this occasion we offer you this haywarikuy, a very special offering.
Praised be Pachamama! Praised be Pachamama!

Juan Bravo Vizcarra's Story

"In 1993, I was invited to exhibit my paintings in Bonn, Germany. Unfortunately, at that time I had just lost all my money. Two credit institutions defrauded me out of my life savings of $17,000. Here, in Peru, these things happen.

"I could not travel to Germany. I knew it would be very difficult to arrange to borrow the money. But a friend who knew of my misfortune said to me, 'Let's go and make a *pago* to Pachamama, so that you have success in the exhibition.' I had always thought of myself as a scientific person and had never personally been a believer in Andean cosmology. Rather skeptically, I agreed to make an offering to Mother Earth. I had nothing to lose.

"We went to the temple at Kenko, ruins outside of the city of Qosqo. My friend prepared the offering, and during the ceremony he encouraged me to focus on having a successful exhibition in Bonn. As is customary, we burned the offering before returning home.

"A few days later, I received a letter from Germany saying they were sending me the money for the air ticket to Bonn and that they would pay the freight charges for the paintings. The price of the air ticket was then reduced by 25 percent, and I was able to leave my family with money. Incredibly, my problems were resolved.

"I was the first Peruvian artist to exhibit in Bonn and the first painter who spoke Spanish since Picasso exhibited there when he was alive. More than 500 people attended the exhibition. I had great success and sold $25,000 worth of my paintings. During the inauguration, they told me that the doors were open for me to exhibit in any city in Europe. I have been invited to exhibit in Amsterdam, Paris, Italy, Norway, Sweden, Austria, and Finland.

"My attitude toward Pachamama has changed. I have begun to see how anything is possible after invoking Her and the apukuna and offering Her gifts from the earth, such as coca leaves, as payment.

"Now, I will be sure to pay homage to Pachamama and send Her another offering before I leave for Amsterdam in October."

7

Andean Cosmology
and Peruvian Healers

The Andean Cosmology

Andean initiations and ceremonies differ from those of the jungle and desert regions. The Andean Quechua have their own traditional healers, and they follow an ancient cosmology and way of life that has been practiced for thousands of years. Cosmology refers to a body of beliefs that any people have about the nature and origin of the universe.

The Andean cosmovision refers to the doctrine of the Andean world. It is a vision of the whole cosmos or universe, all interconnected. Andean cosmology encompasses the general nature of the universe as a whole: what it was in the past, what it is now, and what it is likely to be in the future. It is the totality of the spiritual world of the Quechua people living in the Qosqo and Machu Picchu areas. It is a non-fixed, magical world and incorporates all of Nature.

The Quechua people of the Andes coexist with supernatural beings. The invisible plays a decisive role in their destiny, which is governed by the Uywakke (great, powerful being), the supreme creator of man, animals and plants. Uywakke also governs the apukuna, Pachamama, and Christ, as well as other elemental beings and ancient spirits.

Magic plays a part in a Quechua reality that is never fixed, forever changing. Because of the unknown in their lives, the people may seem ambivalent and pessimistic. There is always the possibility that they may have to adjust themselves by magical means at any given time. They have to appeal to the invisible for favors; their world is never governed by Western concepts of logic.

Despite 500 years of persecution by outside rulers, the Quechua have maintained their traditions and spiritual beliefs alongside their Catholic religion. This combination has produced some specific characteristics typical of the Andean cosmovision.

There was a necessity in the past for the Andeans to practice their tradition in a clandestine way. The Quechua live in a cosmological world hemmed in by pressures of Christianity and Western materialistic tradition. These factors oblige them to hide their cultural authenticity, and they are often forced to accept the standards of the Western cosmology, which is influenced by the Church.

The Prophecy of Pachakútekk

The Quechua regard history as a sequence of worlds, pacha, each governed by a set of assumptions about their order. Each of the worlds, past, present, and future, are connected in the same way, with one separated from the next by a period of time called Pachakútekk (the turning of the world). The Inka state was reorganized by a hero called Pachakútekk Inka, and the European invasion was referred to as a Pachakútekk.

Now the Quechua speak of the coming of the era of Pachakútekk at the end of the current millenia, when great changes will occur. They take this prophecy as a warning from Pachamama about how failure to practice the ancient traditions is affecting the earth and its environment. Pachamama and all her connected beings, runakuna (humans), animals, minerals and plants have forgotten the ancient ways and are suffering for it. In the times to come, material pursuits and money will be worthless. "City dwellers will have only their money to eat."

It is said if mankind helps to heal Pachamama, mankind will begin to heal itself. Pachakútekk will herald the new era when there will once again be light, peace, love, and caring on the planet.

Many other ancient cultures speak of similar prophecies whereby great changes will take place within Mother Earth at the end of this millenium as mankind prepares to move into a higher form of consciousness.

They tell us that all of creation is connected. Ceremony holds the traditions together. When rituals are no longer practiced, then prophecy is told to remind people of what must be done to restore harmony on earth.

The Andean Worlds

According to Andean cosmology, the Andean universe is arranged on three planes of existence. The universe is divided into three "worlds": Kaypacha, Hanakpacha, and Ukhupacha.

Kaypacha is the world in which runakuna, humans, live together with Pachamama, the apukuna, wild and domesticated animals, plants, and all the natural forces such as rain, thunder, and lightning. It is the world of the four elements. There are also beings and phenomena that Taytanchis (God) has placed on earth for the protection and guidance of the humans. The puma or jaguar represents the power of Kaypacha, this world.

Hanakpacha is the upper world of superior energy. Today's Quechua refer to it as the place where Taytanchis dwells. Highly evolved spiritual beings such as Pachakámak, Pachakútek, Jesus, Maria, Christian saints, and spirits of the ancestors reside in Hanakpacha. Men or women in the role of alto misayoq become the mediators between Hanakpacha, the upper world, and Kaypacha, this world.

Students of spirituality may interpret this as a place where beings of a higher state of consciousness, or of a higher dimensional vibration,

This stone carving of a condor in Machu Picchu represents Hanakpacha, the upper world of the Andean universe.

*The three windows of this stonework in Machu Picchu are said to represent
the three worlds of Andean cosmology:
Kaypacha, Hanakpacha, and Ukhupacha.*

abide. From Hanakpacha, the celestial bodies, the sun, moon, and the
stars shine their eternal light on Kaypacha. The condor is one of the three
Andean animal archetypes. It has a view of all worlds from the upper
world and represents Hanakpacha.

Ukhupacha refers to the inner world of Pachamama or the Andean
underworld, inhabited by many types of supernatural spiritual beings in
caves, rocks, and ravines. Some of them are evil and negative characters,
while others are harmless and described as dwarf-like men. They may also
be the spirits of dead Inkakuna and Spanish conquistadors. Ukhupacha
may also be referred to as the inner world of the runakuna, humans

The serpent personifies Ukhupacha. Rivers that run over the earth
enter the inner world in the form of a snake. The serpent ascends and
descends through the three worlds by transmuting itself according to its
relationship with each world (see Chapter Nineteen).

The three worlds are interconnected, and it is possible to pass from
Kaypacha to Ukhupacha through the *kkocha* (lakes), *pujyu* (springs), and
pakkarina (place of origin). One passes from Kaypacha to Hanakpacha
through tombs, special rocks, and crosses. There is a continuous intercon-

nection between the beings of the three worlds, an important aspect of the Andean cosmology.

The Andean concept of the three worlds appeared 3,000 years before the Inka civilization. It has been honored in Peru since the Chavin epoch, 850 B.C.–200 A.D.

Before the Spanish came to Peru, the Andeans had no concept of heaven and hell. They took this idea from the Church, but have adapted it in their own way. To some Quechua, Hanakpacha may be described as heaven; Ukhupacha may represent hell.

In the new era to come, Pachakútekk, there will be a complete interaction and sharing between all people and beings on earth. All will be equal.

The Square Andean Cross

The *cruz cuadrada* (square cross) originated in ancient astrological cults and stems from the Southern Cross constellation chakana, which is seen clearly in the Andean skies.

*The three steps of this stone depict a section of the cruz cuadrada, Andean cross.
Each step represents a plane of existence in Andean cosmology.*

In Andean cosmology, the cross is regarded as the mythical foundation of the entire universe. The square cross embodies all the major principles of Andean cosmology. Its geometric form structured thought and brought order to the religious and mathematical concepts of the Andean world. The square cross is related to Andean mythology, religion, agriculture, and nature.

Ancient builders utilized the Andean cross as a basis for constructing cities and holy shrines. Builders employed techniques based on the geometric designs of the Andean cross in cities and in the sacred plazas of Tiawanaku, Qosqo, and Machu Picchu.

The Andean cross is engraved in the stonework of important ancient temples such as Tiawanaku and the temple of the Sun at Ollantaytampu. At Pisaq ruins and Machu Picchu, three steps carved in stone represent the three Andean worlds.

Traditional Healers and Ritual Specialists of Andean Cosmology

Throughout the Andes the Quechua people are actively involved in haywarikuy, the making and sending of offerings to their traditional Andean gods. The sending of a complete offering or despacho must be orchestrated by a healer or ritual specialist who has received specific training and undergone rigorous initiation. He or she is referred to as a pakko or *yachak*, a man of knowledge, who may be an Andean priest or curandero. A female pakko is called a *laykka*. Pakkokuna is a general name for the Andean ritual specialists, medicine men or women, curanderos or shamans, as they are known in the West.

The anthropologist Juan Nuñez del Prado classifies the pakkokuna into three levels:

Pampa misayoq are herbalists who live in an ayllu and work with the local families in the area. They are trained in the medicinal use of plants, herbs, and coca leaves that contain vital therapeutic value. Pampa misayoq are diviners and they use coca leaves for this purpose. They communicate with nature, carry out simple functions for healing purposes and make offerings to the Pachamama on behalf of the community.

Alto misayoq* is a highly trained and qualified Andean healer or specialist. He serves his apprenticeship with another alto misayoq, and

---

*We have met some female pakkokuna, herbalists, and diviners. However we did not come across nor hear about any qualified female Andean specialists described in the next section. We therefore refer to the following in the masculine.

Machu Picchu, ancient city of light.

The Quechua worship the apukuna (divine lords of the sacred mountains) who are responsible for the well-being of humans, animals, and plants.

View from Machu Picchu of Apu Putukisi, which means "happy skull." This apu jealously guards the sacred city.

The sacred Apu of Salkkantay (Wild Mountain) is 20,574 feet tall.

It is said the Machu Picchu ruins originally were known as Picchu Wanakauri,
"the mountain of origin."

Machu Picchu as seen from Inti Punku,
"The Gateway to the Sun."

Exploring typical living quarters inside Machu Picchu Ruins.

Eastern view from Machu Picchu ruins.   *Patapatakuna: Ancient Inkan Terracing.*

P'isaq ruins—
Intiwatana: Temple to the Sun.

Machu Picchu viewed from Waynapicchu, "Young Mountain."

The sacred rock in foreground was contoured to mirror Sacred Apu.

Willkamayu: Sacred River known as Urubamba in the Sacred Valley of the Inkakuna.

Nevado Veronica (Wakkaywillka), at 17,875 feet,
overlooks the Urubamba canyon and controls the fertility of the Sacred Valley.

The sacred valley of the Inkakuna gives forth the earth's choicest maize.
Inkan nobility worshiped the sacred land for its fertility.

*Community near to Chincheros where the Quechua abide by the ayni system,
"Today for you, tomorrow for me."*

*Picturesque Andean community near Qosqo,
where rituals to the Pachamama and apukuna are practiced.*

Since ancient times, the work ethic of the Quechua has been
"Ama sua, don't be a thief; Ama llulla, don't be a liar; Ama kkella, don't be lazy."

Quechua homes constructed with the natural materials provided by Pachamama:
stone, adobe, wood, and ichu grass for thatch roofs.

Mother Earth is seen as pure and sweet in providing Her nutrients, giving us maize, potatoes, kiwicha, and lima beans. We must take care of Pachamama.

Quechua farmers cultivate crops on these ancient Inkan terraces near P'isaq where they practice the rotation of crops each year.

Water: Power of the Andes.

Sara (corn): Sacred crop of the Andes.

*A Quechua campesino transporting the corn stalks
from fields that are inaccessible by car.*

*Group of campesinos harvesting maize in Yucay.
They look like walking bushes as they carry their loads to waiting trucks.*

Campesino leaving for work in the morning with his plowing tool pulled by oxen.

Young boy from Patakancha collecting the wheat to be threshed.

Farmer with his chakitaklla (foot plow).   *Woman tending her seedlings.*

Campesinos singing and working in unison using chakitakllakuna.

Woman selling akkha (chicha), an alcoholic beverage made from maize, a holy food.

Andean women from Willok community,
enjoying a brief respite from their daily chores.

Outdoor sales display of chicha morada, a blue corn drink that is delicious and sweet,
entices passersby to stop for refreshment.

Hundreds of varieties of Andean potatoes exist today.
Potatoes were exported to Europe when Spanish arrived nearly 500 years ago.

Sara (corn) also is grown in many varieties.
It is considered the nourisher of life in past, present, and future.

*Pachamama provides a variety of magnificent fruits
from sub-tropical farms near Machu Picchu and Quillabamba.*

*Cereals and legumes are indigenous to South America.
Quechua farmers barter them for other crops and supplies.*

The Quechua People of Qosqo and the Sacred Valley of the Inkakuna.

*A gathering of Quechua women and children
wearing their colorful traditional clothing.*

*Carol and Rómulo sharing some happy moments
with Pachamama's children of the Willok community.*

*Doña Jacinta smiling at the new dawn,
another day of work.*

*Juana, a young woman
preparing for her marriage.*

*Felicia is weaving a blanket of alpaka wool. She is an expert at creating the
multi-colored designs, a craft that has been handed down for generations.*

Pachamama's Children.

Two sisters visiting the popular Sunday market at P'isaq.
The style of dress differs in each community.

*Inés, wearing a round montera (hat)
from the village of Patakancha.*

*Varayoc, the young mayor, carries a vara,
an ancient staff symbolizing his authority.*

On market days, Quechua women elaborately decorate their hats with fresh wild flowers.

Although working in the fields of an isolated village at 13,000 feet, where no tourists visit, this woman still wears her traditional clothing and a hat decorated with fresh flowers.

Young Quechua mother secures her wawa (child) on her back with a colorful lliklla (shawl).

A ritual specialist from a mountain community at 14,000 feet prepares and sends an offering: a coca k'intu of three leaves to the apukuna and Pachamama.

Coca leaves connect the Quechua to the divine energy. They are chewed with llipta (lime ash) to activate the alkaloids which maintain the health of the people.

Pampa misayoq (Quechua healer) reading the coca leaves.

Ninety-three-year-old Faustino Navarro Espinoza is the country's leading expert on the Kkechuwa language. He has been a practicing ritual specialist since he was a child.

Haywarikuy is an offering to Pachamama and the apukuna.
Here it is set out in a special ceremony.

*Rag dolls made from ancient woven fabrics are
buried with the dead to show rebirth and afterlife.*

*Behind Machu Picchu, in the Ahobamba valley, are many caves filled with the remains
of Machukuna (ancient beings). These include enormous skulls and bones.*

The pure energy of Machu Picchu attracts seekers from all over the world who come to meditate and renew themselves.

Authors Carol and Rómulo marvel at the quality and varieties of sara, the sacred corn of the Inkakuna.

when he is ready, he dedicates his service to a special apu in a ritual initiation called *kkarpay.* The apu gives him his special "star" to instruct and guide him.

Within the alto misayoq hierarchy, there are three levels. As the alto misayoq attains more knowledge, he moves to a higher level. He begins as the *ayllu alto misayoq,* serving the community. He then becomes a *llakta alto misayoq,* where he serves the village, and finally becomes *suyu alto misayoq,* administering the entire region. He conducts divination and healing ceremonies in which a *kkowi* (guinea pig) may be used for diagnosis. He is able to communicate directly with the spirits of the mountains and he must follow instructions received. Misuse of power for his personal gain will cause him to lose everything he has attained.

Visit to Alto Misayoq

A visit to an alto misayoq in the suburbs of Qosqo is different from the ceremonies in the countryside. Local Quechua in need of healing patiently line up outside the modest home of a recommended alto misayoq. At a specific time, they are shown into a small, bare room lined with wooden benches.

The alto misayoq enters, greets the people in Kkechuwa and Spanish and sits next to a table on the far side of the room. The faces of the visitors clearly show they have come for help and not out of curiosity.

An assistant lights incense, and smoke soon fills the room. The lights go off and the room is plunged into complete darkness. People immediately begin to pray aloud, asking for protection from their saints, Jesus, Mary, and their sacred mountain apukuna. Christianity and Andean traditions interweave. The tension mounts.

Suddenly, there is a bang and the loud scraping sound of fluttering wings. A draft of air rushes through the room and a large bird or even condor appears to be in the darkness of the room. The shaman's ability to leave his physical body has been universally represented in art forms by the condor because it dwells in both worlds of Hanakpacha and Kaypacha, and acts as an intermediary from God, bringing messages through the apukuna, to the people. He is called *apuche, apukondor.*

The Kkorikenki is a mythological bird of colors from the Amazon. It is said to be "the one who has all the knowledge," and talks to the Andean people through intermediaries. Although it has the name of a hummingbird, it is not regarded as one. The mythology of Kkorikenki is similar to that of the Quetzal bird found in Central America. Ancient Mayan chiefs used the brilliantly colored Quetzal feathers as a symbol of power, gained from the wisdom of the bird.

A high-pitched voice or strange-sounding speech comes from the direction of the alto misayoq and identifies itself as a well-known apu. The apu may be male or female. It invites the visitors to ask questions. Participants quietly pray for protection while waiting their turn. Each person's problem is discussed and a solution offered. At times they are asked to stand up in the darkened room to receive special healing, and a spark or flash may be seen coming from their direction. The presence of many beings is felt. When everyone has had a turn, the voice of the first apu bids farewell and takes its leave as further activity and scraping sounds are heard. Another apu identifies its presence.

A visit to an alto misayoq resembles a trance-channelling session in the Western world. A medium is present, spirit speaks, questions are asked and answered. In the Andean setting, the session is dramatic, with darkness and incense adding tension to the atmosphere. As it comes to an end, the lights go on and people quietly leave. Payment is voluntary, small donations are accepted and no one in need is turned away.

Kurak akulleq, distinguished chewer of leaves, is the highest level of healer or master in the Andean priesthood. He has spent his lifetime studying in preparation for this position. The initiate has to have first completed the highest level of alto misayoq. When he is chosen as a successor to a Master, he then must submit to a rigorous initiation.

Andean Initiation

Initiation takes place in the glaciers of the highest Andean mountain peaks and nevadas where the energy of the earth is concentrated. Initiates go alone, and in solitude learn to see, hear and receive true wisdom and power from the Andean Gods.

Two of the most revered mountains are Awsankate near Qosqo and Salkkantay south of Machu Picchu where the apukuna of these mountains are regarded as the most powerful. Initiates also travel to the snow peaks of Qoyllur Rit'i.

The Andean gods order the initiate to undergo a test of life and death. To prepare himself, he must abstain from sexual activity and fast for a period of time, chewing only coca leaves. If the Gods have not chosen him, the lightning bolts in the mountain peaks will kill him. It is said that many initiates are called, but few survive this ordeal.

The novice waits for the right moment to receive his initiation. Three bolts of lightning strike him. The first bolt hits him and he is destroyed and broken into pieces. The second bolt puts him together again. The third gives him back his life and with it special gifts of power received from God.

There may be some scientific basis for this aspect of the tradition. Three separate strokes for a bolt of lightning have been identified: the leader stroke, the pilot stroke, and the return stroke.

Lightning begins as a relatively weak and slow leader stroke from a cloud. The tip is luminous and may travel in strokes and forks toward earth. Often, as the leader approaches the ground, a pilot stroke rises from the ground to meet it. This is followed by a much more powerful and rapid return stroke from the ground to the cloud. The physics of lightning may explain the appreciation by the kurak akulleq of being struck three times, especially if the mediator's sensibility has been heightened by his state of altered consciousness.

Arnold van Gennep in his well known *Rites of Passage*, identifies three dynamics of human transformation and describes the three phases of the journey of initiation: separation or severance, threshold or transition, and incorporation or return.

The initiation of the kurak akullek follows van Gennep's definitions exactly. During the severence phase, the alto misayoq prepares for the ordeal that he is about to face. He leaves behind his family and social world and sets off alone to the high glacier peaks to undergo his initiation. He has abstained from sexual activity and fasted for a period of time. His physical and mental bodies are well-prepared. For days he chews only coca leaves, placing himself into an altered state of consciousness. Alone and in silence, the initiate renews his vision.

The threshold is a time when the limits of the self are recognized, and a territory is entered where the boundaries of the self are tested and broken. The alto misayoq must survive the onslaught of freezing, unpredictable weather conditions, with no food or shelter. Some initiates are said to go into the snow without clothing. The alto misayoq is tested again and again by the wind, the rain, and the snow. By being alone he learns to see, feel, and hear anew. He receives awareness of the way of the Andean gods. His ultimate test arrives when he is struck three times by a bolt of lightning and survives.

Incorporation means the initiate returns to society in a new way, with a new body and a new life. As kurak akullek he has reached the highest levels of mastery. He possesses special healing and psychic powers and the ability to interpret dreams. He may bear some kind of physical defect from the strikes of the lightning.

It is, however, difficult to meet with the great initiated masters, whom we refer to as kurak akulleq. They do not desire to become famous or involved in the commercialization of spiritualism that is popular with tourism in Peru today.

Many alto misayoq who have not reached the true mastery level of kurak akulleq endure the initiation ceremony, whereby they claim to fulfil its terms. They often participate in the popular pilgrimage of Qoyllur Rit'i and undergo their initiations in her snowy peaks. Joining others who had previously passed through the initiation, these initiated alto misayoq are now qualified to aid in the healing passages of life and death of the Quechua community.

Peruvian Healers

Westerners visiting Peru often seek out traditional healers or shamans, a term that is common in the West but not used by the people of the Andes.

Throughout the country are a multitude of healers, with styles and techniques as varied as the scenery. Some are authentic, others are not. Since pre-Inkan times medicinal and hallucinogenic plants have been known to the Andeans and used for healing, as well as to connect with the spiritual world.

The Kallawayakuna, famous healers throughout the Andes, come from the mountains north of Lake Titicaca on the Bolivian side. They work with thousands of plants from the altiplano and the jungle. Their descendents, the Kollakuna, were physicians to Inkan nobility and possessed healing abilities and knowledge of esoteric secrets that mostly are forgotten today.

Healers from northern Peru and other desert areas are referred to as curanderos. They use tobacco, alcohol, oils, herbs, and San Pedro cactus as medicine in their healing sessions. The hallucinogenic San Pedro has been used in ceremonies for thousands of years to assist participants in stepping out of their ordinary reality into extraordinary realms. Slices of the cactus are boiled in water for several hours and other plant ingredients are added. Some of the liquid is swallowed by the healer, his assistants, and the person to be healed.

Healers from the Amazon are called *ayawaskeros* and they work with the *ayawaska* or yage plant called banisteriopsis caapi, which in Kkechuwa translates as the "vine of the dead." This refers to the prepared hallucinogenic beverage as well as the main plant ingredient. The drug is a potent hallucinogen used to induce colorful visions, diagnose illness, and obtain knowledge. Heal-

These amulets and healing objects are used by the Kallawayos, healers from the Lake Titicaca region, in their practice.

ers also use tobacco as an adjunct to the powerful and visionary hallucinogenic plants.

In Inkan times, the willka tree was considered sacred and grew on the subtropical eastern slopes of the Andes. A hallucinogenic powder was made from its seeds and inhaled through a long tube. The recipient held it in his nostril while an assistant blew into the tube from the other end. Inkan priests used willka to induce visionary states during which they discovered the cause of illness and conversed with spirits and gods.

The late healer and ayawaskero Alejandro Jahuanchi conducts
a special ceremony at the P'isaq ruins.

The Urubamba River was known to the Inkakuna as the Willkamayu (sacred river). It is also called the Vilkanota. Wilka is still used by Amazonian tribes but is not currently employed by Quechua healers in the Qosqo and Machu Picchu areas.

Westerners are drawn to study with Peruvian healers who invite them to participate in all-night ceremonies held in exotic locations away from city limits. These ceremonies usually are attended by locals who come for healing purposes. Most genuine healers have undergone many years of study and personal initiations, where they received specific psychic powers and healing gifts.

Initiation ceremonies in the jungle or desert regions of Peru are generally different from those held in the Andes. In the former areas, the healer, curandero or shaman, after preparation and fasting for purification, generally drinks a liquid made from various plants. He thus enters into an altered state of consciousness where he leaves his everyday world and enters into an unstructured, chaotic realm that is hidden from the observers and participants. Hallucinogens transform messages in the unconscious into revelations for the conscious mind.

Through trance journeys into the cosmos the healer learns to live in both worlds, material and spiritual. He seeks knowledge and power for himself and for others during journeys described as "soul flight."

During these journeys, the healer is able to see and converse with invisible beings, supernatural elements, and animals that dwell in non-human realities. Some may be helpful, others are malevolent.

When attacked by powerful elements as ancient spirit ancestors or animals such as the puma and other ferocious beings, the healer is said to acknowledge the presence of negative forces, meet them head on and surrender to their power. He thus overcomes his fear of death.

The healer communes with animals that become his allies. He receives their energy, takes on their powerful attributes, and learns things that are out of reach of ordinary human consciousness. He is able to return from the "dark place" and serve as a medicine man. Negative aspects are transformed into knowledge, and knowledge becomes wisdom which can be used by the healer for the benefit of the community.

Regular healing sessions are held, and healers explain that sick people are those who linger in a place surrounded by negative or dark forces.

Healers and medicine men in the Qosqo and Machu Picchu areas of the Andes are known as pakkokuna. The specific term used for ritual specialists are pampa misayoq and alto misayoq. Hallucinogenic plants are not generally used in the Andes and coca leaves are the most important medicine.

Healing Ceremonies

Each healer practices in a unique style with methods shaped by his own experiences and cultural beliefs.

The time is specifically chosen for ceremonies which may continue for hours through the night. Healers like to work during a full moon when the energy is very high.

As the ritual begins, the medicine man meticulously lays out a ceremonial cloth called a *lliklla* on which is placed his personal collection of sacred power objects. Participants sit in a circle close to the earth, Pachamama, and prayers are offered to the ancient spirits and all connected beings that dwell inside and outside of Her.

The healer calls on the four directions, symbolizing the universe, or circle of life and knowledge. Each direction is represented by different elements, including the three animal archetypes; *mach'akkway* (the serpent); the condor or puma; sacred plants; seeds; minerals; the four elements (earth, fire, water and air); or the body, mind, and spirit. In all ceremonies, these elements are interrelated and interconnected.

In the Andes, medicine men turn to the surrounding apukuna asking for permission to proceed and for guidance and protection for the ceremony. They call on the assistance of invisible beings from the three Andean worlds: Hanakpacha, Kaypacha, and Ukhupacha.

Healers work with groups or individuals to transform negative energies so the true self can arise. No specific directives are given and each participant perceives a personal experience and takes from it his own conclusion.

The melodious voice of the healer's singing fills the night air, while offerings are made to the sounds of drums and rattles. Coca leaves, tobacco or medicinal plant infusions are injested, and the rhythmic beat of the drum induces altered states of consciousness. Chanting moves the singer and participants away from their habitual roles of perception and unites the healer with the beings around him.

Songs comprise a variety of melodies and ancient words, or the language of animals, plants, spirit, or ancestors. High energy bonds the group; messages and visions are received.

During the ceremony participants may see supernatural beings, encounter the puma, fly on the wings of a condor, or embrace the wisdom of the serpent. Much depends on the scene that is created by the medicine man. Throughout the ritual, the healer and his assistants work on balancing energies, controlling the beings of the supernatural world, and assisting people who have come to be healed.

8

Shrines; Sacred Sites; Mystery Schools

The Quechua pray to spirits in the mountains, caves, rocks, springs, and rivers; to the Sun Inti, the Moon Killa, to stars, and all elements of Pachamama. They honor and respect sacred sites in the mountains and valleys of the Andes, and believe that by surrendering to the higher forces their spiritual lives will be enriched and their health and well-being assured.

The powers found in nature and the power of prayers are important to everyday life. The seasons and rituals connected with them gives the people a sense of their place in the scheme of things. The Quechua experience the harmony between the connected inner and outer worlds.

Wakakuna

A *waka* is a shrine or altar and refers to any sacred object or location. It may be a burial place in the country, a mountain with a cave, an unusual rock or something as simple as a pebble, for which people have a special respect.

Wakakuna, like the apukuna, can be personal, local, regional, or national. As people approach the wakakuna they may feel the energies.

Andeans connect with the divine energies through these wakakuna, and these energies help and guide them.

A Story: The Sacred Temple in the Jungle

"When I was learning about orchids I traveled to the jungle, where I met with a man who offered to show me a special variety. I followed him into the dense vegetation and after some time, to my surprise, we came upon a huge stone, an unusual sight in the flat Amazonian terrain.

"The jungle man respectfully walked up to the stone and placed his forehead against it. He stayed in this position for the longest time, apparently tuning into the stone. He seemed to be in a deep sleep. I quietly watched and waited.

"He woke up and told me he had found the place where this special orchid grew. He said, 'I went into the rock and I traveled to many beautiful areas, and I now can recognize where to find the right orchids.'

"I asked him what he was talking about. He answered, 'Aurelio, this is my special temple, my waka. I come here whenever I need to know something and to see whatever I need to see.'

"This man of the jungle who loved the beauty of orchids led me to the exact location where I found the orchid I was seeking."

—Aurelio Aguirre

Apachita

Throughout Peru today, one sees little mounds of pebbles or sticks. They often are found at the top of mountain passes and are called *apachita*. Travellers may also feel the energy shift as they approach the apachita and place a pebble on the mound as an offering. They give thanks to the apukuna and Pachakámak, the Creator God who assists them. Eyes may be raised to the sky and lowered to the earth. An eyelash may be pulled out and blown toward the sky as an offering.

*This waka (holy shrine) at
Machu Picchu is a temple to Apu Putukusi
in the background.*

A traveller who has carried a pebble a long way may place it on an apachita at the top of a mountain pass. He symbolically leaves his burdens behind with that pebble and is able to go on his way free of his problems. The Quechua usually offer the deities whole or chewed coca leaves, which are prized by them both. Besides the pebbles, they may also add a stick or fistful of earth to the mound at the side of the path.

Visitors hiking the Inka trail, Salkkantay, or any high mountain pass will see these apachitakuna.

Wak'arumi

Rocks always have been revered and considered sacred, and all the famous ruins are built on and around unusual rock formations. Andean people understand that rocks have special energy and are there for more than their physical beauty.

To the Quechua, the *wak'arumi* are ancient sacred rock tombs. The forces in those stones have the potential to be dangerous and are therefore

respected. If a man wants to build a house and needs to move a wak'arumi, he must first make an offering to receive permission from the ancestral spirits inhabiting the rocks. If he does not, the stones may become angry and cause the people in the house to get sick.

Cequekuna and Sacred Sites

In Qosqo, anthropologists and archaeologists have described the *cequekuna* as forty-one invisible energy lines originating at the Kkorikancha Temple. They radiate out of the city in four directions, with a variety of sacred shrines and sites situated along the lines. These are the waka-

Many sacred rocks are shapes of sacred apukuna in Machu Pichu.

kuna built on vortices that accept incoming energy and radiate energy out from one waka to another, some great distances apart.

It is known that in Inkan times observations of the sun were made from one waka to another. The Inkakuna had an advanced system of astronomy and a unique ability to read annual cycles of the sun. The Inka calendar was essential to the agricultural cycles.

It is said that all sacred sites are connected with others throughout the planet by invisible pathways of energy called ley lines, which are the same as the cequekuna that originate in Qosqo. Ancient cities and temples throughout the world are built on lines and vortices of energy extending over hundreds and thousands of miles.

Ley lines are straight, but may undulate gently over distances. They exist above and below the earth and vary in width and intensity of energy.

The life force of the earth which radiates from her ley network is intimately bound up with the life force of the sun. There is a close connection between Inti, the Sun, the lay network of the earth, and the health or life force of all the natural realms that inhabit Pachamama.

In the Andes, the ancient people paid attention to the *cequekuna* (ley network) by placing their sacred wakakuna in such locations for the physical and spiritual well-being of their health as well as the enhancement of their crops.

The ancient Andeans knew that the earth and solar system were part of a far greater galactic and cosmic system in which there were many sensitive energy relationships crucial to the existence and growth pattern of Mother Earth. They dedicated temples to the sun and carved stone monuments that are referred to in modern times as Intiwatana, hitching post to the sun.

Structures were built so that different patterns of light would form within, according to the solstices and other periods of rising and setting of the sun and moon. Today, instruments can measure the energy inside ancient temples of stone where profound shifts of energy can be felt. Scientists with sonar equipment have detected different vibrations within the stones at different times of the day and year. At certain equinoxes, specific ultrasonic sounds are emitted. In some circular structures Geiger counters have registered unusually high radioactive output given off by the stones, and infrared photographic equipment has shown rays of light beaming up from them.

Builders of Stone Temples

In the Andes, there are further topics being addressed by both the Quechua people and those who come to Peru to experience her special energy and anticipate the enrichment of their spiritual journey and enhancement of the knowledge they seek.

We acknowledge and respect the Inka civilization and its place in humanity and history, but there are questions whose answers take us further back in time than the written word or ceramic fragments, questions that have not been answered adequately by the scientific community.

There were many civilizations in Peru prior to the Inkakuna. Archaeologists and scientists are still trying to figure out how the temples were constructed without the invention of the wheel or steel implements.

Historians date the beginning of the Inka empire to the twelfth century. The Inka emperor Pachakútekk is credited with orchestrating the building of great stone temples and rebuilding Qosqo 300 years later. Ceramics found at Machu Picchu date back to that period and it is known that builders came to the area from all parts of Tawantinsuyu.

However, claims by the scientific community that the Inkakuna built all the magnificent temples in the Andes in the fifteenth century and moved blocks of stone weighing up to 200 tons from quarries miles away, remain open to doubt.

It has been suggested that parts of the incredible cities of stone were constructed thousands of years before the Inkakuna, when there existed a more sophisticated civilization with command of technologies we do not understand and cannot reproduce.

Sacred stones in Machu Picchu.

Two American scientists, John Anthony West, an independent Egyptologist, and Dr. Robert Schoch, associate professor of science in geology and geophysics at Boston University, have spent many years investigating the great Sphinx in Egypt. They have suggested the Sphinx was carved 10,000 years ago, before Egypt became a desert, making it thousands of years older than previously thought. Their research showed the Sphinx probably had a different head that became eroded by heavy rains. American geologists have agreed that the evidence presented by these scientists is convincing, and the new facts mean that much of history needs to be rewritten.

Egyptologists still claim the Sphinx was built by the Pharoah Chefron 4,500 years ago, and the head is said to resemble his face. They based their facts on information taken from hieroglyphics dated 5,000 years ago.

The new evidence of West and Schoch indicates that Chefron probably remodeled the Sphinx. This contradicts the findings of Egyptologists who have attacked these findings as an "American hallucination." There are no records of civilizations 10,000 years back.

In Peru, there were no written records to be deciphered. The recently-discovered treasures of Sipan, from the Moche period in Peru, date back 2,000 years. Ancient and sophisticated ceramics, exquisite weavings, high-quality gold and silver objects and intricate bead work have been excavated from many sites and are known to be thousands of years old.

As yet there is no scientific proof, as in the case of the Sphinx, but it appears possible that the original, huge stone temples in Peru were built thousands of years before the twelfth century when the Inkakuna ruled.

When the Spanish arrived in Peru 460 years ago, they destroyed rooms filled with historical information stored on khipukuna, a complicated system of tied knots, which could only be read by trained Inka readers. Perhaps the khipukuna told the history of the ancient builders. West and Schoch also were intrigued by the method used by these ancient cultures to move massive blocks of stone, weighing up to 200 tons, in the construction of the Sphinx. Modern engineers, utilizing the latest high-tech machinery, acknowledge having trouble moving such gigantic blocks of stone.

Over the years, it has been suggested that ancient civilizations utilized sound vibrations to move gigantic blocks of stone. The Bible, esoteric texts, and spiritual teachings have portrayed ancient man as having had the ability to tumble down walls or move objects utilizing the vibration of sound.

American scientists recently have demonstrated that sound can affect matter and lift objects, confirming that ancient cultures could have possessed technologies based on vibration of sound. These scientists now recognize the possibility that ancient builders understood acoustic principles and incorporated them into their architecture. In attempting to answer the question of whether sound could levitate heavy objects, scientists at the Space Age Research facility outside Chicago refer to acoustic levitation as a "non-magical way of floating an object in mid-air using very loud sound."

They say that "having one or two sound sources and a reflector, the sound bounces off the reflector, and, on its way back down, the two sound fields pass through each other. In that region where there is interference of the two sound fields there are little wells where you can actually levitate small objects the size of a pea." Today's science can levitate a small rock in this way.

This now provides the scientific community a clue as to how ancient people, such as those who built the Sphinx and stone temples throughout the world, could have raised and fitted together massive stones.

Recent scientific findings in Egypt show that we are descendents of an unknown, early civilization capable of incredible technological feats. The same could also apply to the Andeans. It is possible that thousands of years ago ancient builders of Peruvian temples, such as those in Qosqo, and sections of Machu Picchu, Ollantaytampu, Saksaywaman and others, were in command of a technology that utilized vibration of sound. These temples, with stones weighing up to 200 tons, could have been raised by sound vibrations and fitted together with precision.

Like the Egyptologists, experts on Peruvian archaeology have yet to acknowlege the possibility of ancient builders in Peru who used advanced technological abilities. Ideas such as these are regarded as revolutionary and are discounted and ridiculed by the scientific community.

As the mysteries of Peru are unveiled and evidence becomes more convincing, these ideas will become more acceptable by researchers in Peru. The stone temples in Peru stand as testimony to the existence of technologically advanced cultures.

People are being drawn from all over the world to the sacred sites of Peru, where the energies are regarded as the purest. Books and ancient texts refer to amazing cities of gold hidden in the Amazon Jungle or buried under Lake Titicaca.

In the Andes there is talk of hidden pyramid chambers and secret groups, and it is common to hear esoteric discussions taking place in meetings among Quechua professionals and businessmen of Qosqo. Visitors hear about mystery schools reportedly situated in the heart of the Sacred Valley of the Inka and ask to be taken there.

A sacred sun dial in Machu Picchu called
Intiwatana, "hitching post to the Sun."

Andean Beings of Light

In the Andes, students in esoteric schools of thought meet. It is said that millions of years before the civilization of the first Andeans, highly evolved spiritual beings conveyed electro-magnetic energy from the universe to feed earth civilizations with spiritual energy.

Earth was said to be a space station where space ships from the cosmos could land and set off again. Huge monuments and temples of stone were built on special vortices of energy. Highly evolved souls were incarnated in these holy places and guarded the wisdom throughout the ages. Masters and priests of the sun travelled between the worlds; civilizations came and went.

Since ancient times, the Sacred Valley of the Inka was known as the center of the four corners of the world. At the very early stages of the cult of the Inka, women were looked upon as guardians of secret knowledge, and priestesses were instructed in esoteric wisdom that came from the stars.

Andean *ñustakuna* (princesses to the sun) were positioned to radiate the feminine energy out to the planet. (The Chinese word "yin" now is

A condor, messenger from the Gods, flies by the most sacred peak of Salkkantay, where ritual specialists go for their ultimate initiations.

used universally to describe feminine energy. By contrast, the Himalayas were said to radiate a masculine energy, "yang.")

Golden discs representing the sun were reminders of their god-like origins. They used a language of symbols and served in temples of the sun at Titicaca, Kkorikancha in Qosqo, Machu Picchu and other cities hidden deep in the Andes. Energy paths connected temples of the sun to sacred sites of other ancient civilizations, such as the Mayan and those from Tibet and Egypt. Beings were able to travel from their invisible world into the visible world as we know it today.

It is said that all these civilizations were in constant contact and communication with the sun, moon, and all elements of the earth. The temples were connected to the seven planets and the seven main chakras, energy centers of the human body.

Over the millennia, mankind settled into the bosom of Mother Earth, forgetting his connection to other planets, forgetting ancient secrets and, eventually, becoming third dimensional beings.

Andean masters remind us that we are part of the universe and are connected to all things. The mysteries of the universe are found within us, but through the millennia, we have forgotten who we are, where we came from, and where we are going.

Enlightened masters of cosmology say that we have only to remember. We are multi-dimensional beings, functioning in many levels of consciousness and dimensions simultaneously. At all times we are able to tap into different levels of information. Some of the information we receive may come from the lower psychic, or astral, realms, which may be deceptive, cause confusion, and block our progress toward remembering who we are. We are warned that any information, regardless of the source, that draws humanity's attention to negative situations on earth, inciting fear or worry, is not from the realms we choose to receive information.

Spiritual seekers in Peru aspire to receive wisdom that comes from illumined Beings of Truth, those masters in the spiritual hierarchy that are from the highest dimensions.

The Peruvian Creator Gods Wirakkocha, or Teksiwirakkocha, and Pachakámak come from the highest dimension of Hanakpacha in Andean cosmology. Hanakpacha includes ascended masters such as Jesus or Buddha who come from a place of love.

Spiritual seekers also seek information coming from their own God Presence, which is known as the I AM, who is one with the all-encompassing presence of God.

Mystery Schools

Mystery schools exist on the earth plane and on different dimensional levels within this existence. Beings of a mystery school exist in a vibratory rate that may be too high for most people's perceptive abilities. One may be standing in the spot of the most sacred mystery school and not know it is there.

People who are drawn to mystery schools in Peru are those who have gone within. It is said that masters and priestesses still guard mysteries in the Andes and Amazon. If they wish to invite certain people to a secret place or gathering and the person is ready, he or she will be led to it. Those of like mind and similar vibrational frequencies gather together to learn. Visitors often are drawn to certain areas in the Andes. One need only sit quietly in a place that feels special or comfortable. An exchange of energy takes place and each person receives the energy that he or she needs.

We live in third-dimensional bodies. While meditating, sleeping, or walking in the Andes, the higher self may choose to go to a mystery school to receive lessons. Souls are set free to fly that journey while their third-dimensional bodies are engaged. The mystery school also can be described as a place where souls come to look for God.

> A truer vision one seeks is often held within
> the confines of the soul. Only there can true
> expansion manifest into enlightenment.
> The Schools of Mystery, the Mystery Schools,
> lie outside the conscious realm of ones knowing
> heart—yet reside within the secret most part
> of self that is truly the most "mysterious" and
> seemingly unattainable.
> If you would visit the Mystery School, you
> should be willing to unfold that secret most
> part and embark upon a journey of self-knowledge.
> Not many have the strength, the gift of love-
> of-life to journey thus. If you would seek to
> know who truly you are, tis not a mystery at
> all. The greatest truth is Who-You-Are.
> You are God, Loved and anointed by Him to
> journey and to come home.
> Seek this truth and all Mystery ceases to
> exist.
>
> —Judy Sibrian with "Ezekiel"

Generally the traditional Quechua campesinos have little conversation about cosmological concepts or hidden mystery schools. They live their days connected to Pachamama, breathing with Her as one breath, moving in rhythm to Her pulsating heartbeat, kissing her moist soil, sharing Her secrets with Her other children, the birds, animals, cornstalks, dewdrops and spirits flowing inside of all things. The Quechua live their connected lives in the present moment.

9

▶ Water: Power of the Andes ◀

Water symbolizes the eternity of life for the Andean people. Where there is water, there is life. Water always has been venerated in the Andes, and myths concerning water abound in the explanation of the origins of life and the world.

The Creator God Teksiwirakkocha identifies himself as coming from the sea. Lake Titicaca was represented as the sea, where life originated. It is believed that the llama and alpaka came from the sea together with the humans.

Bodies of water still play a definite role in the Andean cosmovision. Sources of water are in themselves sacred, and springs are regarded as entrances to the inner earth, Ukhupacha. It is believed that waters coming from sacred mountains take on the powers of the earthly source and the waters are used in ritual ceremonies at sacred sites.

Sacred waters running from the fountains at Tampumachay outside of Qosqo and the Island of the Sun at Lake Titicaca, as well as at other ancient sites, are said to be healing. At these sites three fountains represent the three Andean worlds of Hanakpacha, Kaypacha, and Ukhupacha.

In Andean spirituality, the main energy centers of the body are *chaki* (soul of the foot), *qosqo* (navel), *sonqo* (heart), and *ñosqo* (area above the forehead). Water acts as a transformative agent, and by placing sacred waters on these areas, the energy centers of the body are opened. Ancient, forgotten memories may come to the surface, and contemplation of these memories assists people in letting go of personal aspects that no longer

The sacred water fountains at Tampumachay represent the three worlds of Andean cosmology.

serve them. They may, therefore, move on to the next step in life. Waters from the sacred springs act as a gateway into the innerworld of humans.

Immersion in water is an ancient healing practice in the Andes. All the ancient ruins were built with a series of ceremonial baths, and mineral waters and hot springs are found throughout the Andean areas of Qosqo and Machu Picchu. The Quechua believe the power of mineral waters or hot springs cleanses and purifies the body and soul. They feel Pachamama's loving embrace when the hot mineral water surrounds their human bodies.

Regarded as a fertilizing agent of the Andean mountain gods, water is the life-generating force throughout the universe. Subterranean streams said to communicate with each other exemplify the all-embracing influence of Pachamama.

The ancient canals that are found in the valley areas of Peru are important for the next season's productions and are still used by the campesinos today.

Agriculturists have maintained water-worshipping rituals. In August, Quechua farmers from the areas of Pisaq, Calca, Urubamba, and Ollantaytampu summon ritual specialists for dedications to water. They send a special offering to Pachamama to ensure the rains come to fertilize the earth and for seeds to sprout and grow quickly so they will be protected from the enemy: *chijchi* (hail).

In October the Quechua celebrate Uma Raymic, the festival of water, to ensure the rains continue to water the first crops that are planted.

Mayu

Mayu (river) or *ch'aska mayu* (river of stars), is the Quechua name for the Milky Way, which is known as the "river in the skies." The Quechua believe the waters of the earth are in constant contact with the water that circulates in the skies.

The mayu is equated with the Willkamayu, which is commonly known as the Urubamba River. It is believed that the waters of the Willkamayu are carried from earth into the sky and then into the cosmic sea which encircles the earth. The waters pass underground from the west and rise again in the east. As the Milky Way moves slowly through the sky above the earth, it deposits water throughout the skies. The water returns to the earth as rain and flows into the rivers, which in turn lead back to the sacred Willkamayu River.

The Power of the Andes: Rómulo's Story

 "Whenever possible, during my years of study at the University in Qosqo, I would catch the local train back to our family farm near Machu Picchu, where I would help my family work on the land. One November, about sixteen years ago, I arrived at the house and found no one at home. My mother and sister had left early with a worker to check on our livestock grazing in the *puna* called Mesada at an altitude of 14,500 feet. It was my parents' property and a day's walk away.

"I quickly changed my clothes, packed food and coca leaves and set off in the same direction, hoping to catch up with them. I walked through dense vegetation, sweating from the pace I kept, chewing coca leaves and drinking the icy waters from the rivers that came down from the snow peaks of the Nevada Sallkantay. After four hours' continuous walking I still had not reached my mother. When I paused to eat I saw a *lluth'u* (bird similar to a partridge) that lives in the *monte* (wild area) nearby. According to Quechua belief, seeing a lluth'u is an ominous sign. I became concerned about my mother and sister.

"One and a half hours later, I saw fresh footprints, and with great relief soon found them close to the river we had to cross before climbing the mountain. After exchanging greetings we crossed the river on stepping stones which led to a sandy island in the middle of the river. It was beautiful and peaceful and we decided to rest and relax in the sun.

"I suddenly noticed that the waters had risen above the stepping stones. To my horror, the river began to swirl around the island. Rocks, boulders, and logs crashed onto the rocks around us. We were stranded.

"My mother, who knew about the ancient ways of the Quechua people, began to put her practices into use. Grasping a k'intu of coca leaves, she called upon the apukuna to stop the fury of the river. She raised the k'intu three times, from the ground to the heaven in the direction of the sun. She called to the Sun God, and begged him to make sure the river would not harm us. She continued with her ritual for another few minutes. We joined in with our own k'intu of coca leaves. Upon ending the ritual, as is customary, we buried all the leaves of coca at our feet.

"Within moments the raging river became calm. We were able to cross over to the other side of the bank and continue on our journey. At dusk, a few hours later, we arrived at our destination. I kept thinking about the river and the fury it unleashed at us. Living in the Andes had taught us to respect the power of Nature. The lluth'u was a warning sign that something was about to happen. I thought about my mother, who had spent her life honoring all the forces that exist in the Andean world. What was the force that I had just witnessed? I marvelled at the power of my mother, who, in her belief, was able to placate such a fury.

"We attended to our livestock. Two days later we returned home from the puna. We saw that the river had completely returned to its usual pace."

10

Ritual and Ceremony;
Agriculture

Andean campesinos, without modern technology, have learned to farm in altitudes of over 12,000 feet, where they must work in bitterly cold weather, torrential rains and hail storms, and deal with the dangers of lightning and flash floods.

Paulo Delfino describes thirteen ecological zones in Peru. Five are in the Andean area and four of those are used for agriculture. The fifth zone incorporates the glaciers. The Quechua cultivate a wide range of crops suitable to their respective climates and ecological zones.

Hundreds of varieties of potatoes are grown in the Andes, and the campesinos can be seen cultivating the high *andenes* or *pata patakuna* (terraces) that have been there for centuries. The University of Qosqo seed bank has 160 native varieties of potatoes from which sixty hybrids have been produced. From those, unlimited variations of solanum tuberoses have been cultivated throughout the Andes.

In the inhospitable and seemingly barren puna, they cultivate a special variety of potato called *ch'uñu*, which is dried and can be stored for seven to ten months. They also grow high altitude grains such as *kkañiwa*.

In the temperate and subtropical valleys known as the *ceja de selva* (brow of the jungle), the Quechua grow bananas, coffee, beans, rumu or yuca, *palta* (avocado) and a variety of fruits and vegetables

Crops deplete Pachamama's energy and take nutrients from Her soil. The farmers practice agronomy, the science of crop rotation. In order to restore balance to the earth, they rotate crops of corn, wheat, and alfalfa and know which are best suited to follow others on the same piece of land.

All family activities are related to their agricultural needs and a day in the life of the Quechua is long and filled with hard work rendered by men, women, and children.

Ceremonies and Rituals Related to Agriculture

The Quechua are immersed in nature all of the time, and ceremonies and rituals acknowledge their interconnectedness with her. Ceremonies fit

into an annual cycle according to the agricultural season, and performing them guarantees their connectedness. All activities, prayers, offerings, songs, dances, and feasting help to keep Pachamama in balance and restore harmony on earth.

Each new agricultural activity is accompanied by traditional Quechua rituals and ceremonies to honor Pachamama. The agricultural cycle usually begins in August and continues throughout the rainy season. May and June signify harvest time, which is of the greatest importance to the campesinos because the efforts of the year's work culminate at this time. It is a dry season and many other activities such as housebuilding, outdoor

Isolated communities live at 14,000 feet in the puna, (high grassland), where herds of llama graze.

weaving, and lots of traditional festivities take place.

The Quechua also celebrate a variety of Catholic festivities to honor various saints. Certain Catholic prayers are offered, but the ceremonies tend to be distinctly Andean and attention is directed to honor the Pachamama and the sacred apukuna.

Suyunakuy

Suyunakuy is the way campesinos cultivate their fields. A date is set for a group of Quechua farmers to help a neighbor plow his fields for the planting of maize, potatoes, beans, wheat, and other crops in the practice of ayni. Promptly at dawn, the men gather with their

Terraces were used by the Inkakuna for a variety of crops sustained by an efficient irrigation system.

chakitakllakuna (foot plows) and *lampas* (long shovels) over their shoulders. The host greets his guests and offers them mugs of akkha. In good spirits they set off and climb up into the hills to the plot of ground to be worked on.

The owner of the land asks the men for a volunteer to take charge of the day's work, and he is called the *kkollana* (*capitán* or *majordomo* in Spanish). His assistant is the *kkaywa*. The kkollana takes the lead and the kkaywa works at the end, pushing and encouraging the men from behind. He checks on their work and notes their mistakes. Workers later may be ridiculed in front of members of the ayllu for their errors.

*In following their system of ayni, Quechua campesinos
help each other plant and harvest.*

Before beginning work they make hallpay (the ritual chewing of the coca leaves) and then, facing toward their apukuna, they offer the k'intus of coca leaves to the deities. The laborers, called *lamperos*, get into a straight line and, with their shovels, strike the ground together. When several men are plowing together, they move in unison, leaning on their tools, pushing and digging to the rhythm of their songs.

At midday the women bring them food and an abundance of akkha to drink. The day of work ends with chants and the singing of *waynukuna* (Andean songs). The men return to the home of the host, where he puts on his enormous *sillukuy*, a colorful poncho worn only on special occasions. They are joined by the women and children and the celebration begins.

They all drink akkha, there is music and dancing and everyone makes fun of the kkollana, teasing him about his day's work. They sing to him, insulting him in jest. Because of the akkha, things get to be very lively and boisterous. They eventually return to their own homes.

Sara Tarpuy

For centuries, a special ceremony has initiated the beginning of the season for sowing maize and other crops; this is called the *sara tarpuy* (the sowing of the maize). It connects the people with the Pachamama to ensure that She produces an abundance of crops.

A few days before the sara tarpuy, a simple ceremony takes place in which coca leaves are offered, incense is burned, and the women take care of the *muju akkllay* (the selection of the seeds to be planted). This is an important assignment and strict rules are followed.

The woman who chooses the seeds must have abstained from sexual activity for five days prior to selection, must be

Lima beans are part of crops in Quechua's subtropical and temperate climates.

in her fertile period and, therefore, must not be pregnant or menstruating. If these conditions do not prevail, the woman might interfere with the germination of the seeds and Mother Earth would be upset.

Maize seeds are chosen from the many varieties that exist. They may be *parakkay sara* (white maize), *kkello sara* (yellow maize), *ch'ekkche sara* (purple maize), *ch'ullpi sara* (maize for toasting), or one of countless others. Once chosen, the seeds are placed inside a ceramic bowl which then is placed under the care of a *kuhuru* (guardian spirit). This will remove any spell that may have been cast with evil intention.

The day of the sara tarpuy is very important. At dawn the workers congregate at the house of the owner, who is called *chahrachikuy* ("he who works the chahra"). They begin the day with hallpay and k'intukuna as during Suyunakuy, and the sowing of the maize begins. The men dig the ground but it is the feminine essence, the women, who must place the seeds in the Mother Earth.

Saramama

The Quechua must provide sufficient maize to last the year, so harvest time is important. They believe that all plants have a mother. They dedicate a variety of the rituals to the mother of the maize, Saramama.

The farmer selects the finest cob of maize, places it in a special container for this purpose and wraps it in a *lliblla* (a woman's shawl). This is the Saramama, a living being, a mother, who has grown to maturity inside the body of Pachamama. Soil, sun, wind, rain, and human beings are embedded in her very nature. She nourishes the people who tend her. She is connected to and dependent on all which sustains her.

Saramama is watched over for three days. Songs called *harawikuna* are dedicated to her. She then is examined for insects and worms and "asked" if she has sufficient strength to last the year. If she does not look good, she

Señora de Lizárraga grinds maize for soup
on an ancient Inka stone.

is burned and another is selected. Saramamakuna are also cornstalks dressed as women with skirts, shawls, and pins, or special stalks that have produced many cobs or have unusual shapes.

Miska

Harvest time calls for great joy and celebration among the Quechua people. Important ritual steps are taken to honor Pachamama. The harvest of the first crops is called *miska*.

Ch'allaskka is a special ritual for beginning the miska. When the first crops ripen, the head of the chahra hands over a jar of akkha to the oldest woman in the community, who raises it toward the setting sun and in a high voice calls on the apukuna and Pachamama to ask that the crops continue to grow well. In a circular motion she sprinkles the akkha in the direction of the apukuna.

T'inkaskka is the ritual whereby the head of the household receives another jug of akkha and, with permission of those present, walks into the cultivated area. He takes a fist full of earth, kisses it, and lifts his head toward the mountains while invoking the great apukuna. He thanks the sky for bringing the rain that moistened the soil. He thanks Pachamama for having made the seed germinate, for having nourished and ripened it. He sips some akkha and sprays the earth with it. He drinks the remainder of the akkha in the cup. Each one in turn repeats this action and drinks the akkha, because if the *t'inka* is not honored by each man, a fine must be paid.

The harvest of the first crop calls for a community celebration with a special feast after the ritual of ch'allaskka and t'inkaskka at sunset, to show appreciation to Pachamama.

Banquet of the Miska

The finest Andean food is served at the miska feast. There is hank'a, kkowi, *torrejas de maíz* (corn pancake), rice in a yellow sauce, cabbage cooked with potato, and a stir-fry of green beans, onions and cheese, red pepper chile sauce, and stewed beef. Ample akkha is served to wash it all down.

The chief chef fills a plate with each item from the menu and the head of the house takes the plate out to the cultivated fields. Three helpers accompany him, one taking the mug of akkha, the other the k'intu

The Quechua are immersed in nature, and their lives reflect this interconnectedness with her.

of coca and the third a glass of alcohol. They stand around a small hole that was previously dug fifty centimeters deep. The one with the akkha takes a fistful of the earth, which he then kisses three times. They spill the akkha into the hole, tip in the plate of food, pour the alcohol over it and place a k'intu of coca leaves on top. They cover it all with the earth and return to the feast. By doing this, the Pachamama will receive the first serving of all the food. The Quechua make a toast to a good year and enjoy the abundant feast.

Robinson Jeffers, who lived on the Big Sur Coast in California, wrote in 1934 that humankind, with its intellectual systems and grand designs, had become "a little too abstract and a little too wise." He said: "It is time for us to kiss the earth again." The Quechua people have never stopped kissing the earth and loving Pachamama.

Kkowi (guinea pigs) are a popular food for the Quechua.
The animals are also used for healing.

Kkowi

In almost every Quechua home in the countryside, and in many homes in the city of Qosqo, an area is set aside for the raising of kkowi (guinea pig), known in Spanish as *cuy.* These animals are clean and quiet and they come out of their dark corners to retrieve scraps of food and weeds their owners feed them. On special occasions an older male kkowi is chosen and swiftly killed, skinned, washed, stuffed with herbs, placed on a long stick and roasted in an oven or open fire. Kkowi serves as a main course for all festivities and is regarded as a special treat for families and guests.

Roast kkowi is similar in taste to poultry and is wonderful when cooked fresh. To prepare it, the cook skillfully grabs two or three male or non-reproducing female guinea pigs about ten months to one year old and places them in a closed basket. She or he asks permission from the dieties to kill the animals and offers a prayer for those that remain, requesting they continue to reproduce abundantly in the future.

The chef swiftly kills them by snapping their necks and places them in boiling water to enable them to be skinned easily. The entrails are removed and the kkowi is washed well.

He or she then grinds together cumin, pepper, salt, a few varieties of crushed garlic cloves and leaves of the herb *wakatay*, which grows in the Andes. Wakatay is an important ingredient that enhances the taste of the kkowi and is said to prevent digestive problems after eating the meat. After mixing the ingredients together with a cup of vegetable oil, the kkowi is placed in a bowl, basted with this marinade, and left in the sun for two hours.

The cook then roasts the kkowi in an open dish inside an oven until tender, or if there is an open fire, skewers the kkowi onto long sticks and places on hot wood embers, turning often until cooked. Kkowikuna cooked on an open fire taste delicious, especially when served with *uchukuta*, a hot, spicy sauce, or nuts, cilantro, parsley, toasted maize, and hot peppers.

Immediately after the meal, the Quechua chase it down with a tot of cañazo or good alcohol. Kkowi are high in protein and cholesterol. The alcohol counteracts the effect of digestion problems that one may experience after eating this rich meat.

*A variety of landscapes offers the Quechua
many agricultural opportunities.*

Tákke

Tákke is a *chokkllo* (corn cob) with tassels that have been divided into two or more parts during the formation and growing of the plant. The chokkllo that grow from it are called children. The biggest corn is called the Mother. Joined together they are called tákke.

When a family's first-born is a girl, this is considered a tákke for the home, and is a promise of abundance and prosperity.

Sara Huñuy

At harvest time a ritual is made for the safe transfer of the crops to a spacious place of storage. This ritual is called *sara buñuy*. A plant that has produced two or more chokkllokuna is selected without separating the chokkllokuna from the stalk. This stalk is decorated and the leaves are folded down and braided to the bottom, ending with a cross which may be blessed by the head of the chahra. One of the sons of the farmer carries the cross on his back and accompanies the harvest to its storage place.

Hail, Snow, Lightning

Chijchi (hail), rit'i (snow), k'akya (lightning) are referred to as three terrible beings. They are, in fact, three brothers whose deeds are malicious, spiteful and capable of destroying the crops. The pakkokuna are called in to make offerings to these deities in order to appease them.

A Story

 A man was walking in the Andes near Awsankate. At twilight he was caught in a sudden storm. He was surprised to find himself outside a well-constructed residence. He knocked on the door; an old woman opened it and he asked her if she would be so kind as to put him up for the night. She agreed to do this, but on the condition that at the first ray of dawn he would leave the house without making any noise. She told him she had three sons who were very ill-mannered. Her sons were called Chijchi, Rit'i, and K'akya, the last being the most bad-tempered of the three.

The old woman found her visitor a corner to sleep in, and as he climbed into his space he heard the loud noise of hail falling outside. The mother quickly covered the visitor with a *raki* (an earthenware tub used to ferment the akkha). She warned the man that her son was entering and he was not to make a sound. He even had to breathe as little as possible.

119

Frightened, the man followed the instructions of his hostess and he lay quietly beneath the tub. However, he became curious and lightly lifted the tub. He was able to see that in the room there stood a large hailstone in the shape of a man.

A short while later, the second son Rit'i banged at the door. He had brought some vicuñas loaded with products he had taken from the fields of the farms he had destroyed with snow. The visitor peeped again and saw a large snow man in the room.

Suddenly there was a loud crack and clap of thunder. Once again the mother opened the door, this time for her youngest son. Remembering the warning the old woman had given him, the traveler did not dare try to lift up the raki. He was able to see through the crack between the raki and the ground. The woman closed the door for the last time. An intense, brilliant flash of lightning filled the room.

At the first ray of dawn, following the instructions of the mother, the man climbed out of his hiding place without making a sound. As he crept away from the corner, he saw the raki change into a rock. He hurriedly opened the door and stepped outside. He headed down the path and, feeling relieved, he looked back. The house he had slept in was no longer there, but had changed into an enormous cave.

—Translated from a Spanish story
By Juan Nuñez del Prado

Many Andean legends have supernatural themes that emphasize nature's dangerous potential, and the elements are considered deities to be respected. Ancient temples were constructed and dedicated to the natural elements. Worship of God and nature was important, and it was never done from the confines of church-like structures. Temples built to worship nature were always open.

Campesinos farming in the high altitudes of the Andes frequently must contend with storms of snow, hail, and ice.

*According to Quechua philosophy, the mountain deities are
a protective force against the elements.*

The Quechua believe the apukuna, mountain dieties, guard herds of
animals on their slopes. Their most notable pet is the *ccoa*, a malevolent
cat-like animal with phosphorescent eyes who brings lightning and hail,
and who usually is seen with hail running out of his ears and eyes.

The ccoa is an active, angry spirit and greatly feared. The intimation
of this song is the singer believing the cat-like bull to be a form of the
ccoa who caused the storm and is calling out to the apu. The bull's owner
appears as a horseman to carry him to a place of safety.

The Ill Wind and Other Evil Influences; Death

Machu wayra refers to an intangible negative force or energy, an "ill wind." The Quechua describe this as a sudden, unpleasant sensation that may be perceived alone or in the presence of others. Sometimes it is a momentary feeling that passes; sometimes the victim may be physically affected and steps must be taken to rid him of the "ill wind."

The force is believed to have originated from the fetus of a woman who aborted either intentionally or spontaneously. When a woman aborts, she must call an Andean pakko or curandero to hold a specific ritual to burn the fetus. The ashes of the fetus are capable of causing illness and even death to others if not disposed of carefully.

Some people purposefully send the machu wayra to others. They call on the services of the yachak, who prepares an offering with the fetus of a hen or pig along with other items in order to send evil to another person. When the intention is to send evil, it is black magic or sorcery.

Getting Rid of Machu Wayra

The Quechua ask for protection from the Pachamama and make Her a haywarikuy. They may need to bring in a ritual specialist to assist them in ridding themselves of machu wayra. There are many ways to do this.

Ruda

The plant called ruda grows in all parts of Peru. A branch of this is lightly rubbed all over the head, body, and extremities of the affected person. The branch or leaves are burned, making the noise of small firecrackers, and a strong odor is released. Within minutes of performing this ritual, the negative energy of the machu wayra will leave.

Garlic as Protector

Garlic is commonly used as a condiment in the Andes. The more common types are large cloven yellow garlic or white garlic with small cloves. Bunches of garlic are hung and hidden in corners of homes to counteract the incursion of the negative energies of machu wayra and all evil spirits.

When Andean people walk through their mountains and large storm clouds appear, they chew some cloves of garlic and blow toward the clouds. The clouds then mysteriously move away and the weather improves.

Healing with Kkowi

The Quechua healers, shamans, alto misayoqkuna, and curanderos all utilize the healing powers of the kkowi. When a person becomes ill, the healer passes the animal over the patient's body from head to foot. The healer offers special prayers that initiate the removal of the illness, then proceeds to remove the skin of the kkowi while it is still alive. Bruises found inside the animal represent the pains of the patient that were transferred energetically to the kkowi during the ritual. The healer inspects the chest cavity of the animal to see if the patient's problem was in the heart area. The patient is now cured.

Souls of the Living and the Dead

There are many beliefs concerning machu wayra and the souls of the living and the dead. It is believed that the machu wayra has the ability to capture the souls of people, to cause them to go into shock, drop their energy level, and disturb their sleep patterns. Sometimes people become unconscious or paralyzed.

A yachak or Andean healer must be consulted, and it is his or her task to find the cause of the suffering and assist the person's soul to return to normal.

A Law Student's Remembrance: Gladys's Story

 "When I was a little girl of nine, my abuelita (grandmother) became very sick. Abuelita adored my four-year-old brother, who never left her side. She would share with him all the foods, such as soups and juices, my mother had prepared for her to make her well.

"Abuelita died a few months later, and two days after she was buried my brother became sick. My mother took him to see all the doctors and specialists in Qosqo. No one could help my brother. He got sicker and sicker; he would not eat and became very thin.

"Eventually my mother went to see a pakko, an old woman who read coca leaves. She said the boy was under *chayka*, a type of spell or negative force that had been instigated by my deceased abuelita. It seemed that my abuelita wanted the boy to go with her when she died. The pakko told my mother the doctors would never be able to cure him, but that she could, if my mother was prepared to follow instructions exactly.

"First, the old woman ordered a special haywarikuy to remove the chayka. At midnight on a Monday, the pakko and my mother carried my brother to the cemetery where Abuelita was buried. They sent off the offering and the pakko then chanted special prayers calling on the spirit of Abuelita.

"My mother was told to plead with Abuelita to release the chayka on her son and to tell her how much she was suffering because her son was so sick. The pakko then took some dirt from the graveside, mixed it with special herbs and rubbed it all over my brother's body. This process was repeated again at midnight on Tuesday.

"My mother then was told to make a quantity of akkha and offer it for sale from the house. She was to place my brother to sleep on the floor of the doorway, and as people came in to buy the akkha they had to step over the boy to get the akkha. They then carried their purchase out the same way, and as the buyers left, they carried away the illness of my brother.

"This was repeated until that Friday night; already there was a great improvement in my brother. Thirty days later, he was healed. His appetite returned and he could eat, and two months later he began to walk again.

"He is now an adult in perfect health. The major change we noticed was in the color of his skin, which up to age four was light. After the work with the pakko, his skin turned dark and has remained so to this day."

Death

The Quechua believe that *wañuy* (death) is an ending only as concerns the body. But for the soul, physical death is the beginning of a new journey into the formless world, with transformation that leads to rebirth. To die is to return to the womb of Pachamama.

Ancient burial sites in Peru contained bodies wrapped in the fetal position, buried in communal caves along with friends and relatives who had gone before.

The Quechua venerate their dead out of love and respect for what they have given to the living. They believe in maintaining contact with the ancestors and feel connected to them in many ways. The bones of ancestors that lie in the body of Pachamama are transformed into plants and rivers, mountains and living creatures. They are a part of human beings as well. Death gives birth to new life as the seed sown into the bosom of Pachamama.

Quechua pakkokuna believe that at death a person's soul leaves the body and wanders for five nights in animal form. At the end of this period, the soul of the good person goes to Hanakpacha, the Andean heaven. The soul returns to the cemetery each holiday and goes back to the house where he lived once a year. After five years the soul disconnects from the family forever. The soul of the bad person goes to Ukhupacha (the underworld or inner earth), where it is condemned to wander to all the places where he or she committed sins in life.

Funerals in the Andes follow Christian traditions. A burial service is attended by a Catholic priest and followed by a period of mourning.

Symbolic Death

Throughout the ancient sites in the Andes, one finds large, carved, flattish stones referred to by archaeologists as funeral or death stones. They believe they were used to prepare the bodies for burial.

Healers from all parts of Peru come to visit the ruins at Machu Picchu and conduct healing ceremonies at special sites. There is a large funeral stone at the highest point of the ruins, near to the original entrance. Three steps, symbolizing the three Andean worlds are carved into the side.

Ten years ago I joined a shamanic journey led by Alberto Villoldo. We were accompanied by the late Don Eduardo Calderon, a curandero from Trujillo. Eduardo invited participants to lie on the flat surface where he "read" each person's energy field and performed healing work to balance their energies.

"Eduardo believed the canoe-shaped stone, carved with rings and pointing to the west, was utilized in ancient times by initiates undergoing a symbolic death. Eduardo recited the prayer: "May the winds of the south take the canoe to the regions of silence and death and then back to life." Legend says the spirits of the dead would pull the canoe, with the initiate lying on top toward the sunset. The person's spirit returned from the east, where the sun rises, and new life emerged. People would return as Inkakuna, children of the Sun.

Recently, Jade, a visitor to Machu Picchu, christened the funeral or death stone "The Sunboat."

She wrote the following verse:

Sunboat

> Stone of the Sun
> Carry me toward the light;
> Let me spread my wings
> like the condor
> and love my path on earth.
>
> Snake, great teacher,
> Reveal me thy wisdom;
> teach me to heal.
> Become part of the healing force
> that enlightens creation
> On my path to the Sun.

"The Sunboat."

A Special Funeral Service at an Andean Chapel in the Sacred Valley of the Inkakuna

 In April 1991, a group of twenty women from South Africa came on a Magical Journey to the Andes and stayed at the then Alhambra, a picturesque colonial-style hotel situated in the heart of the Sacred Valley.

As we prepared to leave Qosqo one morning, we were informed that the mother of one of the women had passed away in South Africa. Flights to Africa went weekly, and there was no way that Ida could return in time for her mother's funeral.

The Alhambra has a beautiful chapel amidst flower-filled gardens. A decision was made with the man who then managed the hotel, our friend Tito Lizano, to hold a memorial service that afternoon to give Ida the opportunity to bid her mother farewell.

The gardener presented Ida with a small bouquet of flowers in her mother's favorite colors. We asked Ida to close her eyes and relax on a carpet in the center of the chapel. We sat in a deep meditation and women in the group offered their special prayers. Ida was asked to silently call her mother to her, and talk with her and say good-bye. When she indicated that she felt complete, we all began to sing "The Psalm of David: The Lord is my Shepherd," which was the group's favorite song.

Suddenly, there were three loud knocks on the large, heavy Spanish-styled doors that were closed shut. An icy cold energy filled the chapel sending chills down our spines. Immediately after, the two doors dramatically swung inward, wide open. Startled, we all looked toward the doors. The cold energy seemed to move out through the doors. Outside, moving above an opposite building in the courtyard was a huge, round, brilliant, white light. We watched it slowly start to rise and move toward the heavens. A faint drizzle was seen in front of the dazzling light as the spirit of Ida's mother was taken on her journey to the light.

The women were overcome with emotion. Tito, the manager, was awestruck. Neither he nor Carlos our guide had ever seen anything like it in their many years of living in the Andes. Later, Tito explained that it was not possible for the heavy doors to open by themselves. He had personally closed them and there had been no wind outside. There was no outdoor light in that position. It was indeed a remarkable experience.

For the Andean Quechua who maintain a deep sense of connection to their cosmology and the spirit world, a phenomenon such as this would not be extraordinary. It would be readily accepted for family members to be visited by the spirit of one who has just died to bid farewell.

More Evil Influences

Visitors to the Amazon enjoy the luxury of flying directly from the major cities, but for the average Peruvian, traveling by road is the only link between dense jungle and the outside world of commerce.

About thirty years ago the state decided to build the first roads leading from Qosqo into the Amazon forest, but no sophisticated machinery was available—not even tractors.

Teams of men loaded with picks and shovels carved roads that wound through steep Andean passes. Workers cleared rocks by hand and dynamited tunnels through granite mountains to enable them to drop down into the Amazon basin below. Many lives were lost during the dangerous construction of these roads.

Workers hacked and cleared away dense vegetation with machetes to gain entrance to the magnificent unspoiled rainforest. They wove paths through terrain that was flooded continuously by the powerful Amazon waters during the rainy season.

Today, there is constant traffic on the roads between Qosqo and the jungle. Huge trucks ferry fruit, vegetables, and wood. The narrow roads cannot support two vehicles at once, and convoys must head in one direction toward the jungle on Mondays, Wednesdays, and Fridays, and return on the other days to avoid the difficulties of passing on treacherous roads.

In rainy season, as one descends to the jungle, roads worsen because of tropical downpours. Subterranean rivers appear and undermine the roads from underneath, washing them away. Drivers must stop to build up the road with stones and mud before they can continue.

Natural rivers wash away the banks and mudslides block the roads. One cannot go around anything because of the thick jungle or deep gorges on either side. Passengers patiently sit and wait for a bulldozer to come and clear the obstructions; truck drivers may be stuck for a week.

Not all visitors to Manu can afford the plane costs. If they elect to go by truck, they must contend with a road filled with potholes and, as they descend into the jungle, they are subjected to heat and mosquitos. Tracks that lead to the river where boats are available often are flooded, and visitors must wade up to their knees in water and mud to get through.

Nestor Lizárraga's Story

"I grew up working hard on my family farm at Machu Picchu. I loved adventures and taking risks, and if I decided to do something, I would do it.

"I qualified as an accountant in Qosqo, but a few years ago found myself out of work. I decided to go into the lumber business and travel to Kosnipata, near to Manu National Park in the Amazon. I was not familiar with this area.

"A few times a month we would drive to Kosnipata via Paucartampu and Pillawata on a Monday, Wednesday or Friday. We took passengers into the jungle by truck, and the next day returned to Qosqo with lumber.

"One journey, my compadre Freddy and I left Qosqo at ten o'clock in the morning. After driving through Paucartampu and Pillawata, we approached the little village of Patria. Driving on those bad roads required great concentration, and Freddy felt tired. He stopped the truck, made himself comfortable, and went to sleep.

"I went to sleep leaning against the doorway of the truck. A few minutes later, I felt something touching me. It felt as if hands were moving across my body. I began to shudder as I tried to call for help, 'Freddy, Freddy.' My cry was within me, and the sleeping Freddy couldn't hear.

"I was between my sleep and awake state, not asleep, yet not awake. I was calling to him with all my force trying to alert him, and, as I snapped fully awake, I still felt the hands over me. They were grabbing me, grasping me at my throat.

"'What happened to me?' I wondered. It was completely dark and there was no one on the road. The doors were closed and Freddy was sleeping deeply.

"I opened a window and looked back at the people sleeping in the storage area above the truck. I started to hear groans and moans coming from the sleeping passengers.

"'Ay, Ay, Ay.' Frightened, I shook Freddy and told him to get up.

"'What happened?' he asked surprised.

"'Look, listen, they are all complaining, as if they are all having a nightmare.'

"'I told Freddy what happened to me, and he immediately said that he, too, had felt a hand grabbing him. He tried to assure me that it was nothing.

"'Lets get out of here,' he said. He had rested, and so we drove into Pillkopata at about eleven o'clock that night.

"I will never forget that feeling. It was the worst sensation of my life, and it frightened me. I had physically felt the hand touching me all over, and for me it was something supernatural. I had never thought about these kinds of things; neither did I believe this could happen.

"I told my story to my brother-in-law, who also drives a large truck to carry wood from that area. He told me that one time while he was entering Kosnipata it began to rain strongly. He hadn't brought the canvas cover for the truck, and, since he was carrying passengers, he decided to stop and rest inside the tunnel to protect them from the rain. He said nothing happened to him, but as soon as the passengers in the truck fell asleep they all began to groan 'ay, ay, ay,' calling for help.

"He said one of the passengers woke up startled and shouted, 'Vamos, vamos! Let's get out of here!'

"He asked, 'What is going on? What about the rain?'

"The passenger replied, 'Never mind, let's go, let's go!'

"A few months later, I was traveling to Kosnipata with an assistant, whom we called Zorro (fox) because he was half brown and had a sharp wit. I had always liked to travel next to an open window, but since my first experience with the grabbing hands, I had become a bit nervous. I preferred to be near to the door, should I have to escape, so Zorro sat between the driver, Emilio, and me.

"It was about two o'clock in the morning when we decided to rest, about twenty kilometers from Pillawata. We were all tired from struggling to fix flat tires, but I could not sleep and was smoking a cigarette. I was worrying about getting safely to Kosnipata.

"Then the sleeping Zorro began wailing, 'ay, ay, ay!'

"'What happened, Zorro?' I asked.

"'I felt someone pushing me. I thought I was falling out the door into a ravine below.'

"I laughed at him and thought, 'This Zorro is a character.' We smoked until I became tired and began to doze.

"Suddenly I was in a nightmare. I started to groan, and what had just happened to Zorro hit me. I felt like the door was opening and I was falling into the ravine below. I was calling, 'Zorro, Zorro, grab me!' But he didn't hear.

"When I woke up, Zorro began to laugh and laugh, saying the *jefe* (boss) was just like him. We decided we could not sleep there; it was cold. We had a cigarette, woke up Emilio, and left.

"After my previous experience, when I first felt the hands on my body, we had loaded the truck with lumber at Kosnipata and prepared to return. Freddy stopped the truck where my nightmare had struck the previous night and exclaimed, 'There is a reason you had a nightmare here.' We had parked inside an area filled with wooden crosses placed inside the earth. We had been resting inside a cemetery.

"After hearing my brother-in-law's story, and then witnessing another strange experience with Zorro, I began to talk to the local people about these events.

"It is said that many people died during the construction of the roads, which were built by manual labor. To get through the mountains, workers used small sticks of dynamite and placed them into little holes in the ground. Three tunnels were built this way, bit by bit. They would

The chapel at the old Alhambra Hotel in Yucay.

place dynamite in a hole, advancing little by little. It is said that when they lit the dynamite they couldn't measure the distance and never allowed enough time to escape.

"Those who come from that zone claim that hundreds of deaths occurred in that area through the careless use of dynamite, and there were many accidents with rocks falling. Workers entered areas without ropes and disappeared in the rubble. Cadavers were completely inaccessible and remained in there forever.

"The roads are so difficult to drive that at times drivers fall asleep at the wheel, and it often is impossible to retrieve the bodies. Each year on that route, at least one truck goes off the road and overturns.

"Many people have died working on the roads, in the tunnels, and in subsequent accidents, and their bodies were never retrieved. Locals believe their souls, trapped in those areas, are still grieving. Travelers stopping there often experience the disturbingly realistic nightmares, and it is believed those trapped souls are trying to reach them and pull them down, too.

"These experiences scared me, and I could no longer rest or sleep en route to the jungle. I retired from working in that haunting zone."

▼▼▼

Ancient Beings

There are many caves in the sacred valleys of the Andes, some of which are filled with ancient human remains. These are known as *machukuna; so'ka machukuna* for the masculine sex, *so'ka payakuna* for the feminine sex. They are said to be the first inhabitants of the area.

During their time of life they worshipped a Copper Sun, whose light was dull and opaque, as well as the moon, Killa. These machukuna had so much power they tried to conquer the Copper Sun God, who then decided to destroy them with *ninapara* (a firestorm).

The wise ones of the machukuna warned the others what was going to occur. It is said they hid their riches and quickly built themselves houses of mud and clay called *so'ka wasi,* where they were confined forever. Others fled deep into the caves where they lived until the end of their days.

Ñaupa Machukuna: A Story

There was a time when the sun did not exist. There were men living on earth whose great power of thought made them capable of moving rocks, and they could reshape mountains with a single ray of thought they beamed out. Killa shone in the half light and poorly illuminated the activities of these beings known as *ñaupa machukuna.*

One day Ruak the Creator God, who was chief of the apukuna, offered to empower them. The arrogant machukuna exclaimed that they didn't need his help because they were already omnipotent.

Irritated by such a haughty answer, Ruak created the sun and ordered him to rise in the sky. Frightened and almost blinded by the brilliant light, the machukuna sought refuge in small houses and caves. The heat of the sun dehydrated them and caused their muscles to dry up.

The machukuna continued to live in their caves, and to this day can leave their places of refuge only when the sun sets or when there is a new moon.

—Story in Spanish by Juan Nuñez del Prado

The Quechua are wary of exploring caves with the remains of machukuna, as they are believed to emanate an evil energy that causes illness.

One evening we visited a Quechua home with a group of women. The conversation was of the Quechua belief in the machukuna. Women from villages far apart tell identical stories about machukuna who are reported to visit women sleeping alone in the house after their husbands have gone off to work in the early morning hours.

The machu appears to the woman in her half-sleep state and talks to her as if he is her husband who has returned home. The machu lies next to her in bed and impregnates her. Her husband returns from work that evening and she finds out that he never returned early that morning. She then realizes that she has been visited by a machu.

The baby is born and comes into the world with a terrible odor. It is ugly and black in color. There is no flesh on the body, and within no time the baby dies. There is no doubt that this creature comes from a machu and not from another man.

An Adventure to the Caves of the Machukuna

Rómulo and I were discussing the Andean concept of ñaupa machukuna. He revealed that as a boy he had been to caves with skeletal remains of these beings. He had seen giant skulls and huge femur bones, and he offered to take me there.

We went back to his family chahra, a farm behind the slopes of Machu Picchu, and we had a conversation with his mother. Señora de

Lizárraga confirmed what Rómulo had said and told us more about the caves with the remains of the machukuna.

For the past eighty years the Lizárraga family had known of the existence of the caves on their private property. No one had entered the caves nor interfered with the skulls. As Quechua people, they knew of the significance of the site and chose to leave the area undisturbed. Rómulo's father had passed away and the family had long since given up trying to farm the land near the caves, which were a good eight-hour hike away from their farm on the Urubamba River.

We planned to go the next day at dawn, but due to rain we had to postpone the trip because it would have been too dangerous to hack our way through the dense vegetation. The weather was perfect when we finally set out a week later.

Señora de Lizárraga prepared a special bundle of different grains to take to the caves as an offering to the spirits of the ancient burial site. Accompanied by Rómulo and Julio, the older brother, and knowing both were armed with *kuchunakuna* or *curvos* (machetes), I looked forward to this venture with great trepidation. Images of slippery paths and poisonous vipers slithered through my imagination.

The first three hours of hiking were pleasant. Paths followed the banks of the picturesque river and plants were in abundance. Rómulo and Julio explained the medicinal value of the flora and the uses they had observed when growing up. As we approached the high mountain slopes, the vegetation thickened. We kept climbing and the brothers maintained a steady pace, hacking at the tall grass stalks, bushes, and vines ahead of us.

We arrived at a large, flat rock that overlooked the entire valley. The two men had been looking for this landmark. The plan was to make our offering of coca leaves to the Pachamama and apukuna there. The rock was crawling with the largest ants I'd ever seen. The men quickly started to burn some dry brush while I hopped from one foot to another in the hope that the ants would not have a chance to climb up my legs. The smoke chased the ants away in no time.

The three of us held hands for a moment and asked for permission from the ancient spirits of the valley to enter the next valley where the caves were. We each took turns offering a k'intu of coca leaves to the Pachamama and local apukuna. The k'intus then were placed into the ground and covered with earth. We rested awhile and the men chewed the coca leaves.

The men debated which way we should go. Apparently they recognized nothing. Everything was completely overgrown and there were no tall trees as landmarks. We tried walking in several directions. Julio walked into a hornet's nest and was stung on the lip. Without complaining, he continued to walk in front. The vegetation was now three times my height and there were walls of bushy scrub and vines everywhere. Julio was shaking his head as if to say we weren't getting anywhere. He went off in another direction, and I was thinking, "Come on Rómulo, find the caves, find the caves."

Suddenly, Rómulo started to move forward, and I followed him. Within moments he walked right up to the caves. He excitedly pointed to the locations of some others nearby and Julio quickly came to join us.

I stepped up to one of the caves and then crouched down to peer underneath. The entrance to the cave was a few feet tall and about ten feet wide. From the outside we could see a few very large skulls, long, bulky femurs and other bone fragments.

The men took out a small bundle filled with wheat, kinúwa, and corn their mother had prepared and we set out the offering to the spirit ancestors of those caves. The men offered their silent prayers, and I gave thanks for the protection we had received and for being allowed to see the remains of the machukuna.

The energy around the caves was intense, and the air had not been disturbed in many years. Rómulo said there were many similar caves in the area but the men looked uneasy. It had not been their intention to enter the cave, and we had not brought flashlights. Now that they had shown me one of the caves with the skulls, it was clear that they felt it was time to leave.

Following our tracks out was easy, and it was downhill most of the way back. At one point I looked up into the distance and Rómulo confirmed what I saw. It was an old Inka pathway leading from behind Machu Picchu across some other mountains and into the valley we were leaving. Perhaps Hiram Bingham and subsequent archaeologists never found a great quantity of ancient remains at Machu Picchu because these civilizations buried their dead in the valleys away from the sacred cities.

Back at the farm Rómulo mentioned how extraordinary it had been for him that day. He said he was just about to give up on finding the caves and suggest we turn back when he felt as if something was pulling him forward. The next thing he knew, he had arrived. I smiled. Soon after, I had the opportunity to ask an old spiritual teacher about the remains we had seen. I was told they were indeed very ancient and in fact pre-Inka.

▼▼▼

14

Andean Handcrafts; Traditional Dress

A dazzling display of colorful dress and high quality *artesanía* (handcrafts) greet visitors wherever they travel in the Qosqo and Machu Picchu areas. The Quechua have retained their traditional style of dress and intricate art of woven textiles, knitted clothing, and hand-painted ceramics. They use a wide variety of fibers from the llama, alpaka, and vicuña for weaving and knitting blankets, wall hangings, rugs, sweaters, hats, gloves, and ponchos.

Artisan markets are filled with colorful hand-knitted *chompakuna* (sweaters) with wonderful ethnic designs made out of wool, alpaka, or synthetic yarn. Llama hair feels rather coarse, while baby alpaka, which comes in natural colors of white, brown, gray, black and tan, is soft to the touch. Vicuña hair is silky and luxurious but rarely available since the animals are a protected species and the price is prohibitive. Women are seen spinning and weaving while others walk around weaving long, colorful belts on a hand loom.

The Quechua make exquisite ceramic items. Around the square in P'isaq, in the Sacred Valley, villagers hand-paint ceramic bowls and pottery, decorating them with intricate, traditional symbols unique to that area. Children can be seen in small family workshops, painting beautiful ceramic beads used for modern earrings. These are sold inexpensively to tourists.

Each market in the Qosqo and Sacred Valley area has a section on *hampi kkatu* (traditional medicine). Besides selling items for offerings, the

Quechua sell amulets made of ceramic or stone. They usually are carved in the form of animals and are used for fertility as well as good luck and protection. Quechua artists sell a variety of picturesque watercolor paintings depicting typical Andean scenes.

The traditional dress worn by Quechua women today is a mixture of styles from pre-Spanish days and Spanish Colonial peasant dress. Women wear Panama-type hats made from woven palm fibers or, depending on their village, traditional, decorated flat hats made of wool with colored fringes hanging from the brim.

Under the hats, they wear their hair in two long braids fastened in the back with a long ribbon. They wear full, gathered skirts called *mélkkhay* or *melkkhay*, made from wool cloth called *bayeta*, or dark colored cotton. On festive occasions women wear many layers of skirts and a *lliklla*, a traditional handwoven shawl held in place by a *tupu*, a decorated pin. They tie a carrying cloth called *kk'eperina* on their backs which enables them to carry heavy loads. Younger women often carry their babies, tightly swaddled in cloth, inside the kk'eperina.

Quechua men generally wear Western-style clothing. Some wear a *kutun* (man's shirt) made from factory woven cotton and pants of bayeta wool. Traditional men wear a vest called *chaleco* and a brimmed hat called *montera*. *Ch'ullukuna* are multi-colored hand-knitted hats often decorated with buttons. *Varayokkuna*, mayors or appointed heads of the ayllukuna, can be seen carrying a *vara*, a wooden staff with a beautifully-decorated silver tip.

Most of the Quechua wear *usutakuna*, sandals made from rubber tires or leather. They find them durable and practical for walking through the mountains and working in the fields. Since ancient times, men and women have worn small woven pouches called *ch'uspakuna* to hold coca leaves.

Each district has a distinctive pattern for a poncho with characteristic colors and patterns. Lyn Meisch in her book, *A Travelers Guide to El Dorado and the Inca Empire*, quotes a study done by experts, saying that it takes about three to six months of work to spin, dye, prepare the warp and loom, and weave a traditional poncho found in the markets of P'isaq and Qosqo.

The weaver receives about four cents an hour for his work, not including cost of supplies. If the weaver was to receive the legal American minimum wage, the price of the traditional poncho at today's rate would range between $1,300 and $1,600. If visitors knew this, they might be more inclined to pay the Quechua a fair price for their work, rather than bargain them down to almost nothing as is often the case.

15

Stories, Singing, Dancing; Insults; Festivals

Storytelling is the ancient form of education in the Andes. It has played an important role in the passing down of tradition from generation to generation. Stories still are told in villages throughout the Andes, where they are the connecting thread between the traditional culture, Pachamama, and all her nature.

Stories keep the Quechua in touch with the creative forces of the universe and remind them how humans, animals, and the natural world all link into one dynamic, interconnected force of life. Supernatural beings and animals often are seen as mirrors of the human world. Stories illumine the past, origins, and ancestors.

They help the Quechua maintain and restore balance and harmony as they travel through the changing cycles of life. The modern world has not yet encroached upon the Andean world. Stories offer the Quechua a sense of identity and enable them to proudly define their place in the world today.

In Chapter One, we explained some of the difficulties in translating Kkechuwa stories into another language. Only experts of the Kkechuwa language can come close to capturing the essence of the narratives, whose meaning may differ from village to village. Campesino tales with good translations into Spanish are available.

The Farmer, the Llama, and the Condor

There was a farmer who had many llamas, but a condor always ate them. One by one, the condor ate the llamas. The farmer was very upset and one day he thought of a scheme to trap the condor. He grabbed him and pulled out all his feathers until he was completely bald. Then he let him go.

Some time later, an official arrived at the campesino's house, accusing him of stealing clothes and ordering him to present himself before the local authorities. The farmer wondered who could have stolen the clothes and why the offical came to him. He paid no attention to the official and ignored his summons.

The sacred llama is often part of Andean folklore.

A few days passed and this time the officials sent a warrant for his arrest. Indignantly the farmer said, "From whom would I take anything? I have never robbed anyone nor stolen anything," he cried. Once again he ignored the warrant.

The highest ranking officials came with another document and told him to accompany them and bring the clothes he had stolen. Again he denied the accusation saying, "What clothes? I have not taken any clothes. I only pulled feathers out of the condor and let him go. I punished him for destroying my herd of llamas."

"In that case," said the official, "it is the feathers you have stolen. Bring them with you."

They led him away and made him walk a far distance into the hills. After many hours of walking, they arrived at a house and went inside a sort of room. Impossible as it may seem, sitting in a circle were many condors. In the center of the circle he saw a condor without feathers, shivering from the cold.

The king of the condors began to interrogate the farmer. "Why have you robbed this man's suit?"

"I pulled out his feathers because he ate my llamas," he tried to explain.

"Have you brought back the clothes to return to this powerful condor?" he asked.

"Yes, yes, I have brought them," the man cried as he handed over the tied-up bundle of feathers.

With great haste, the plucked condor began to put his feathers back into his body. When he had finished dressing himself, the condor king reprimanded the man.

"Don't do this again. Is it understood?" Without punishing him, they let him go.

—Narrated in Kkechuwa by Gregorio Ccoyo Ch'ipa
To Cecilia Granadino, 1992.

Songs and Dances

Andean fiestas and ceremonies are vibrant with characteristic songs and dances, as the Quechua always have been a singing and dancing people. All aspects of daily life are transmitted through songs called waynukuna, which are of pre-Spanish origin and have been passed down orally for centuries.

In Inka times the *amau'takuna* (wise men) recited short narratives to instruct children and remind them about their traditions as a people. Notable events were put into verse by the poets and set to music by musicians. After each triumph they composed new songs to celebrate the achievements of the Inkakuna. Songs and dances were accompanied by drums, flutes, clay and shell trumpets, gongs, seed rattles, and various kinds of bronze pipes and rings.

In the Andes today, waynukuna within each area take on their own specific characteristics and style. Each ceremony has a different combina-

Carol tape records Quechua children
singing at school.

tion of music, poetry, and dancing and may contain expressions of love, humor, sorrow, and tragedy. Members of the family and friends participate in waynukuna which play an important part in all Andean celebrations and festivals.

The rhythm and beat of an Andean song is an unforgettable and remarkable experience in melody and expression. Sounds alive with images echo movements in nature, with whom the Quechua have a harmonious relationship. Waynukuna capture the songs of the valleys, the sounds of deep gorges, roaring rivers cascading from sacred peaks, and golden sunlight illuminating the maize fields.

While walking through the Andean mountains with a condor or hummingbird hovering nearby, the Quechua never see themselves as alone. Waynukuna portray how animals, birds, and humans all exist together and are seen as friends, their love, joy, and sorrow shared. Some songs may seem nonsense, but they are filled with meaning by the way they are sung.

Folkloric songs from the villages are original and cannot be interpreted by outsiders. Music that expresses mythology, mountains, and moonlight cannot be understood by those who live in cities far away from nature. Andean music is created by a village that sees the whole world as a living being.

With music comes dancing, and Andeans take the opportunity to further express their artistic ability. It is common to see shy, quiet campesinos join the dancing and transform into lively, uninhibited, gyrating beings, free from work and worry. For that period of time, the dancer experiences freedom and joy. The dance frees them from limitations and allows them the opportunity to take charge of every aspect of life.

Dance creates energies that help Pachamama to balance and harmonize the energies of earth and sky. Dancing brings the mind and body into perfect harmony; it clears and aligns the energy fields. The dancer becomes part of nature, and nature becomes part of the dancer. Each village has its own style and variation, each festival its own music; different music has its own instruments.

The Quechua mastered the guitar and mandolin brought to Peru by the Spanish, and adapted the instruments to their own music. The *charango* (Andean mandolin) is a very popular instrument with many variations in size and numbers of chords. The sound of the charango cries for the indigenous Andean people with the same force and haunting sounds of the *kkena* and *pinkuylla* (flutes). Music enhances the spirit of the gathering.

Harawikuna are sung by groups of women at special gatherings, funerals, and harvest celebrations. The women's voices reach a high pitch that is

Ernestina is a talented kkena player from Aguas Calientes.

impossible for a man. The vibration of the final note guarantees that no element of the earth or celestial skies has not been reached by this final shriek.

Javier Garrafa and His Music

 "This music is an inheritance from the Andean gods manifested through me. While playing, I feel the force of nature and know I am part of it, and it will always continue this way.

"My family comes from Apurímakk where there is a tremendous force of energy. I have always lived in the Andes.

"Pachamama deserves to be respected; we must do it, not just talk about it. We are making Her sick. Visitors who come here are also causing this sickness. They are poisoning our plants. Bayer is a German company selling insecticide and fertilizer to our people. We the Quechua, want the foreigners to reflect on what they are doing to our people They must not be selfish with their power and vanity. Tell that: Please don't contaminate the Quechua world. Do not exploit us. Reflect on this.

"The Quechua campesinos are connected to the earth, which is good. We must focus on returning love to the earth and the earth will give us wisdom. We must breathe pure air and we must eat pure products and food. We must respect Pachamama and her waters which are everything, pure energy. Please let us harmonize everything on Pachamama.

"To talk about this chokes me up, it is too personal. I put all my energy into my songs. What I want is to transmit this energy to others."

"The builders of these ancient cities were specialists in music. They made mathematically perfect constructions by utilizing the combined sounds of their special ancient musical instruments."

Faure Dueñas Peña

Faure Dueñas Peña is Peru's foremost kkena player, whose finesse with the Andean flute has touched the hearts and souls of thousands of people. He also is a highly acclaimed lecturer and composer. At Machu Picchu, in August of 1994, I talked to Faure about the Andes and his music.

*Javier Garrafa experiences the forces
of nature when playing his music.*

Faure's Story

 "I am Quechua, born in the city of Qosqo. From the age of five I lived close to the earth, explored ancient caves in the Andean hills and played inside the nearby ruins of Saksaywaman. These places lured me with their mystery, and there I would feel strange sensations, a particular kind of energy or heat.

"The Andean world is filled with naturally spiritual and affectionate people. I loved to stay with the campesinos and share their rich, traditional lives. I would observe them sending their despachos, offerings, in homage to the Pachamama, apukuna, sun, and moon.

"At the age of ten, I began to study classical guitar. I entered the Conservatory of Classical Music in Qosqo and continued to study in Lima for seven years. I was developing a unique talent for this instrument.

"But something drew me to the haunting sounds of the kkena, the first pre-Columbian instrument of Andean Peru. The kkena was used by Mochican, Nazcan, and other ancient cultures thousands of years ago. Its music reflects the psyche of all humanity of Tawatinsuyo, the complete Andean world extending from Argentina to Colombia.

"While formally studying the guitar, I kept returning to this ancient musical instrument, the kkena. Slowly it revealed itself to me and beckoned me to become part of the Andean community. I felt as if this world, this nature with its special energy, had been placed into my soul. It seemed to tell me that I had been chosen for this work.

"Whenever I returned to Qosqo, I practiced in the countryside and at Kenko, Saksaywaman, and other sacred sites. While playing and composing in these surroundings, I was aware of the presence of the Andean gods, and I felt deeply connected to nature. I was part of the Andean cosmos, Kaypacha, Ukhupacha, and Hanakpacha. I lived in two realms, the external and internal worlds, the spiritual and the material. For me, the most significant always was the spiritual.

"I continued to play the kkena, learning from my own apprenticeship with Andean nature, and I had developed my own technique when I began to teach at the Lima conservatory.

"I play for the National Symphony of Peru and, in the big cities, classical music tends to be more European and rather closed.

"By contrast, the Andean expanse of music is quite complex. Chromatic scales, half steps of the musical scale, were practiced by ancient Peruvians. Instruments of the past, such as the wankar, tinta, alzon, antara, and the kkena, are more than 5,000 years old.

"They have an immense range of complicated scales, and the rhythmic patterns of Andean music are hard to play. The Inkakuna composed their music with great rhythmic values consisting of five quarter notes per measure. Musical composers from Qosqo now write music similar to that which probably was played thousands of years ago.

"At the end of 1994, I played in the first concert for kkena and orchestra in Lima, in a program consisting of three movements. The first part, the lively *wayno*, is an exceptional erotic genre. It is syncopated in such form that does not exist much in European music, and is therefore difficult for the musicians of Lima to perform.

"The second, a slow movement, is the *harawi*, called *jarawi* by the early Spanish. The third movement is a *kasawa*, which is more lively with a religious and war-like character.

"This ancient scheme of music is completely different for today's musicians, and movements are complicated and problematic. Conductors of great city orchestras are familiar with only three quarter or four quarter rhythms, and often they omit this genre of music entirely.

"The kkena deserves to become recognized at the symphonic level. It must be played by great artists and accompanied by accomplished musicians. I believe this music soon will reestablish itself and attain the prevalence it enjoyed during the Inka Epoch.

"Performing at Machu Picchu is very different from playing with the symphony orchestra. At Machu Picchu, I close my eyes and feel the unique purity; I play for the people.

"Machu Picchu visitors from the outside world often seem superficial and materialistic when they first arrive. But after spending time in the Andes and hiking through the ruins, they appear to absorb our culture and spiritual influences and they evolve. They tap into our three Andean worlds, which are most perfect, and these interconnected cosmos transform the materialistic attitudes of the unenlightened visitors to those of a higher consciousness.

"Strange things happen when one plays music in the midst of this strong Andean energy. I have watched people listen and observed them transform. Many times they leave crying. The music is connected to the spiritual world, and its pure energy transforms something in their hearts and connects them with nature, especially here at Machu Picchu.

"People often say to me, 'You, playing here? You should be in the concert halls or educational institutes where you belong. What are you doing here?' They seem to frown upon my playing in a public place.

This is the site where Faure performed
his Machu Picchu concert.

"But I tell them it is not the fact that I am playing here that is important, but rather that something greater has called to me. I come into the ancient city and play, and I leave with this energy.

"I believe my playing at Machu Picchu is a form of service which introduces the world to this music in its intrinsic setting. People in the crowded dining areas stop eating, turn, and listen. The vibration reaches them and they carry this sound, this message in their hearts. They take home a cassette because they want a reminder of this ethereal experience.

"For me, Machu Picchu is a sanctuary, a very sacred place. Only God knows what it really is, and no one can decipher it. I see it as a monastery, a place of rituals and ceremonies dedicated to all the Andean gods who are adored by my people.

"Inside the ruins I play the kkena and interweave with this world, as the music is an integral part of the creation of this holy place. The creators were born with these instruments, and I endeavor to recreate that part of the ancient life and carry it into the present.

"The lives of the ancients were integrated with the healing sounds, and in parts of the jungle near Iquitos, healers cure with vocal sounds. They practice biphonic, triphonic, quarterphonic, and pentaphonic sounds and use the tones to heal. They cure the sick with songs and instrumental music.

"The builders of the ancient cities were specialists in music. They made mathematically perfect constructions by utilizing the combined sounds of their special ancient musical instruments. The vibration of this sound would enable them to transport and carve the stones. Music carries an impacting energy. It is said that supernatural forces helped man build fortresses such as Saksaywaman and Ollantaytampu by utilizing sound. Great structures of rocks appeared here and there, and strong energy forces came from a concentration of sound.

"One night I entered Machu Picchu alone to pray for a Quechua porter who had been killed carrying a load on the path leading toward Machu Picchu. I began to pray for the porter, when suddenly my concentration was broken by the sound of large boulders falling from the mountainside near Intipunku, the gateway to the Sun. Rocks crashed noisily, and fire and sparks framed their figurations. I became uneasy and began to play the kkena. The stones immediately stopped falling.

"Music, precise and important, always has played a role in the Andes. The Andeans played special harmonics from dawn to dusk for worshipping nature, for women, war, agriculture, plants, astronomy, life, and death. They had music for the simplest things to the most extraordinary. The Andeans had music to mold and entwine into each moment of their lives.

"I will always return to Machu Picchu to replenish my soul with the spirituality and energy. I feel the protection of the apukuna that surround me. I am rewarded with a force and vitality that help me to play my music throughout the major cities of the world."

Insults

Exchanging insults among the Quechua is a form of recreation. People gather around as competition grows between insultors. Each tries to make the other appear ridiculous.

Improvisations give prestige to the insultor, whose object is to triumph over his rival. For someone who has a great sense of humor or a flair for irony, insulting may provide an opportunity to show off his talent.

Sometimes insulting is done in formal groups or shouted from a distance. A decision is made as to the kind of insults to be given. Pornographic insults are considered vulgar and regarded as too easy to give and not enough of a challenge.

Some examples of mild insults commonly used by the Quechua are the following:

Salka—It means wild, but refers to someone who fawns over another to win favor.

K'ullu uya runa—A shameless scoundrel.

K'umu K'umu—This refers to someone who acts nice to a person, then behind their back does something to hurt them.

Pamuco—A fool, an idiot.

Chachara uma—One with curly, wavy hair; these people are often teased.

Ch'iputiñawi—A person who has tiny, beady eyes like a chicken.

Festivals for Fun

Andean rituals related to the agricultural calendar (see Chapter Ten) are followed by festivities.

The Quechua campesinos joyfully celebrate additional festivals with Christian origins. These have been restructured by the Andean community, and few people can tell of their religious significance. Traditional stories, music, and dancing are blended into festivities throughout the Quechua farming communities and the villages of the Andes.

The Festival of Carnaval

Carnaval or *pukllaytaky,* means "let's play" and is celebrated each February. The Carnaval festival is of pagan origin in Europe, and the medieval "Christians" mixed Catholic and goddess-worshipping rituals to celebrate fertility rites of ancient times.

Parties take place in Andean towns, and it is a popular time for commencing courtship among the Quechua youth. In the days following Carnaval, the young man "robs" his sweetheart, who willingly allows him to take her to his house to meet his parents (see Chapter Sixteen) .

Campesinos living on farms away from the towns use the festival as an additional ritual of gratitude to Pachamama for Her potato harvest. In the countryside at dawn, a senior member of the family goes to the field of papas (potatoes), taking with him akkha, kañiwa, ground maize and *misk'ikuna* (candies). In the afternoon, all members of the extended family connected to the chahra gather at the farm to make the t'inka ceremony with coca leaves.

The owner of the first parcel invites two or three men to accompany him and they select the finest potatoes. The chosen potatoes are called *mamapapa.* They bring them to where the rest of the family waits, and place them on an *unkhuña,* a small cloth of beautiful colors decorated with flowers. They kiss the potatoes, spill drops of wine, sprinkle them with candies and leaves of coca, then together call on the Pachamama and dieties and pray to the Father and María.

The owner of the next parcel of land does the same and repeats the act. By the time the sun sets, all the parcels have been honored in the same manner.

Everyone then goes to the house of the one who has the *carguyok*, the honor of being the host for that year, where food is prepared for the group. If the farmers have cattle, senior members of the family may offer inheritances to their children. In the evening a pakko sends an haywarikuy to the Pachamama, giving thanks for the crops and asking for health and fertility for the inherited cattle.

This festival also reenforces the solidarity of the family and their respect for ancient traditions. The joyful celebrations that follow offers them a respite from the heavy agricultural work of which they are part. There is music, singing, dancing, feasting, and legendary drunkenness.

Campesinos use the festival of Carnaval to offer gratitude to Pachamama for abundant harvests.

Festival of the Cross

Cruz Velacuy, the significant Festival of the Cross, is held on the third of May. On top of the Andean hills the Quechua erect huge crosses made of wood or stone to protect the villages. Most communities and farms have small chapels where they place crosses that have been around for generations, and men, women, and children decorate the chapels with fruit and flowers from the fields. They adorn the crosses with embroidered "clothing" and illuminate them with long decorated candles. The Quechua watch over the crosses all night while praying, singing, and dancing.

On the morning of May 3, priests are invited to conduct a solemn mass and villagers throughout the Andes bring their decorated crosses to the farms and town squares. The majordomo, the head of the family, carries the cross which is then blessed by the priest.

Families who have the carguyok prepare a special feast. If they are affluent enough, a cow may be ceremonially slaughtered for the occasion and the meat roasted on an open fire. Generous portions are served with potatoes or yuca and offered to all the guests. The rest of the day is celebrated with joyful singing and lively dancing to traditional music. An endless supply of akkha is offered and guests are free to drink until they drop. A successful party raises the prestige of the host's family in the community.

Love and Marriage in Quechuan Tradition

Courtship

A Quechua man may compliment a woman in the following way, as relayed in a popular folksong: *Qanmi kanki sonkko sua, misk'i, simi, ch'aska ñawi imaymanan kkampa munaycha* (You have stolen my heart, you speak so sweetly, your sparkling eyes shine so bright, all of you is beautiful.)

The Kkechuwa language is filled with beautiful, expressive, and humorous sayings, such as *Permanentichata ruachipusayki ch'achara wallpa hina purikumaykipak* (I'm going to curl your hair to show you off with waves in your hair. Everyone will want to look at you.) This popular *waynu* is sung to men and women with curly hair, who are often good-naturedly teased among the majority of Andeans with straight hair. It is the suitor's way of showing pride in the one he loves.

The following is a beautiful Kkechuwa song translated into Spanish, and then English.

> Ama urpichay ama sonkkochay
> ripuyta yuyaychu
> sonkkoykka hatun rumi hina ñit'i sunkiman
> ripuskkayki ñampi chaypitak wakkayniy

No te vayas paloma mía
no te acuerdes del camino,
mi corazon como una peña
te caería en el camino,
como un río mi llorar
te llevaría.

Don't go, (little) dove of mine,
don't think of the road ahead,
(for) my heart would fall like a boulder
in the middle of your journey
and my tears (weeping) would sweep you
away like a river (in flood).

The Chalina: Rómulo's Story

"When I was fifteen years old, I accompanied my mother on a two-day walk to the Yanaoka in the high Puna. Each year my mother contracted workers from that area for our farm.

"My mother, from the Yunes subtropical zone, arrived with gifts of coffee, coca leaves and trago (alcoholic drink), cigarettes, and tropical fruits. We were welcomed during the February Festival of Carnaval. The village was preparing for the celebration that night when young and old would get together to sing and dance. I was introduced to my mother's campesino friends and their children, and soon I was part of the singing and dancing among the young people.

"A young girl attached herself to me, staying by my side and holding my hand all night. I was young and shy, but I realized that she was expressing her 'love' for me. At midnight she opened a pouch around her neck, took out a chalina and gave it to me. This was a scarf beautifully woven in many colors. I took it and, in my innocence, put it into my pocket. When the party ended I joined my mother and we went to sleep at friends. The young girl looked upset and returned to her parent's house.

"At breakfast the next morning when I casually showed off the chalina the girl had given me, my host jumped up and said, 'young man, this chalina has great significance. You obviously appealed to the girl and she gave it to you as a sign of her desire for love and sexual initiation. You made an agreement with her by accepting the chalina. Did you sleep with her?'

"When I assured my host that I had not had any sexual contact with the girl, he told me I would have to go immediately to her house and meet with the whole family and her other potential suitors. I was to publicly announce that I had accepted the chalina without knowing the consequences.

"My mother and I took gifts of coca and trago. We were greeted by the family and given a special meal. I declared I had accepted the chalina without knowing the custom and I now understood its meaning. The girl was not taken by me and I was returning the chalina so that she may find another suitor. I regretted I could not accept the commitment.

"The family understood and my mother and I returned to our farm across the mountain with the workers we had set out to find. This was my first encounter with the custom of love."

The Chalina

When young Quechua girls begin to have desires for sex and matrimony, they begin to weave a chalina. They use multi-colored threads, and whenever they have spare time they work on their chalina. As they weave, they think about who it will be given to and they wait for one of the special village festivals and celebrations. There they will choose a young man and then hand over the chalina. This indicates the young woman wishes to have a serious committed relationship with this person. Once accepted, the couple goes off to consummate their relationship.

The Serenade

In many cases boys do not receive a chalina, but they, too, may have desires for a sexual relationship with a young woman. Serenades are sung to loved ones in the Andes, and beautiful songs alternating in Kkechuwa and Spanish are offered with great feeling.

In many Andean regions, a young man of sixteen or seventeen learns to play a musical instrument such as the *charango* (an Andean mandolin made of wood). He learns different songs to serenade and develops an understanding of the music and different instruments. This is an indication that the young man wants to fall in love and have sex. At a suitable celebration, the young man will find a young woman he is attracted to. He uses the charango to woo and court the young woman he desires by serenading her. If she desires him, she will allow him to capture her and take her off to another place.

The Doll

In some regions a young man will arrive on horseback or on foot at the home of the girl he has fallen in love with. He brings a special doll with him. Around the doll's neck the suitor has placed a card or letter with all his credentials written down. Her acceptance of the doll is an agreement to a committed relationship.

The Commitment

The decision having been made, the couple goes to the girl's parents to talk about their union. The parents immediately call on the parents of the young man and arrangements are made. The two sets of parents exchange a bag of coca leaves called *ch'uspa,* and this interchange signifies mutual agreement by the in-laws. This leads to the next phase of courtship.

Sirwanakuy

Sirwanakuy (to serve one another) is widely practiced in both rural areas and the cities of the Andes. Once the arrangement is made between parents of the couple, the couple moves in with one of the families and helps the in-laws in whatever is most needed. A child is soon conceived, and whether they have a legal civil marriage or are married in the Catholic Church or go through no ceremony seems to be relatively unimportant. The couple and children they have are accepted by both families. After two years of living together, the law offers the woman the same rights for herself and the children as those of women with legal ties of marriage.

Dreams

Moskkoykuna (dreams) are regarded as important messages that guide Quechua men and women in their daily lives. They believe certain images and symbols that appear in dreams have a great deal of meaning. Andean healers often are assisted in their work by the information they receive in dreams. The following common dream symbols are interpreted in the same way by different villagers in the Qosqo and Machu Picchu areas.

Maize (*sara*)—Signifies wealth and money that one will receive from another.

Dog (*alqo*)—Be careful, someone may steal something from your home or take money from you. If it is a small dog, the thief will be someone from your family and if a large dog, it will be a stranger.

Clean water (*unu*)—A sign of good health.

Muddy water (*kk'ata unu*)—One may acquire an illness.

Salt (*kachi*)—You will cry for an unspecified reason.

Someone naked (*k'ala siki*)—Someone is speaking badly of you.

Chord or rope (*wask'ha, tintu, wijuju*)—Some kind of journey or work will be undertaken.

Sheep or guinea pig (*uwija, kkowi*) or any furry animal—You will not accomplish your plans.

Fox (*atoq*)—Good luck.

Hen (*wallpa*)—Bad luck.

Flower (*t'ika*)—Someone is pregnant, or perhaps you are, if you are an eligible woman.

Fruit (*sach'a mijuy*)—You will give birth to a son.

Snake (*amaru* or *mach'akkway*)—You have acquired negative energy or an "ill wind."

Mouse (*kkechi*)—You will obtain money.

Rat (*huk'ucha*)—Something bad will happen.

Thorns, spikes (*kiskakuna*)—Indicates witchcraft. If the spines enter the body, the witchcraft will succeed. If it doesn't enter the body, it won't succeed.

Going up a slope or climbing a mountain (*wichayman puriykka allinmi*)—You are advancing well and will achieve what you are seeking. Downhill is the opposite.

Andean Food of the Gods; Medicinal Plants

Pachamama has produced an amazing variety of edible and medicinal plants in the Andes. Since ancient times the Andean people cultivated tuberous plants such as papakuna (potatoes), of which hundreds of varieties exist; ulluku (a small type of potato); cereals such as maize, kiwicha, kinúwa (quinoa) and kkañiwa; and legumes such as *tarwi* and *habaskuna* (beans). The subtropical valleys near Machu Picchu produce *uchu* (peppers), *rumu* or *yuca* (a delicious root that is boiled), *rakkacha* (similar to a carrot), *llakjón* (tuberous root), coca leaves, *inchiskuna* (peanuts), *pákkay* (leguminous fruit) and *chirimuya* (fruit), and many others.

The Andean people's diets were mainly vegetarian and these crops were capable of sustaining many different populations. When the Spanish conquered Peru they immediately exported potatoes and corn to Europe and the rest of the world. However, a great number of delicious and nutritious plants indigenous to South America were ignored and remain relatively unknown to this day. In some Western countries, Andean food products are beginning to appear in the food stores.

Kinúwa, Kkañiwa, and Kiwicha

Cereals such as kiwicha (amaranthus candata), kinúwa (chenopodium quinoa) and kkañiwa are indigenous to the Andes and referred to as "Food of the Gods." They contain 10 to 25 percent protein, which is much more than is contained in the imported grains such as wheat, flour, and barley. They also contain important quantities of calcium, phosphorus, and magnesium.

One of the proteins in kiwicha is called lisina, and it is known to enhance sexual potency and promote strength and virility. Inka men were known to be strong and it was common knowledge they were fearless fighters who had sexual relations with many women. Their strength and sexual prowess was attributed to their consuming large quantities of

kiwicha in many different forms. The Spanish found out about the value of kiwicha, and when they understood it could give the Andeans strength and revitalize them, they prohibited its cultivation in Peru and replaced it with wheat and *cebada* (barley) imported from Europe.

For more than 450 years kiwicha was forgotten, but due to an efficient Inkan storage process, archaeologists were able to retrieve seed from old sites. There has been a recultivation of this plant in central and northern Peru and in other countries.

Recently, the National Aeronautics and Space Administration (NASA) discovered that kiwicha is an excellent food low in calories and cholesterol, and it has opted to include it in the diet of space voyagers.

The Sacred Valley is home to fields of grains and cereals. Kiwicha is shown here.

Sara

The discovery of sara (corn) has intrigued scientists all over the world. It appeared in the Andes more than 4,000 years ago and is a hybrid cross between theosinti and a perennial grass in the *cia* family.

To the ancient Andean people, sara was a gift from God. It was regarded as the most sacred crop of the Inkakuna. Golden replicas of corn cobs were found in temples and sacred sites such as the Kkorikancha temple in Qosqo and, according to the local people, at Machu Picchu ruins before Hiram Bingham arrived.

Sara is the nourisher of all life—past, present and future—and is offered

Sara was considered a gift from God, according to the ancient Andean people.

to the dieties and ancestors. She is part of Pachamama and all things and is called beautiful by many because all aspects of her feed life.

Akkha

Akkha, or chicha as it is known in Spanish, is still one of the most important drinks for the Quechua people. Prepared at home, germinating maize kernels are ground and cooked to form a thick, beige-colored, fermented drink. Akkha is served to all guests and workers who come to work in ayni, and it plays an important part in ceremonies and festivals.

Germinated corn is the essential ingredient of akkha.

Before drinking akkha, the Quechua first offer some to Pachamama to thank Her, and trust that the seeds within Her will germinate like the corn seeds used in the akkha.

To prepare the akkha, the individual will select maize kernels of the finest quality and place them in a large bowl. She will then keep them damp for eight days, adding water so the grains germinate to three centimeters. Once germinated, they are dried in the sun, ground with a stone pestle and mortar, and boiled until well cooked.

After cooling, the Quechua will place a clean basket made of straw on top of a *raki* (a large ceramic bowl) and strain all the liquid from the boiled maize through the basket, keeping the residue back from the maize. The liquid is stored for forty-eight hours until it ferments into an alcoholic substance. Some women mix the akkha with alcohol made from sugar cane or with malted beer to accelerate the fermentation and enhance the taste.

The akkha is served in large mugs called *kkeros*. One of the curative properties of akkha is the prevention of problems with the prostate gland in older men. It is also known to augment the production of blood, and is a diuretic. This knowledge encourages the Quechua men to consume large quantities of akkha whenever possible.

Akkha for Sale

If a household wishes to sell akkha to passersby, they hang a long pole outside the door to which is attached colored strips or a bundle made from red or blue nylon or plastic. Visitors to the Sacred Valley of the Inka notice these poles as they drive through the countryside.

Chicha morada is a refreshing drink made from purple corn. A jelly-like dessert called *mazamorra morada* is also popular.

If a basket is hung in the doorway it announces to passersby that wheat and corn breads are for sale. When banana leaves are hung from the door it indicates the sale of coca leaves.

Pákkay, Purutu, and Tarwi

Pákkay (inga adenofila) is a leguminous fruit that has been used since ancient times in Peru. It feeds nitrogen back into the earth. Purutu (phaceolus vulgaris) is a bean, a legume high in protein. It, too, fertilizes the soil with nitrogen, and farmers grow it between their maize crops. Tarwi (lupinus mutabilis) contains 47 percent protein. That is double the protein of red meat. Moreover, the plant fertilizes the ground where the campesinos plant because the roots produce nitrates.

Recent studies in the biology department of the

A Quechua woman sells akkha.

San Antonio University in Qosqo show that tarwi, used as a food, breaks down cholesterol in the body (Departamento de Biologia de la Universidad de San Antonio del Cusco, UNSAAC, 1993).

Kkora Hampikuna

Kkora hampikuna are common medicinal plants. Thousands of varieties grow in the different ecological zones of Qosqo, the Sacred Valley, Machu Picchu, and Quillabamba. Medicinal plants are widely used and the campesinos benefit from their therapeutic properties.

For Sprains, Twists, Blows, and Fractures

Soltake solta (citacanthus sp)—A parasite that grows on top of trees. It binds (solders) torn ligaments and fractured bones together.

Chi'llka paukar or *challwa chilka* (baccharis sp), *cháman* or *chama* (baccharis floribunda)—As with soltake solta, all act as anti-inflammatory agents. Arnica helps to activate the three plants.

Yawar ch'onkka (enothera rosea)—An antibiotic and anti-inflammatory.

Since the Quechua may be hours or days away from medical help, they take care of themselves by using a wide variety of plants that grow locally.

Using a stone pestle, they grind together as many of the above herbs as possible. A little water is added to form a paste as well as a small amount of urine, and if available, the ground and dried meat of a poisonous snake to add vitamins. A cupful of wheat is ground and added to form a stiff paste binding all the medicine together.

The mixture is heated to a tolerable temperature and cañazo (alcohol) is added. The paste is applied to the injured area, covered with paper and then bound with a strip of bandage for a minimum of twenty-four hours. It sets like a plaster cast. The treatment is repeated for the next few days or until swelling is down and the injury is better.

Burns

Llantén (plantago hirtella)—Bite the leaf and place it on the wound. It cools the injury. Replace the leaves frequently.

Yerba de cáncer (stachys herrerae epling) —Dipped in boiled water, it cleans injuries and acts as an anti-inflammatory agent.

Matico, mokko mokko (piper elongatum)—Anti-bacterial plants that work like penicillin. Bite and chew the leaf a little to activate it and then place on the injury.

Other Medicinal Plants

Uchu (capsicum pubescens)—Known as *rokkoto* or *ají* (hot pepper), is used by the Quechua as a condiment to hot local dishes. It is known to kill internal parasites.

Winkiki (cyperus ferox)—Originally from the depths of the jungle, where the wise men and healers cultivated the plant for its ability to attract people with positive energy to help farmers with their agricultural work. Those with negative energy are repelled. The plant also helps people succeed in their business. It is said that if you pass the leaves in front of the body, you will return to that same place. This plant may be seen growing at Machu Picchu. Sit before it and know that you will return to that sacred city.

Maca: Searching for an AIDS Cure

Maca is a plant containing substances that fortify the immune system. Heberto J. Esparza Borges of La Universidad Autonoma Metropolitana in Mexico claims it could prevent AIDS. Studies by Peruvian and European scientists have shown that the plant tuber contains certain alkaloids that benefit the human immunological system.

Maca is known to stimulate fertility in animals. The ovaries of females that eat the plant are activated, increasing the number of ovarian follicles.

The effect of the plant on the immunological system is an aspect that has drawn the most attention from the world's researchers. Borges says the plant stimulates the hematopoietic system that produces the red blood cells.

At present, scientists from Italy and Germany are trying to determine if maca can help cure illnesses like AIDS, and others that cause deficiencies in the immunological system.

Eaten as a vegetable, the maca tuber is first dried in the sun to remove its toxins, then boiled to bring out its sweet taste.

"Aquicito No Mas"

In the surrounding mountains of the Sacred Valley of the Inkakuna, the Quechua campesinos can be seen walking well-travelled mountain paths to get to their cultivated lands, chahrakuna or local markets where they sell or barter their harvest.

The Quechua generally do not point their fingers as Westerners do when asked directions. They gesture with their chins, accompanied by a phrase such as *Aquicíto no más, mamacíta, papacíto:* "Just a little further, little mother, little father." This could mean anything from around the corner, just a few minutes' walk away, to a three-hour drive, ten miles away.

Rómulo and I were once lost on the narrow, winding backroads of the Sacred Valley after receiving directions from Quechua campesinos. We were looking for a certain pakko, a gifted female healer, and were trying to figure out where to go next when suddenly Rómulo leaped from his car, bounded over a stone wall, knelt down, and picked something.

Excitedly, he handed me a small branch of mint with purple flowers. He told me it was the first time he had ever seen the plant in bloom. According to his mother, it was a very lucky sign and he suggested I keep it in a special place. He took another little branch for his mother.

La Hierba Buena: Señora Lizárraga's Story

"My mother sent me to the forest to find herbs and vegetables she wanted to cook for lunch. I was playing in an area where the hierba buena grew and I saw that the plant had flowers that were purplish. I thought to myself how pretty the flowering herb was and decided the leaves would not be good to eat at this time.

"After gathering some other vegetables, I returned to the house and entered the kitchen. My mother asked me if I had picked the *hierba buena* (mint) and I said, 'No mama, the herb was very mature, full of flowers and not worth using in the soup.'

"My mother looked at me astounded. 'You found the herb flowering?' I responded, 'Yes, mama, they were covered with purple flowers.'

"My mother said, 'Run, return to that place and bring home some of the flowering hierba buena.'

"I ran back to the place and I saw that the flowers of the hierba buena had disappeared. I searched all over the banks of the river. I didn't find a single flower and, puzzled, I returned home without the flowers.

"My mother reprimanded me. 'Why did you not even take one flower when you saw it?' Then she added softly, 'Daughter, it was wonderful luck for you to see those flowers. It is extremely rare to see them and they only appear for a very short period of time. When you become an adult, you will be well served and have many riches.' She was referring to spiritual riches. I was twelve years old, and I ran out into the garden filled with happiness."

▼▼▼

 # Symbols in Daily Quechuan Life

Days of the Week

Each day of the Quechuan week is dedicated to a certain facet of Andean nature. The names of Quechua days of the week represent powerful symbols in the Andean cosmology.

Apuchaw

Apuchaw (Sunday) is dedicated to the apukuna. Apukuna, the divine lords of the sacred mountains, are considered the most important of all traditional deities. The Quechua show the utmost respect to the surrounding apukuna and acknowledge their importance in rituals and ceremonies (See Chapter Three).

Killachaw

Killachaw (Monday) is dedicated to Killa, the moon. Killa is regarded as the feminine essence. She is continually changing and controls the water, flood, and changes of season. The Quechua see her as entering into darkness, and the campesinos are afraid of her. Healers work with the high energy of the full moon for healing and the sending of special offerings. The Quechua are wary of Killa as she waxes, wanes, and disappears. They fear her darkness and know her as birth and death.

Killa is related to fertility, and the Quechua look to her phases for timing various agricultural activities. Seed planting may begin with the new moon and extend to the full moon, when planting is complete. Once the seeds are planted in the Pachamama they are protected by the moon, who also controls the reproduction of different animals. Kkowikuna and hens do not reproduce on full moon.

Atichaw

Atichaw (Tuesday) is dedicated to *ati*, which means power. The Quechua believe that great power comes from rayos (lightning), which can be divided into different types. *Ch'aki rayo* (dry lightning) is regarded as very dangerous and has a loud sound and unusual flash. In Chapter Seven, we described how a qualified Andean priest goes to the sacred peaks to become initiated as a master. He utilizes the power of the lightning and, if he survives the bolts that strike him, he is left with special psychic abilities. He may also be left with physical disabilities as a result of ch'aki rayo.

Rayo is regarded as feminine lightning, which may harm women or carry them away. Because of this, women are not encouraged to remain alone in the pasture fields.

Relámpago is male lightning, characterized by loud thunder claps. It does not strike the earth and therefore does not have the power to kill.

Koyllurchaw and Ch'askachaw

Koyllurchaw (Wednesday) is dedicated to the *qoyllur*, the morning star, and *Ch'askachaw* (Friday) is dedicated to the *ch'askakuna*, the stars.

Stars are the light by which inner awareness is guided. They play an important part in the Quechua cosmology and represent the divine presence. The cosmic power of the stars reaches down and blesses the earthly lives.

After many years of study and initiation, an alto misayoq receives the gift of a star that guides him in all his healing work. The Quechua believe in the ability of the stars to heal.

According to legend, before the sun and moon appeared in the sky, the star *pacha pakkarikk ch'aska* (dawn of the earth star) was the first bright object to emerge. Qoyllur is the name for the morning star, Venus, which belongs to a cluster of Goddesses.

Many Quechua campesinos look to their skies for guidance for the best time to plant, and they do this by determining the position of the brightest star relative to the other stars of the kollka (Pleiades). The kollka is also called the celestial storehouse or a nursery of seeds, and farmers observe the stars on June 24 or August 15 to make crop and weather predictions for the coming year. It is believed that if the Pleiades appear large when they rise, there will be an abundance of crops in the coming year.

Chakana represents the constellation of the Southern Cross, which is seen clearly in the Andean skies. In Andean cosmology it is regarded as the mythical center of the universe. Representation of the Southern Cross appeared at the center of the Kkoricancha altar during Inka times.

Celestial crosses are related to fertility and offer protection for the crops in bad weather. They also are important in rituals and ceremonies.

Gary Urton, in his book on Andean cosmology, *At the Crossroads of the Earth and Sky*, uses the phrase "star to star constellation" when the stars are linked to form inanimate, geometrical, or architectural figures along or near the main path of the Milky Way. He describes the "dark cloud constellations" as the "black areas which appear in sharp contrast to the interstellar dust and distinctly appear as either animals or plants."

It is said that animals of the dark cloud constellations originally came from the puyju (springs) in the Pachamama. The animals were able to descend into the Ukhupacha through the springs and were able to ascend to Hanakpacha by way of the mountain peaks, the apukuna.

Intichaw

Intichaw (Thursday) is dedicated to the Sun, Inti. Ancient Andean legends refer to the importance of Inti. The Inkakuna were considered the children of the Sun and their civilization was based on devotion to Inti. Inti illuminates the path and represents the universal force, supreme cosmic power, enlightenment, and understanding. Inti's rays transmit the divine energy to the world.

Today, the Andean Quechua honor Inti as one of many deities and include it in prayers and offerings. They look to the sun in the sky as a unit of time and make appointments according to where the position of the sun will be. They may arrange a meeting for "when the sun is over Machu Picchu peak."

Where the sun lies on the horizon determines the onset of agricultural periods. Urton says that in some communities on August 1 the sun is observed and, if it is *ch'usu* (small), it is a sign of a bad year. If it is *ransa* (large) the year will be normal and if it is *k'ello* (yellow) it forecasts a very good year.

K'uychichaw

K'uychichaw (Saturday) is dedicated to k'uychi, the rainbow. The Quechua do not necessarily perceive the seven colors of the rainbow as do Westerners. The significant colors for them are *puka* (red), *ancash* (blue), *k'ello*, *k'omer* (green) and *yurach* (white). In Andean cosmology, the rainbow represents a mach'akkway (serpent) which has two heads. It rises up into the sky from a puyju and arches into another spring some distance away. The rainbow is also said to be related to the Milky Way, which arches in the sky at night and is referred to as a celestial serpent.

The rainbows are regarded as malevolent and are said to enter the woman's abdomen through her vagina, causing severe pain. The Quechua say it is dangerous for a woman to urinate next to a spring when it rains because this is when the rainbow enters her body.

Animals of Importance

Traditional people of the Andes have carried on a form of interspecies communication for thousands of years. The Quechua feel responsible for animals and it has always been important to have a good relationship with the animals that surround them. Animals provide food, clothing, housing, and protection, as well as offer insights in dreams and healing ceremonies.

The Quechua celebrate festivals to honor and venerate animals. They respect the animal that is killed and offer a prayer of thanks to the animal for providing them with food.

There are stories of campesinos being killed while trying to save their animals. Domestic animals become members of the Andean families and enjoy their affection. There is a saying, *Si se le pega a un hombre, puede ser que se deje pegar pero si se toca a uno de sus animales, se rebelará con toda seguridad:* "If a man be hit, it could be he let himself be struck, but if one of his animals is touched, he'll surely fight back."

The apukuna are considered the owners of the wild animals and homage is made to them. The Quechua look to the animals for messages from the dieties. Seeing different animals may indicate that perhaps the dieties are asking for an offering or that something is not right. It may signify the presence or absence of rain or the beginning or ending of a season.

The Quechua regard animals as teachers. By observing their behaviour they learn to take on animal characteristics or qualities that will enhance their lives. Observing a field mouse might impart lessons in tenacity, for example.

Today, humans are destroying the protectors of the wild regions. Citizens with firearms and police come to hunt animals for sport and their meat. They claim the animals are dangerous and destroy the crops of the farmers. Those who follow the ancient traditions know it is important to be in harmony with the animals and all connected elements of Pachamama. They know that animals are connected to humans and their presence protects and teaches.

Llama

Historically, the llama was one of the most important animals in the Andes. It was offered to the Andean deities in the form of sacrifice. Llamas provided the Andeans with wool for clothing and dung for fertilizer and were used for transporting products. Llama meat was salted, sun dried and preserved. The word beef "jerky" comes from the Quechua word *ch'arki*.

In the night skies, the llama is one of the most conspicuous dark cloud constellations. It is directly involved with life on earth and assists in the circulation of its waters and the fertility of the llamas. The llama appears in the sky during the rainy season. Llama ñawikuna (eyes of the llama) refer to the two bright stars (A and B Centauri) that appear during the llama birthing period.

Today, the llama is in danger of extinction in the Andes. There is an improved transport system in the Andes, and horses and mules have replaced them in the mountains. The Alpaka has proven to be more profitable because it produces a better wool and has a tastier meat.

The llama must be conserved and valued for the honorable role it played in the ancient world of the Andes. It deserves to be acknowledged as a creature dedicated to the Andean deities.

Atoq

In Andean legends the atoq (fox) is the helper of the mountain deities. In the skies it is represented by Sirius "the dog star." It carries water from the mountains of Awsankate to the Vilcanota River. It is active in twilight, working between the worlds at a time when people die and are born and sleep is deep.

The fox lives in altitudes of up to 15,000 ft. Because it preys on vicuña and sheep, the campesinos regard it as dangerous.

Taruka and Ukuku

Two other important animals in danger of extinction are the *taruka* (deer) and the *ukuku* (spectacle bear.) The Quechua have depleted some of the high altitude areas of wood for fuel, and the deer can no longer live there.

The spectacle bear does not hibernate and needs food from different ecological systems to survive. It searches for bamboo and palm sprouts in the same area where people plant corn. The bear continues to be hunted by farmers because they destroy their crops.

Hanp'atu

Hanp'atu (croaking toads) announce the onset of rain, and the behavior of amphibians and cycles of agriculture are closely connected. The toad is represented in the constellation that rises in the sky during the rainy season, and the Quechua utilize toads in rituals for rain. They also are used by specialists of malevolent practices and sorcery.

Llut'u

The Quechua regard seeing the *llut'u* (animal resembling the partridge) as a bad omen. The female abandons her nest and the eggs are incubated by the male. The eggs have a variety of colors resembling the rainbow and there is an association between agriculture, rainbows and the celestial llut'u. The llut'u pursues the toad through the celestial skies and plays a part in crop fertilization in the rainy season.

*The puma symbolizes power and represents this world, Kaypacha,
in Andean cosmology. This ancient stone is from a private collection
at the old Alhambra Hotel in Yucay.*

Puma

The three most important archetypal animals representing the three
Andean worlds in Quechua cosmology are the puma, serpent, and condor.
The puma (mountain lion) symbolizes power and has been revered by the
ancient inhabitants of Peru for its strength and elegance. In Andean cosmology it represents the present world, Kaypacha, the world where
humans, plants, and animals live.

The puma is a dual entity: a predator feared and killed by man, and
also a deity that is regarded as a strong protector that blends into the territory. In Andean rituals the power of the Puma is evoked and human beings
can utilize it for personal growth. At the present, farmers have killed off
most of the pumakuna and they are in danger of becoming extinct.

Mach'akkway

Throughout the history of the Andes, *mach'akkway* (serpents) have had
great symbolic importance. Stonework of cities and temples from ancient
civilizations bear etchings of serpents, symbols of adored and respected

female deities. Snake goddesses appeared all over the temples of Peru. The yogic and Eastern traditions call the coiled serpent the Kundalini. It awakens in her secret place at the base of the spine and rises up through the chakras or energy centers, toward the head, activating the spiritual life and becoming *shakti* (divine energy).

During Inka times the serpent called Amaru was revered and regarded as the snake of wisdom enlightened by God. In most matriarchal cultures the snake is ubiquitous and all important. It represents the Goddess the world over.

With the rise of male-dominated cultures and their attendant symbol systems, the snake has been converted into a negative emblem. Societies all over the world have systematically killed the earlier supreme deity, the goddess symbolized by the earth-crawling and water-swimming snake, and replaced it with masculine symbols such as the sun and sky, or eagle.

The symbol of the snake shedding its skin is regarded as a process of renewal within one's lifetime. Like the snake, humans must allow the old ways to fall away and the inner bright skin to emerge.

In the Andes, the serpent represents Pachamama and Her inner world, Ukhupacha. The Quechua believe the snake epitomizes the meandering of the river. The river is water, and water is the symbol of life, which is eternal.

In Andean cosmology serpents are associated with all three worlds. They ascend and descend through the three planes of existence transforming themselves according to their relationship with each world. There are two mythical serpents, Yakumama, symbolizing water, and Sachamama, representing fertility.

In Hanakpacha, the upper world, Yakumama creates the rain and is associated with Chokkechinchaw, the bright feline that causes the rains to come. This feline is represented by the constellation known as Scorpio, which announces the summer. In Kaypacha, this world, the rain is converted into a river that runs across Pachamama in the form of a snake.

Sachamama comes out of Ukhupacha, the inner world, in the form of a two-headed serpent. In Kaypacha, it transforms into a tree with its upper head becoming the crown that feeds on flying beings and the lower head the base which attracts the animals of the surface of the earth.

The tree is called *mallki*, which has a double meaning. It refers to a seed that germinates as well as the term for ancestors and mummies. Mallki is a symbol for the two-headed serpent. In Hanakpacha the serpent transforms into a rainbow that fertilizes nature with its colors.

In the Andes today, the traditional Quechua man is at peace with the feminine Pachamama and maintains his ancient connection to Her.

Snakes, however, do not feature in rituals and ceremonies of the Quechua, an absence that may well now symbolize the synchretic union of masculine Christianity with feminine earth worship.

Since they are more active during the wet season, serpents are, nonetheless, still associated with water, wisdom, and fertility. Snakes can be invoked as protectors of a place, and the Quechua people living in the Machu Picchu area today are wary of snakes. It is said that whenever the campesinos tried to plant their crops too close to Machu Picchu ruins, they were frightened off by a large serpent with two horns. They believe this creature is there to protect the encroachment of farmers into the Sacred City. Snakes also teach them to be alert in the Andean territories. Perhaps at a subconscious level, they are acknowledging the continued power of the feminine in their nature-based cosmogony.

Kondor

Kondors (condors) have lived in the Andes for thousands of years. Andean folk as well as visitors always are thrilled by the sight of condors with wingspans of up to ten feet, soaring in the high mountain slopes. They always have played a role in the natural cycle of life and death and are thought to have supernatural powers.

Some Andeans believed the condor carried the sun away at night and back again in the morning. Condors were sacrificed to honor the spirits of the dead. It also was believed the condor came to see if its human following had kept its faith.

The condor epitomizes Hanakpacha, where higher spiritual beings and Taytanchis dwells. Quechua believe condors are symbols of the spirit and if they fly high enough they will touch the life-giving sun. They are messengers from the heavens and representatives of the mountain deities. Seeing them is regarded as a lucky omen.

Living in the Andes: Conversation with Aurelio Aguirre

"I spent my childhood years in the Andean wilderness. My Quechua parents and teachers would tell me magical tales about ancient legends, and I, with a couple of friends, would secretly take off to explore those wonderful places of fantasy.

We would disappear into remote areas outside of Qosqo where no one ever went.

"We entered worlds inhabited by invisible beings. Everything had light and form, and the sounds were incredible. Sometimes we were amazed because nature was singing to us, speaking to us; it was all so beautiful.

"We chatted with the animals; we knew the beautiful insects were intelligent beings who could communicate with each other. If we didn't understand them, we knew it was because we did not know how.

"Throughout my school years I remained close to the Andes. Friends would happily accompany me into the never-ending folds of the snow-capped nevadas where we continued to visit exotic places.

"Something special always has pulled me to the mountains. My connection to the Andes is part of my being, my life. When I walk in the mountains I always feel happy. After each journey I return home like a new man.

"Some people call it energy. It is the power of nature that creates this wonderful experience, and, while in this special state of consciousness, I have seen many beautiful things.

"I have been a professional guide for twenty years. About eight years ago, I was working with a group of tourists in the Qosqo area. A woman,

To the Quechua, water is the symbol of life.

accompanied by her son and daughter, was not able to walk without using walking sticks. After touring the ruins she said: 'Aurelio, I don't know what is happening. I am able to walk.'

"We traveled through the Sacred Valley of the Inka and on to Machu Picchu. At the Sacred City this lady hugged me and said, 'Aurelio I think it is you who made me walk. Thank you for that.' Her two children excitedly added, 'What did you do to our mother? She is walking.'

"I quietly answered, 'Nothing, nothing. Believe me, it is the Andes, the mountains. There is a special power present that encourages people to overcome whatever they find difficult.'

"I understood that at that time. But seeing the woman walk without her sticks made me begin to look deeper. I asked myself, 'What is it that happens here? What about me? Am I a part of it, or is it just nature at work?'

"I thought about this a great deal and finally came to the conclusion that I was, indeed, a part of these things. However, I :elt I needed to develop myself in order to become closer to this kind of experience and fully understand it.

"Up until then, I had often thought that experiences, like the woman walking, were just coincidences. But then I observed that they were consistent. I started to search within, and changes came about. I sat quietly in nature and began to see what was possible.

"When my daughters Caterina and Mariel came to me for help with schoolwork, I would take them for a walk in the Andes and say, 'Why don't you speak to the plants and insects as if they spoke Spanish? Ask them questions. Talk to them, as I did when I was a boy, then listen. Give nature a chance to speak to you. The answers always come.'

"A special experience occurred in my life about seven years ago. I was working with a group of fifteen Italian tourists. They called themselves a 'spiritual group,' and I had not the first idea of what their kind of work was about. I was willing to help them arrange special journeys to renew their energies, to search for the unknown. To me, some of the things they did seemed rather silly, like games adult people might enjoy.

"We were at the top of the mountain at Markawasi, a stark but beautiful power place that always has attracted spiritual seekers and new age hippies from Lima.

"The Italians got up for a sunrise meditation, holding each other in a circle, and I thought they were crazy. I was cooking breakfast for them and, because of the lack of oxygen at that altitude, it was a difficult task. Finally they ate, and I was free. Feeling very tired, I wandered off and went to lie on an unusual rock shaped like a cross. It felt like a very special place.

"Suddenly I was in a magnificent dream. I became this gigantic eagle with a golden aura. I was soaring over the ocean waves. I saw the rocks and high cliffs below me. I could see everything; it was so beautiful. I saw all the nicest places around Markawasi.

"Then, slowly, I felt my eagle body slip into my human body. I felt I was in a deep, deep sleep. I woke up with a start and realized that the Italian group had surrounded me. Some of them were holding me, because apparently I had been rocking back and forth at the edge of a sheer precipice that dropped thousands of meters below.

"The group had seen me, realized I was in danger, and came to gently hold me. They looked startled and asked me about my experience. I was surprised at their happy response to my story. They invited me to join their group and participate in their rituals. I practiced meditation and saw how it could nurture people and help to alter their lives.

"Soon after, I met a female artist from California who knew how to read I Ching coins. She told me she could see my aura and 'feel' things about me. I was curious and wondered what she could tell me.

"She threw the coins and exclaimed that something was unique and had not appeared for her before. She threw them again, looked at me and began accurately to tell me about my life and everything that had happened to me.

"Then she added that it was clear there was going to be a great change and I needed to be prepared. Soon I would no longer be married but I never believed her because I loved my wife. She added that, according to those coins, I would find a job that would keep me traveling. Soon after this, my wife left me and I began a new job which required a great deal of traveling.

"The same lady asked me to write down my name. She said that Aurelio means 'golden, shining,' and comes from Latin. My family name Aguirre means 'eagle.' My name, Aurelio Aguirre, is 'Golden Eagle.'

"As I continue to live in the Andes today, working with visitors from other countries, I have embraced different ways of thinking. This has helped me to see other aspects of my life and understand myself better.

"As did my Quechua ancestors, I now perceive the physical world connected to the spiritual world, and it is one of the nicest things that is happening to me."

▼▼▼

20

The True Discoverers of Machu Picchu Ruins

The Spanish invaders never found the city known as Machu Picchu. In Kkechuwa, *machu* means "ancient" and *picchu* means "summit, mountain top." Some say the city originally was known as Picchu Wanakauri, "the mountain of origin." Construction of the city was never completed, and it was abandoned before the Spanish arrived 460 years ago.

The city was intact up to the beginning of the twentieth century when farmers were growing crops of maize, yuca, bananas, and coffee beans on the slopes of the mountains and along the banks of the river Willkamayu. The mild climate allowed them to grow crops that could not grow closer to Qosqo.

In 1875, Rómulo's grandfather, Angel Mariano Lizárraga, was leasing land at San Miguel along the edge of the Ahobamba River. San Miguel is the area at the foot of Waynapicchu (Young Mountain), which sits above the ruins of Machu Picchu. Angel Moriano Lizárraga had a brother Agustín, who came to help him farm in 1890. Agustín always was searching for additional fertile land to cultivate yuca, *zapallos* (squash), cereal, and coffee.

In 1900, Agustín began to clear land by burning the dense vegetation at Inkarakkay, a valley at the foot of Waynapicchu. One day after burning a great stretch of plant growth, he climbed the cleared slopes to explore an area he'd never entered. There, Agustín found an ancient

Machu Picchu rises from the banks of the Urubamba River.

stairway rising from the banks of the Urubamba River, west of the mountain and leading to a place that is known today as the Sacred Plaza of Machu Picchu.

The fire had burned the surrounding terraces and almost reached the ruins. Agustín was very excited when he saw level areas filled with rich soil, apparently waiting to be cultivated. Then he realized his discovery was much greater: the terraces formed the outer edge of a vast, mysterious city hidden in the jungle.

It appears that Agustín Lizárraga, great uncle to Rómulo, was the first man in modern times to know of the existence of the Machu Picchu ruins. On one of his return visits, he left an inscription on the back of the great Sacred Rock that was inscribed "A. Lizárraga 1901."

Agustín noted the walls of the Inka buildings were perfectly constructed, and he became more excited when he noticed that in each exposed niche there were placed ceramics, tools, and figures made in gold and silver.

The rest of the family got to know about the treasure and talked about the corn cobs made out of gold and other fine items. But unlike Agustín, they had no desire to remove them from the ruins. They knew it was a sacred place and did not want to touch or remove any of the objects for fear of being punished by the ancient beings of the city.

But Agustín was young and rebellious and was more tempted by the treasure than respectful of Quechua traditions. It is said that he removed some beautiful objects within easy reach and sold them to a family of commercial merchants and traders, the Lomellini family from Italy. Years later, this family was known to be the most wealthy and admired in Qosqo, thanks to their secret business with Agustín Lizárraga.

Over the years, Agustín took his neighbors Enrique Palma, Gavino Sánchez, Luis Béjar U. and others to show them the ruins. It is said that when Agustín Lizárraga had a get-together with his farmer friends at his home, he served them wine and the best whisky in mugs of gold and silver. He also showed his friends some of the other unusual objects he had found. Perhaps these men returned to the ruins and also helped themselves to objects that were easily accessible.

Agustín invited Toribio Richarte and Anaclato Alvarez to cultivate the numerous terraces. Together with their families, they established their small chahras in the area that is now the Tourist Hotel at Machu Picchu. Eight years later in 1909, Agustín invited Melchor Arteaga from the district of Mollepata to visit the ruins to cultivate more terraces. Arteaga was a poor man who immediately saw a way to get rich. He began to sell ceramics and gold indiscriminately and boasted about the treasures. Word of this man soon reached Hiram Binghams' ears.

The professor from Yale was looking for the lost city of Willka-pampa (Vilcabamba), which was Mankko Inka's last stronghold in the jungle after the Spanish conquest. In 1909, Bingham met Albert Giesecke, an American born rector of the University of Qosqo. Giesecke repeated stories he had heard about the ruins above Mandor Pampa and suggested Bingham meet a Quechua man, Melchor Arteaga. Accompanied by Sergeant Carrasco, his military escort, Bingham set off for Mandor Pampa.

In the April 1913 issue of *National Geographic*, Bingham wrote of his meeting with Arteago and said, "This Indian rather better than average, but rather overfond of firewater... offered to show me the ruins he had once visited if I would pay him well for his service, fifty cents (1 sol) for his day's labor."

Bingham mentioned that Quechua families were established farmers at the ruins.

"At noon, we reached a little grass hut where a good-natured Indian family who had been living here for three or four years made us welcome and set before us gourds full of cool, delicious water and a few cold, boiled sweet potatoes."

In February 1912, José Gabriel Cosío, a delegate of the Peruvian government, noted Agustín's inscription at Machu Picchu. It also was noted by members of the scientific commission of Yale.

That same year, Agustín died while crossing turbulent waters of the river Willkamayu in what were said to be very strange circumstances. Cosío was instructed to remove the inscription on the Sacred Rock.

We asked Rómulo's mother what happened to the treasure that Agustín had had in his home.

She said, "It was said the treasure he had found in Machu Picchu and kept at home was inherited by his wife Rosa. After her husband's death, she became involved with the Catholic Church. She was encouraged to go to a Sunday confession at the Convent of Santa Clara in Qosqo.

"At the confession she told the priest she had some objects of gold and silver. The priest told her those objects were possessed by the devil and that she must donate them to the convent in order to absolve herself of the guilt. So great-aunt Rosa handed over all the treasure to the convent of Santa Clara in 1913, on the understanding that they would be mounted on the great altar in the church. She was told that her soul would then be saved."

No one knows about Rosa's soul, but the treasure was never seen again.

We asked Señora de Lizárraga how the people felt about Hiram Bingham coming to Machu Picchu.

"I remember my husband, who was a young man at that time, telling me that word went out that a gringo had found the ruins that were filled with 'mines of gold.' The local Quechua who wanted to get work with Bingham's outfit referred to the foreigners as a company of *saqueadores* (plunderers). The gringos had already set up guards in the area and would not offer any work to them."

The locals, Señora Lizárraga said, felt "uncomfortable" watching what belonged to their people being removed by the outsiders. They counted seventy large crates of treasure being carted away from the ruins, and no one ever learned what happened to the objects they contained.

According to Rómulo's father, Bingham had contracted three Quechua youths to take care of the camp. Three months later, they died under mysterious circumstances. Neighbor witnesses from Makinayuk, now known as Aguas Calientes, said they were murdered when trying to take back what had belonged to their ancestors. They were either punished by the apukuna, protectors of Machu Picchu, for removing the treasures in the first place, or perhaps by some gringos.

Even before the Quechua knew anything about the ruins at Machu Picchu, they knew it was a great spiritual center where the *sabios* (learned men) and Andean priests went to commune with the apukuna.

Bingham wrote about using the Quechua in the "construction of the bridge over the roaring river to make a trail sufficiently good for Indian bearers to use in carrying 60-pound food boxes up to camp, and later our 90-pound boxes of potsherds and specimens down to the mule trail near the river."

Controversy surrounds Bingham's "discovery" of the ruins at Machu Picchu. The National Geographic Society underwrote Bingham's expedition in 1912 and 1915. Claims were made over the years by English, French, German, and Italian explorers, and by prospectors, missionaries, engineers, and writers who said they visited Machu Picchu before Hiram Bingham.

Many accusations were levelled against Bingham's claim to being the first white man to visit the ruins. Bingham rebuked all these attacks and denied ever meeting these men or reading their articles prior to "his" discovery. He did briefly acknowledge that "some Indians" knew about the ruins before he got there.

The article, "Fights of Machu Picchu," published in Number 32 of *South American Explorer* by Daniel Buck, denies the

Stone carved as sacred altar to the apukuna at Machu Picchu.

other claims of "white men" that they were the first discoverers of Machu Picchu.

Confirming Señora de Lizárraga's story, Buck writes, "During his hurried inspection of the ruins, Bingham took note of a name and date, 'Lizárraga 1902,' scribbled on a wall. (Both dates 1901 and 1902 appear when reference is made to the inscription.) The following day, Arteaga told Bingham that Agustín Lizárraga, who lived at the nearby San Miguel bridge, had discovered Machu Picchu.

Buck adds that in a letter dated Aug. 8, 1911, handwritten at Santa Ana to Dr. J.S. Keltie at the Royal Geographical Society in London, Bingham made the first announcement of his discovery, writing that he had "found the ruins of a wonderful old Inka city... now called Machu Picchu i.e. old Picchu. It is so difficult to access that no one hereabouts has seen it. So far as I can discover only three Peruvians have seen it (except for a few Indians)."

According to Buck, during a shipboard interview published in the *New York Times* on Dec. 22, 1911, when Bingham was returning to the United States, he proclaimed the members of his expedition "were the first white men to see the remains of the City of Machu Picchu... since Pizarro entered it 400 years ago." (Pizarro never entered Machu Picchu.)

This fine stonework with niches is found in the temple at Ollantaytampu.

The three windows of the sacred temple, behind which
Agustín Lizárraga entered the ancient city in 1901.

Cosío, the official delegate to Bingham's follow-up expedition in 1912, wrote: "It is not true that Dr. Bingham was the discoverer of the ruins, but he did give them fame and archaeological interest. Before he came there, they were frequently ascended, and many people lived there, cultivating squash, yuca, sweet potato, sugar cane, and corn.

"A Mr. Lizárraga, now deceased, knew the site in all its details. On July 14, 1902, by the same road that Dr. Bingham took, a Mr. Sánchez, of Caicai, and Messrs. Enrique Palma and Lizárraga came to Machu Picchu. But, as always happens, they had no scientific or historical interest. They were interested only in hunting for lost treasures they thought were rumored to be buried in such locations."

Cosío added that when he visited Machu Picchu in 1912, Anacleto Alvares, one of the campesinos farming in the ruins, had lived there for eight years.

Bingham hired local Quechua men to build a bridge over the raging river, a dangerous task that claimed lives.

When he began excavation at Machu Picchu, Quechua men from other towns were recruited to work for them. The locals were unhappy because the Yale professor forbade them to enter the ruins, and those who worked in the area soon were tempted to resign. When they were sent into inhospitable areas to find caves to excavate, they came up with nothing and returned cut and bruised from the dense vegetation.

An undercurrent of racism further aggravated working conditions. The men in charge described the Quechua as "lazy and lacking in incentive." Since these workers were not from the area, they did not know where to look for the caves, and no one took into account the Quechua reluctance to disturb ancient burial sites.

The Quechua believed, as they do to this day, that negative energy emanates from the beings inhabiting ancient sites and causes disease and even death. Fear of angering the sacred apu of Machu Picchu, guardian of the "lost" city, was strong enough to keep the Quechua from disturbing the ruins. Even today, the Quechua campesinos show little interest in the many ruins dotted about the Andes. They appear interested only in finding good arable land for cultivation.

Despite his desire to keep local men away from his undertaking, Bingham found himself obligated to employ the services of some of them. The local Quechua, who knew all along where the caves were, quickly revealed the location of nearly all of them in the vicinity.

The new Quechua generation is asking what happened to the treasure from Machu Picchu. It is known that some of the Quechua farmers in the Machu Picchu area removed easily accessible objects of gold and silver and sold them to merchants in Qosqo at the beginning of the century. Señora de Lizárraga has spoken of hearing about the Lomellini family becoming wealthy through these illicit transactions.

Bingham acknowledges in the April 1913 issue of *National Geographic* that he appreciated the opportunity to work closely with a Cesar Lomellini. He salutes "Messrs. Cesar Lomellini & Co., of Cuzco, who for two years have acted as our agents and have placed at our disposal their excellent facilities for handling the difficult situations which arise in connection with the organization and administration of an exploring expedition, and all without charging us any commission or any rent, although we occupied a large room in their warehouses as our headquarters for many months."

Many other Europeans and Peruvians claimed to have visited Machu Picchu ruins before Bingham arrived. If so, did they, too, remove treasure from the ruins? Cosío of the Peruvian government called the Quechua men at Machu Picchu treasure hunters, but Bingham claimed to have found the city intact. He did not say the ruins had been previously disturbed.

Over the next five years, Bingham continued to excavate Machu Picchu and the surrounding areas. It is said that treasure was removed from these sites and sent out of the country under the pretext that they would be studied at Yale University and then returned to Peru. The crates the Peruvian government permitted to leave the country were shipped overland to Arequipa and then on to the port of Matarani. The citizens of Matarani and Arequipa knew the treasures had come from Machu Picchu and went on strike to oppose the riches leaving the country. President Augusto B. Leguía suddenly dismissed the authorities involved, and their replacements immediately allowed the artifacts to be taken away.

Many pages are missing from the books of records, and little research can be done on the ex-porting of crates through

Agricultural terraces were formed at Machu Picchu.

Matarani following Bingham's arrival at Machu Picchu.

Bingham declared that he never found any gold or silver at Machu Picchu. He wrote, "Our collections have all safely reached New Haven. They consist in large part of the bones of the people who built and lived in Machu Picchu, of the potsherds, pots, and bronzes found there, and of the geological, osteological, and paleontological material collected in the vicinity of Cuzco, of geological specimens from other parts of Peru, and of 2,500 photographs taken with the 3A Special and No. 4 Panaram Kodaks."

The Quechua farmers who had seen and heard of gold objects at Machu Picchu before the ruins were cleared and excavated had their own

Magnificent stonework appears in temples throughout the Andes.

ideas about what was in those crates.

It is difficult to point a moral finger at anyone. The subject of the Machu Picchu treasure is an issue of local jealousy and nationalism. In the early years of this century, both Peruvians and Bingham and his colleagues took what they knew was not theirs. (European explorers would probably have done the same as Bingham at that time, had they had money and opportunity.) The Quechua who removed the idols disobeyed the gods they lived by. They didn't concern themselves about selling national treasures that belonged in a museum. Bingham simply had more money; he and his teams of workers were backed by the National Geographic Society, assisted by the Peruvian government and lauded by the United States and the rest of the world. He was able to haul off everything he found, none of which was seen again.

Machu Picchu most likely has been discovered many times over since the last inhabitants of the city, the Inkakuna, lived there. Before Bingham's arrival, those of the local oral culture were not able to let the world know they had stumbled across some strange city filled with beautiful objects.

The elderly daughter of Melchor Arteaga and her family today live in a shack at a nearby railway depot. Other descendants with blood ties to the early Quechua farmers of Machu Picchu continue to live and farm in that area. Señora de Lizárraga clearly remembers hearing the stories of those days.

It was important to Bingham that he step into the territory as a modern-age Columbus and claim all credit for establishing the route to a "new world" of wealth and exoticism. The Quechua probably would have appreciated some sincere acknowledgement of the assistance they gave in the famous rediscovery of the ruins at Machu Picchu in 1911.

The new Quechua generation asks, if Bingham was dishonest about many of his claims, what else about his record is suspect? They request that all treasure that was removed from their country be returned to Machu Picchu and the museums, where it rightfully belongs.

Nearly a century after the Quechua campesinos first visited the ruins of Machu Picchu, and over 80 years after Hiram Bingham's visit, one of his quotes, written in 1922, still remains true for all people:

> *Whoever they were, whatever name be finally assigned to this site by future historians, of this I feel sure: that few romances can ever surpass that of the granite citadel on top of the beetling precipices of Machu Picchu, the crown of Inca Land.*

The Apukuna and the Eighty Mustazas

 We spoke about the main apukuna of the Machu Picchu area. Señora de Lizárraga told us the apukuna of Putukusi and Machu Picchu constantly conversed with each other. They often agreed on ways to protect the people, animals, and plants of the area. Apu Putukusi is east of Machu Picchu and faces the hotel and ruins at the top of the Machu Picchu site.

"Many years ago, Apu Machu Picchu had demanded from Apu Putikusi that he pay him eighty *mustazas* (sacrificial gifts) for allowing him to enter Machu Picchu, the house of the Sun. Apu Putukusi accepted this demand and when the foreigners came to Machu Picchu in 1911 to clear the streets and stairways, many of them died. It was said they died from snake bites or they slipped down the sheer cliffs of Waynapicchu, looking for treasure.

"The Quechua then understood that eighty mustazas meant that Apu Machu Picchu had to receive eighty human sacrifices accompanied by payments and offerings to the apukuna for allowing Apu Putukusi to enter the house of the Sun. Bingham and his people never made the offerings because they were not aware of the Andean cosmology. Bingham packed up the cargos of priceless treasures he had excavated and sent them to Arequipa, Matarani, and then on to the United States. One of the trains carrying the treasure crashed and many people died. There were now more sacrifices."

The Quechua people from the Machu Picchu area understand that Apu Putukusi still requires human sacrifices to meet the total of eighty mustazas demanded by Apu Machu Picchu. They point out that just below the two apukuna there are usually train accidents in which lives are lost, and it is understood that Apu Putukusi is still collecting payment for Apu Machu Picchu.

21

Machu Picchu:
Consecration or Desecration

After each visit to Machu Picchu, I indulged myself with an extended stay on the Lizárraga farm. At night I would lie in bed and gaze up through the window at the silhouette of Machu Picchu Peak towering over a sheer granite cliff, a view not seen from the ruins. Apu Machu Picchu became for me a blossoming presence. It took on life and I found myself communing with it, talking about my projects and asking for guidance and advice.

The local village was called Intiwatana, named for a large "hitching post to the sun" found near the base of the mountain. Opposite Machu Picchu, campesinos pointed out other intiwatanakuna on surrounding mountain tops, all appearing to have some relationship to each other. I believe they were constructed within a special vortex of energy, which one could feel while meditating at the farm below. It was interesting to note that, precisely at the base of this vortex, the government built a large hydroelectric station responsible for all the electrical power used in Cusco and other parts of the country.

Rómulo's mother would invite our Magical Journey groups to spend a few days at her farm. It made the perfect resting place for our Wilderness groups that had hiked and ridden on horseback from the sacred mountain Salkkantay. Amidst the most spectacular scenery imaginable, we would cross two 16,000-foot passes on trails that took us around the glaciers of Salkkantay. On the last day, we would hike down the flower-filled

Aobamba valley into the sub-tropical vegetation of Machu Picchu, arriving at the entrance to the Lizárraga farm.

Visitors would delight in using the oroya to cross the river, eating campesino food, and hiking along trails to study the medicinal plants. We would chat with the locals, many of whom were descendants of the Quechua who had farmed there at the turn of the century, already working the terraces of Machu Picchu before Hiram Bingham first claimed to "discover" the ruins.

I "chatted" to Apu Machu Picchu about my enthusiasm to establish a garden of medicinal flowers where visitors could observe Andean plants growing in their native habitat. Señora Lizárraga offered me a piece of her land, and tempting as it was, I had a strong sense that something was not right and it would be wiser to settle in the Sacred Valley.

In February 1995, the first of natural disasters began in the area around Machu Picchu. Late one night a huge landslide destroyed the entire hot springs complex at Aguas Calientes, just missing the village below. In December that year, our group left Aguas Calientes by bus for Machu Picchu. I stayed back with my son, Paul, who had a rash and needed to get medication. As we headed for the next bus, we were told that a huge boulder next to Machu Picchu Ruinas Hotel had dislodged, and within moments had become a plunging rockslide that swept through the zigzag roads leading to the station below. The bus with our group had just made it safely to the top. Paul and I, with the other tourists, had to hike 45 minutes on a steep trail up the mountain. As we climbed a distance from the slide, more and more boulders bounced off the mountain top. It was three months before the roads were repaired.

Five months later, a large chunk of glacier ice dislodged itself from Salkkantay, producing an avalanche of giant proportions. The avalanche gathered mud and stones as it thundered down the same valley we would travel from Salkkantay to get to the Lizárraga farm. That night, lying in bed at another small farm up the valley, Rómulo's brother-in-law, Eliseo, suddenly heard what sounded like rolling thunder. He yelled to his wife, Clothilda, to run with him up the sheer mountain cliff, and they escaped just in time to watch their home and animals being carried away in the dark. Wearing only thin clothing, they spent the cold Andean night clinging to brush until morning light when they could make their way to safety. A neighboring family with three small children disappeared in the mud, never to be found. Normally a two-day walk, it took the avalanche just a few hours to cover the distance from Salkkantay to the Urubamba below. It destroyed everything in its path, and the force of the boulders

Before the 1998 landslide: the hydroelectric station (middle of photo) at Intiwatana below Machu Picchu, and the Lizárraga farm, to the northeast (upper right).

smacking into the river changed its course, submerging hectares of land that the Lizárraga family had farmed for a century.

Fires raged in the area around Machu Picchu in October 1997, scorching thousands of hectares. At first, the fire was not taken seriously, and emergency crews were brought in only when it began approaching the ruins at Machu Picchu. Flames surrounded the entire ancient city and turned the emerald green mountains into black desolation. The path up to Waynapicchu was closed, and authorities quickly planted hardy bushes to stabilize the mountain cliffs before the start of rainy season.

Soon after, my partner Mark and I were appalled by news that the government planned to build a roadway and dam for the hydroelectric plant up the unstable valley where the mudslide had occurred. We watched tractors and bulldozers strip away the remaining green vegetation. Gone were the orchids, hydrangeas, begonias and impatiens that grew on the banks of the river. Our senses were assaulted with rubble and dust, and the energy of the area felt heavy and unsafe. We had received

This is the same view of the hydroelectric station (middle left) and the Lizárraga farm (upper right) taken after the 1998 landslide.

sufficient warnings from Salkkantay, and sadly I knew it would be the last time I would bring visitors to Intiwatana and the farm below Machu Picchu Peak.

In February 1998, another huge section of glacier from Salkkantay, melting in the unseasonably warm weather caused by El Niño, had separated from the mountain. This created another avalanche ten times greater than the first, which traveled down the same valley. Rómulo's daughter Indira, his niece, and brother Lucho were visiting the farm, and Rómulo didn't know if they were safe. Señora Lizárraga and her daughter-in-law, Joni, had gone to sell fruit at the Intiwatana station and had crossed the river on the oroya only minutes before disaster struck. They had to climb well above the station to escape the rising water. No one knew the fate of those who had remained on the farm.

Lucho was harvesting coffee beans when he looked up and saw a cloud of smoke cannonballing down the valley. He knew something was very wrong and ran back to the house to call the girls, who were playing indoors. Together with his brother-in-law and another worker, Jose, they fled the house and climbed the steep mountain slopes. Within a few minutes there was an explosion and the entire farm shook powerfully, as if caught in an earthquake. The avalanche of boulders and mud dammed up the roaring Urubamba river, churning back and causing the waters to rise almost 100 meters. Three tidal waves of mud rose up and enveloped the farm, burying 150 hectares of land and destroying two double-story homes along with the furnished guest houses used for Magical Journey groups. The waves of mud reversed direction, driving upstream toward the hydroelectric plant and destroying it along with hundreds of buildings and houses in the complex. The foraging river waters rushing from Machu Picchu crashed into the turbulent water trapped below and forced a rupture in the dam wall.

The local train from the jungle, filled to capacity with travelers to Qosqo, was just minutes away from Intiwatana station. As the driver turned the bend a flying boulder crashed into the front of the train and he saw the avalanche hit the river ahead. He stopped the train and hundreds of

The hydroelectric station (lower left of photo) and the Lizárraga farm (middle right) are completely submerged under more than eighty meters of mud.

passengers scrambled up the mountainside seconds before the water burst out from the dam. The flood continued on its devastating course to the jungle, destroying the train, railway line, towns, and farms, taking with it the livelihood of thousands of farmers and severing their lifeline to the outside world. The loss of agriculture and the hydroelectric plant will affect all of Peru for years to come.

Miraculously, Lucho, the girls, and the two men escaped by climbing to the top of the mountain, but it was three days before rescuers were able to cross the river to bring them to safety. Meanwhile after escaping the devastating landslide which buried Intiwatana train station under eightymeters of mud and stone on the other side of the river, Señora Lizárraga and her daughter-in-law sat huddled together at the upper railway switchback, waiting for a train from Qosqo, to take survivors from the area. Señora Lizárraga did not believe that any of the family on the farm could have survived the destruction. Her two young granddaughters had come to celebrate their grandmother's eighty-ninth birthday, and she had left them playing inside the house when she crossed the river to sell bananas at the station. She had played out this ritual every day of her life, and from the few soles earned each day had saved enough money to send all her children to Qosqo to be educated. Proudly, she always would proclaim that her seven sons went to university and obtained degrees. During almost nine decades, she had hardly missed a day selling fruit, tending to her coffee beans and chickens, and cooking for the farm workers.

In disbelief and shock, she watched her life's work disappear under waves of churning mud and tons of debris. She saw her land become a lake and her neighbors' farms vanish along with the homes of all her elderly friends living along the railway lines.

Soon after the tragedy, Señora Lizárraga, now living with her children in Qosqo, came to visit me. It cheered her up to see how many of her Machu Picchu plants were now thriving in our gardens at Willka T'ika. Wistfully, she said she would like to go back and farm at Machu Picchu one day.

I asked her for her thoughts on this tragedy that has taken away everything she has worked for during this century.

"People must understand that all of Machu Picchu, the Intiwatana, and the hydroelectric plant are protected by the apukuna, the powerful mountain deities. The apukuna have become angry because they were insulted by the locals and skeptical foreigners. Many people want to climb to the snowy mountains such as Salkkantay, Huamantay, and Palkkay without asking permission from the apukuna or the Kamak, creator of man. These gods have been offended by those who fail to acknowledge them and do not send their offerings.

"There are people who wish to develop the area, and they do not understand that, since ancient times, this land has been preserved as sacred. It was to be left only for the wise ones whose spirits control the region. The guardian spirits do not want roadways or industry, or people who pollute the land from Chillka (the start of the Inka trail) to Aobamba (the valley behind Machu Picchu). These are sacred areas. It was there the deities had built the ancient city of Machu Picchu. The caves you visited (see Chapter 13) where you saw remains of the gentiles, the ancient beings, belong to the guardians of the valley of Aobamba. Close to the caves, teams of workers began tearing up the land to build a road. Engineers drew plans that would require hauling in building materials. They were going to lay giant tubes to erect an even larger hydroelectric dam in the heart of this sacred land. Authorities ignored the first landslide, which came down as a warning from Salkkantay over a year ago. The engineers who planned this construction were unaware of the caves and failed to respect the spiritual beliefs of the ancient ones, the *naupa machukuna*."

According to the belief system of the Quechua, Pachamama has sent warning after warning to the people of Machu Picchu. Salkkantay, the most powerful of all mountain deities, has spoken yet again, this time with a vengeance that cannot be

Doña Robertina, a resident of Intiwatana, sits above the valley where her family farm was destroyed by the landslide..

ignored. Our stories gathered from these people will live on, but many of the places I wrote about exist no more. We must ask ourselves if this is an example of the enormous price to be paid for not respecting Pachamama, our Mother Earth. Most tourists visiting the ruins at Machu Picchu still remain unaware of, and unaffected by, this tragedy that has taken place on the other side of the mountain.

22

Alicia Chacon:
Story of an Andean Healer

"My name is Alicia and I am a curandera Andina, healer or *laykka*, a female pakko. Everything I have learned has been passed down from my ancestors. My great-grandfather and my grandmother also were pakkokuna, and they taught my father, who taught me. I was the only daughter among eleven sons, and when I was born there were signs on my body signifying that I was chosen to do this work. On my forehead there were the red marks of a small chakana, the Andean cross representing the Southern Cross. On my wrists you can see the markings of the eyes of a llama, and there are the markings of a larger chakana in the center of my chest. My father anointed me in an Andean ceremony called *unuchakuy*, taught me special prayers, how to read coca leaves and maize, and gave me the knowledge of the four directions, *tawakkuchuy*.

"Growing up, I was different from others and never really had friends. My father would say, 'I will take your left hand, and you will continue walking to different places.' He would tell people, 'My daughter has the knowledge. When I die, I will leave her to take over my work and help you.'

"*Noqa wañutiyka wawan hapinqa lloqè maquiyta.*

"*Paymi necsinka tukuy hampikuykunata.*

"As an apprentice to an Andean healer, I was put to three tests. The first was to master working with the kkowi, guinea pigs used as diagnostic tools in the country, where there are no x-ray machines. In a special healing ceremony, I pass the kkowi over the body of my patient. I must keep it alive while removing its skin in order to examine its insides. The kkowi

203

absorbs the illness of the patient so that I can 'read' whether the patient has suffered a blow, a broken bone, or has heart or other organ problems.

"For my next test I was taken to the mountain Sallkkantay, which is considered the most powerful protector. The correct name is Sallkanchay, the wild one, and it is the second highest glacier in the region. There, I had to drink three cups of the blood of a condor to receive its power. The condor represents another powerful god in the Andes.

"Finally, I had to learn by heart all the special prayers I was given in Kkechuwa. These secret ancient prayers are given only to the initiated and never shared with other living beings. With knowledge of these secret prayers, I was given the powers to become an Andean priestess, to work as a healer in the villages.

"My belief system is pure Andean. Our special gods are the sun, the moon, the rainbow, the stars, and the lightning. No other gods can replace these. We never use Catholic prayers, but rather our own, for in this way we can heal our people with complete faith. I follow a religion that is for myself and for the people of my village.

"I never imagined that I would have contact with people from another country, and believed that my work was going to be only for me and my people in the Anta pueblo. For three years I had been living together with my husband in Qosqo, and only recently did I tell him about my work. I realize this may have been a little selfish to keep what was pure Andean wisdom from others, but it is only now that I feel comfortable to share with outsiders what I know to be true. As I get to know more people, I will show them what is the true Andean spirituality.

"Recently I had the opportunity to go to Machu Picchu. There I observed how people were making a mockery out of the Andean gods, the apukuna, and Andean spirituality. It made me upset to listen and see how people were putting on a show for the express purpose of making money. I saw self-anointed people dressed up in fancy clothing, calling themselves Andean shamans after growing their hair long and tying it into ponytails. They did not know how to send an offering; they were throwing coca leaves here and there, moving sticks in their hands and fooling around. What they were doing was sacrilegious, and all of this was disturbing. I never saw anyone at Machu Picchu work in the way of a true Andean priest, and I now understand that most of the guides do not really believe in these things.

"It is my destiny to work with true spirit and help people. Always, I will keep working with what is mine, what is me. But when I hear there are initiations being offered to foreigners in the Andes, and that people

Alicia with author Carol Cumes, working with the healing energies of stones.

believe they, too, can become high priests or shamans in just a short time, I know this is false. To become a true shaman or *hampich*, an Andean curandera or pakko, is a lifetime of work. You are chosen for this role at birth and must be committed to the life from a very young age.

"Our Mother Earth needs an offering in the form of foods that grow and live within her. We must offer the finest products to her that she has given us. Coca leaves are never thrown around. They are part of the haywarikuy, the offering ceremony, which is made up of special Andean elements. Included in the offering is the coca k'intu (see Chapter 5). The finest coca leaves must be selected and placed in threes, in a specific sequence, and in the order of the apukuna surrounding the area. Often when people ask for help from Pachamama and make incorrect offerings, they do Her harm. These ceremonies should be performed only by qualified people who are born into this work, live for this work, adore the earth, and are happy.

"The mountains, rocks, and stones are my friends and companions; they are my father and my mother. It upsets me when rocks are destroyed or blown up by dynamite, as if they are destroying a person. We see that happening around Machu Picchu, where mountains are burning and rocks are falling because the people no longer adore nature.

"Recently there was a problem with a tourist from Germany. She had taken a stone from Machu Picchu to her house. It was just a simple stone, but as soon as she arrived home everything began to go wrong and her life filled with problems. She returned the stone to her guide in Peru, saying that it was a terrible stone and he should not look upon or touch the stone because it was evil. The week the guide had the stone he, too, began experiencing problems. He asked another guide to take it back to Machu Picchu, but this one also could not manage the journey and he gave it to another, who then began to suffer. And so these guides came to consult me, through my husband. They warned me not to look at or touch the stone. I told them not to worry, for I knew about these things. I told them that this stone was an *ariska, salkkarumi,* a 'wild' stone, which had not been healed. It had never been touched by other people and belonged inside an Inka tomb. It contained a special oxidized acid that could harm a person.

"First, I cleansed the people who brought the stone. Then I looked at the stone and smelled it. It had an old and wild smell. I kept the stone with me for a week and healed it. A month later I took it to Saksaywaman, where I 'planted' it and asked the apukuna to receive the stone, which it did. Now that I am beginning to have contact with persons from other countries, I always warn them to be wary of stones for often, if the gods of the Andes, the apukuna, have not received a payment, then visitors will not be able to remove them. Stones have their own places in ancient sacred sites and should not be taken because they might become disconnected from their spiritual home. Before removing a stone, one must see whether it is made of quartz and whether it will bring good luck or bad. Stones made of quartz are not so dangerous because they can be cleansed easily.

"I wish to tell people to adore and appreciate what is nature. The Andean mountains are filled with spirits, and these apukuna are our spiritual gods who will protect us and keep us from harm. We must not destroy the vegetation, the trees, the animals. People who are using spirituality to make money by offering false ceremonies are causing harm to Pachamama. The spirits of the Andes are strong and they are becoming angry.

"Within me is the desire to teach what is truly Andean and what is real, so that people will not be deceived by false masters. I have been encouraged to give talks to those who are interested in Andean culture, and I would like to begin by demonstrating true offerings and teachings about Andean herbs.

"Andean offerings, haywarikuy, are not only for the farmers, but also are sent for people in business, for the house, family, and for general well-being. All these offerings are made to the gods. I do not make the offering

Offerings and ceremonies given at Machu Picchu should only be done by qualified people who are born into such work; anyone else is considered sacrilegious.

on my own, I share it with the people, and I want everyone to participate. I also say the prayers aloud in Kkechuwa because I want them to be heard by everyone.

"To understand what a true haywarikuy is, one must focus upon it with positive thought and prepare it while in a deep meditative state. The last time I observed people sending an offering at Machu Picchu, everyone was dressed in white. It is not necessary to wear white clothes because our Andean gods receive us just as we are. To send the offering, we must give thanks to the mountains, to the flowers, to the birds, and to the river, for this is very powerful to us. At the same time, we must reflect on Hanakpacha, the world above; Kaypacha, this earth; Ujhupacha, the world below, or inner world. (See Chapter 7.) We must acknowledge that we are connected to everything, the apukuna, the rainbow, and the moon.

"For the Andean people, Machu Picchu is one of our apukuna, the mountain spirits, our gods, as are the other mountains that surround our villages, such as Apu Putukusi or Apu Saksaywaman. While growing up, I heard from my father that Machu Picchu was a sanctuary of the Inka. Occasionally he went there to make an invocation to the apukuna, because below Apu Machu Picchu there is a concentration of what is the

spirit of the Andes. Our religion began long before the Inkakuna constructed Machu Picchu and lived there.

"Andean healers have no real need to know about the temples and
sacred cities. Their belief is in Mother Earth and all spirits of nature. This
spirituality was there before the Inka came and continues to exist. All
places in nature are sacred, and none are more sacred than others. The
same applies in other areas where there are sacred cities surrounded by our
apukuna. Normally we go to the mountains near our own communities
where we can establish contact with our apukuna. Each village invokes the
spirit from their area. There are, however, some great apukuna such as
Salkkanchay and Ausangate, who command more respect than others and
control an entire region."

I asked Alicia if she believed the apukuna spoke directly through the
medium of an alto misayoq (see Chapter 7), directly to people during special sessions.

"I'll tell you a story. One day my father told me he had heard about
people who had some communication with the apukuna. He did not
believe it and said it was not true. He took me to visit this man who
called himself an alto misayoq, and we were shown into a big room inside
his house where there was a large table set with food. Before we entered,
my father said we must each hide a flashlight inside our coats. The alto
misayoq and his assistant began the session and told everyone to be quiet.
They said there would be no light entering the room, and everyone began
to pray in the dark. We listened while they prayed with Catholic prayers.
Finally, we were told that the apu was coming. We heard the sound of rain
followed by the sounds of wings flapping. My father told me that in one
second we should switch on our flashlights, and we did. The alto misayoq
had a bag filled with sand, which he was throwing against the roof. Under
the table his assistant held the wings of a condor which he was flapping.
My father shouted out that they were deceiving the people and taking
money from them for nothing, and he made sure that the two men were
banished from the village.

"The apukuna do not speak directly through these people in this
way, they speak to you spiritually through your mind and being. You don't
hear them converse. You feel a sensation through your body and might
feel weak as if you were going to faint and fall to the floor. Thereafter one
becomes a vehicle for the expression of their will.

"When sending an offering, I concentrate hard on the apu, and as I
connect spiritually I feel that something strange is happening inside my
body. Some people begin to shake while establishing contact with the

spirit of the apu. If you have good faith, you will receive help through the offering."

The concept of ayni is innately Andean (see Chapter 4). I had come to see that the sending of an offering was a manifestation of the spirit of ayni, an expression of the spirit of devotion and belief in the mutuality of nature and life. I chatted to Alicia about this, and she said:

"Ayni is the process of giving to others what they need, and when the giver in turn needs something, it will come back to him or her. The intent of ayni is to give rather than have the expectation of receiving. Ayni takes place when you send offerings to Pachamama and the apukuna because you need their energy and power in order to work and not feel bad. You give the apukuna your offerings and in return they will give you the energy you need. Ayni is an exchange of living energy.

"Give to Pachamama for love, not because there is an ulterior motive. The people in the mountain communities are living close to Mother Earth in their daily life. They do not have anything else closely connected to them. They receive everything from the Mother Earth, the plants, crops, and water, and so deeply imbedded within their consciousness is a reverence for Her importance. Thus, they continue to give Pachamama their offerings and thanks.

"As a healer, I work with good faith and help others who are ill, morally and physically. I use words that will lift their morale and encourage them to believe in themselves, so they will be able to overcome their illnesses. When people come to me with a grave disease, I work with them spiritually and we do a focused meditation. First they must talk about all that has happened in their lives, then they must focus on themselves to remove this illness. In diseases such as cancers, I work with a type of mud taken from the earth in special areas where there are springs. I place it into an earthen container, mix it with special Andean prayers, then spread it over the body. It is important that the person hold the positive idea that he or she will be cured. Whatever problems we have, we must not hide in them or dwell on them. We must believe that we can overcome everything, and that nothing and no one can do us harm. We can do anything by allowing the apukuna to help us think positively."

With these words from Alicia, I feel that I have traveled the full circle in my journey to Machu Picchu. I appreciate the truth about Andean spirituality and I have walked the path of my destiny. I began my journey searching for the Andean truth and I was satisfied that I had found it in the mountain people. Alicia's words ring true. That is what it is, that is all that it is, and that is all that it needs to be. We come as visitors to the Andes. Let us come with respect to the children of Pachamama, in a spirit of self-respect. These people have stayed close to their own roots. We can learn from them to end our own alienation from nature, not by distorting their traditions and beliefs, but by rediscovering our own heritage of respect rooted in the same Mother Earth. We are, after all, only visitors to Her planet.

Afterword

The Legacy of Pachamama

Andean cosmology has directed human life in the region for thousands of years, and the Quechua people have handed down their traditions and spiritual beliefs in oral form for generations. It is vital that Westerners appreciate the Quechua way of life as a valid and positive way of relating to the world and not demean or dismiss it as primitive superstition. What might seem ludicrous to the European mind is, in fact, a working philosophy for the Quechua. Their belief system works in the context of the Andean people and land.

Westerners can learn much that is good and applicable to their own culture from these "alien" traditions. They can observe the Andeans' unwavering love for Pachamama: a respect for nature and all her powerful forces; an understanding that all things are interconnected; and the practice of ayni, the gift of sharing, that makes the arduous farm work possible.

We are reminded that families remain intact and that their members feel valued as part of a large and festive community. The generosity of these people is impressive, as is their capacity to relax, sing, dance, and feast after the hard work is done.

This book may trigger a journey of awakening, whereby we begin to look inward to discover our own purpose in this lifetime: who we are, why we are here, where we are going, and what we are connected to. We need only allow the process to unfold. Rather than attempt to take on the Quechua belief system as our own, we may adapt the principles of Andean cosmology to the philosophy of Western society.

Steps leading to the sacred temples of Machu Picchu.

The possibility that visitors to the Machu Picchu and Qosqo areas might "try on" the Quechua people's sacred customs and ceremonies in an insensitive manner is a source of concern for some inhabitants of the region. A discerning reader will not be surprised to know that unqualified specialists from Qosqo and so-called spiritual seekers from other countries are packaging and offering pseudo-spiritual journeys of initiation for commercial purposes. Our reprise of the history of the "discovery" of Machu Picchu is reminder enough that the human spirit, whether issuing from a famed North American university or an "unknown" indigenous farm, stretches to embrace many impulses of the baser "animal" nature.

What is significant for our purposes is that the Quechua belief system is sometimes interpreted by profit-motivated individuals as a "product" with saleable value: it is true that Andean cosmology offers something desirable that Westerners might be willing to buy into. We recognize the desirability of a world view that stresses tolerance, kindness to nature and all other living beings, and respect for the wisdom of beloved forebears. We sympathize with the native holders of this attitude who are offended by attempts to commercialize a richness of spirit and heart that is impoverished by unworthy thoughts of financial exploitation.

Our position is beautifully symbolized by the following prayer. It was given to us by a Peruvian spirit who represents an immortal human soul no longer burdened with temptations the body demands to be fulfilled. The prayer advises that each of us, during our allotted time on earth:

> *Walk through this place as a visitor. Respect all things you come upon and you will be respected. Respect all people you come upon and you will be honored. Pray to all the gods you come upon and you will be accepted. He who honors the traditions of all ancient people and all contemporary people has no enemy. You are caretakers of realization. Realization by any name is the awareness that you are God. The feeling of great understanding is Love. The man who attains God is the man who walks each day as though he is on a vacation from heaven, the vacation on Planet Earth in Human Body, the journey called reincarnation. It was never meant for you to establish residency here. You were meant to taste here, and to enjoy yourself in its rituals and sacraments, with wisdom to experience the passion, anger, joy, love, peace. Yourself in the presence of the great trees that are forever green. You are but a visitor to this body, to this planet. The gold you seek, the house you build, the relationships you form are only for experience to keep, to help keep you forever weaving the experience called you.*
>
> *I come to you from a world that is within you, that awaits you, that brings you to my world through the gate of dignity, self-respect and self-love.*

It is easiest, of course, to feel that world of dignity, self-respect, and self-love steal into the soul when the body is walking the Sacred Valley of Peru or climbing the purifying thousands of meters of the ancient Inka Trail into the clouds ringing Machu Picchu. That feeling of journey and arrival is so powerful that it pulls many Westerners away from their smog-filled cities to the grassy highlands of the Andes time after time, to lose and then find themselves in the bottomless gaze of a pair of soft black Quechua eyes, or the patient regard of Pachamama.

We have woven into the pages of this book a context for that potential spiritual union of self to world and to self. Its format appeals to the Westerner's analytical (written) approach to understanding the inexplicable realities outside his libraries. The truths it attempts to convey appeal to the spirit-gods that live in each human being, wherever the apukuna have deigned to set that person's feet on the path to a higher realization.

Clear skies around Apu Machu Picchu.

Sacred Journeys to Peru

For information on sacred journeys to Peru led by author Carol Cumes, and on Willka T'ika, a Medicinal Flower Garden and Retreat Center located in the Sacred Valley of the Inka, Peru, please write to:

Magical Journey
915 Cole St., Suite 236
San Francisco, CA 94117
888-PERU-070
info@travelperu.com
www.travelperu.com

In Peru:
Casilla Postal 70
Urubamba, Cusco, Peru

Appendix A: The Kkechuwa Language

To know the Peruvian Andes is to know the Quechua people. An understanding of the Kkechuwa language will open the doorway into their fascinating world.

Kkechuwa, in Spanish written as Quechua, is the beautiful, living language of the Andes. It is rich in expression and imagery; power resides in the sounds and vibrations of every word. In the Andes of Peru, the name of every sacred peak, landmark, town, river, animal, plant and every aspect of nature is in the Kkechuwa language.

Faustino Espinoza Navarro, of the Quechua Language Academy in Qosqo, is an expert on the Kkechuwa language and an Andean ritual specialist. He informs us that the origins of the Kkechuwa language can be traced to prehistoric times when the inhabitants of the Andean valley in the Qosqo region were called Kkeswakuna. They interpreted the sounds of nature to create a language called Kkeswasimi, which Espinoza believes is the correct name of the Kkechuwa language.

At the time of the Spanish invasion in 1532, Kkechuwa was the language of those indigenous to the region of Qosqo. It was also the administrative language of Tawantinsuyu, the immense Inka Empire that included most of what is now Ecuador, Peru, Bolivia, northern Chile, and northwestern Argentina.

During the Inka period, the language's full name was Kkeswasimi, *simi* meaning "mouth" or "spoken tongue." Kkeswasimi consisted of two categories: Kkhápakksimi was used exclusively by the rich and powerful Inka lords and royal families known as the children of the Sun; Runasimi (human speech) was spoken by those considered to be the children of the Pachamama, the Earth Mother. They lived in the countryside, away from the sacred centers and had no formal educators. Runasimi was the official language of Tawantinsuyu.

Runasimi or Kkechuwasimi, or Kkechuwa as it is known today, varies in each region; this language is spoken in Qosqo, the former Inkan capital, and is widely understood and regarded as the purest. Sixteen million people in Peru, Bolivia, Ecuador, and northern Argentina still speak this indigenous language, more than any other native tongue surviving in the Americas. The language continues to spread throughout Andean countries.

The Western world was introduced to this complex language by the writings of famous chroniclers in the centuries following Spanish arrival in Peru. They offered a wide variety of interpretations in their attempt to document the Kkechuwa names and the Inkan way of life.

They described an annual ritual in Qosqo when the people would rid their city of illness, suffering, and evil. The inhabitants cleansed and purified their bodies by fasting and abstaining from sexual activity, while the sick, lepers, cripples, and dogs were sent out of the city area.

Various dates were given for the same ritual. According to the chronicler Inka Garcilaso, the ritual was called Citua. Another chronicler, Molina, from Qosqo, named it Zitua. Yet another, Martín de Murúa, referred to it as Itu, and Barnabé Cobo called it Situa.

As one can see, both the original language and facts on the Andean traditions were clearly distorted over the years following the Spanish occupation of the Andes.

Learning Kkechuwa

It is difficult to learn Kkechuwa. Words are long and have a unique pronunciation and definite rhythm. One word in Kkechuwa might require a long description in Spanish. There are a multitude of words and pronunciations. The letter "k" may be sounded in several different ways. The absence of a slight click turns "a gentleman" (*werakocha*) into "a lake of grease" (*wirakkocha*) or "the gate of the rainbow" (*k'uichipunku*) into "the door of the pigpen" (*kuchipunku*). To speak Kkechuwa implies a deep understanding of the texture of things. In Kkechuwa there are no words that imply doubt such as "perhaps" or "maybe." Each word expresses a definitive vision of reality.

Kkechuwa is part and parcel of the natural world. Espinoza explained that the word *kkeswa* was taken from two sounds produced by nature in the Andes. During the rainy season, when great boulders were loosened from the mountains and began to slide down the slopes, they produced the sound "kkess." As they fell to the bottom of the ravines where the rivers flow, they sounded as "waa." The boulders blocked the ravines and dammed up the rivers. In time, the water pressure burst the dam, sending huge boulders with uncontrollable force down the rivers. As the large stones ground smaller ones into sand, the clear sound "kkess" was produced. The bumping of the rocks that continued to tumble down the river created the "waa." The word for "ravine" in Kkechuwa is *kkeswawayk'o*.

Many of the language's words are taken from the animal world of the Andes: the llama, for example, clearly says "llaam llaam;" dogs bark, "alqo alqo;" and the Taruka deer says, "th'aru, th'aru" as it runs. Other words are related to the sounds of weather: *k'akya* is the clap of thunder produced by lightning, and *para* is the sound of falling raindrops.

Traditional Quechua people used the sounds woven into the names of objects or elements to summon the power of those objects. Humans, animals and all elements of nature were condensations of sound, solidified vibration. The Quechua sounded the names of apukuna (mountain lords), animals, rain, roaring rivers, and all elements to evoke their power and converse with them.

In the sixteenth century, Padre Domingo de Santa Tomás wrote about the Andean language, compiling and publishing the first grammar and vocabulary text called the *Lexicón o Vocabulario de la Lengua General del Peru*. He referred to the language as Kkechuwa.

The use of the word Quechua as a name for the language was possibly the result of the Spanish mistaking the word *kkeswasimi* (language of the valley) for the name of the language. Apparently the word *kkeswa* was easier for the Spanish to pronounce than kkeswasimi. Eventually, the Spanish language adopted the term Quechua, with characteristic Castillian spelling.

Ninety percent of the current population speak Kkechuwa. In the rural areas it is spoken everywhere and is the language of everyday interaction. During the reforms of President Juan Velasco (1968–1975), the Peruvian Government declared Kkechuwa an official national language. Government changed and Kkechuwa now is recognized for official use only in areas where it is widely spoken. Due to lack of government interest and support, the language is not taught in schools or in the countryside of the Andes where it is spoken. Few teachers are fully bilingual.

Kkechuwa continues to be passed down orally from generation to generation. It is the first language that all the children in the farming communities of the Andes learn to speak.

In *The Language of the Inka since the European Invasion,* author Bruce Mannheim refers to "Spanish being the language of the dominant sector and Quechua, the language of the dominated." He considers Kkechuwa an oppressed language, and notes that the Quechua people must maintain a working knowledge of Spanish. They need Spanish to deal with administrative paperwork and to defend their legal claims in court. The Quechua often have to protect their basic production resources and their land from outsiders, former landowners, and scheming bureaucrats.

Spanish also is needed for those leaving their traditional communities to seek temporary urban work in order to earn cash for goods that can be bought only in stores. Rural parents believe their children must learn Spanish in school in order to move ahead in the future. For the past 500 years the Quechua have accepted the fact that they must use another language as a condition for their survival.

The Quechua still have great ambivalence toward Spanish-speaking people and find it an intrusive social system with values that contradict the order of their world. Without any political organization, the Kkechuwa-speaking Andean people have maintained themselves as a spiritual nation and through the medium of their own language have proudly reinforced their traditions, festivities, agricultural ceremonies, and connectedness to Pachamama.

In our search to find the correct way to spell the Kkechuwa words in this book, we discovered there is no uniform way of writing the language. Experts on the Kkechuwa language and members of the Quechua Language Academy in Qosqo are still debating the form and method. Linguists do not all agree with the revised Resolución Ministerial Act of 1985, which presents a standardized alphabet. However, they all agree that it is more important that the feeling of the words be preserved.

Espinoza says, "Padre Jorge Lira had a great understanding of the sounds and forces of nature. His Kkechuwa dictionary is the best ever written; there is no other like it. Other Catholic priests hated him and wanted to kill him because of his love for the Quechua people and their language. When he died, they would not let his body into the cathedral. Padre Lira was one of the best preachers of the truth in the Andes."

We have chosen the spelling used by Lira in his dictionary of Kkechuwa-Español. The late author José María Arguedas wrote that Lira dedicated his life to the study of the Kkechuwa language with an intense love for the Quechua people and their culture. He inspired their confidence and faithfully recorded their words.

It was no easy task to preserve the singing quality and characteristic intonations of the Kkechuwa speakers. Lira was able to gather folk tales and bring the expressive folklore with its oral flavor into written Spanish. Linguists agree that Lira was one of the most renowned investigators of Runasimi and his method is most acceptable and similar to that used by linguists, historians, naturalists, ethnologists, sociologists, and all lovers of the Quechua world.

In 1941 Lira wrote in Spanish that: "Language is the lighthouse that unlocks the dark secrets of history, allowing its vibrant light to penetrate and illuminate the dead monuments that lie in tombs language was destined to conquer. In the same way that the sun takes over the purity of blue skies and triumphs over palpable darkness, language goes before the human race to light its way."

*Kkechuwa-speaking children are given Spanish textbooks in a
village school at Patakancha, high in the Andes.*

An Elder Inka Speaks

Professor Faustino Espinoza Navarro is a world authority on the Kkechuwa language, a renowned teacher and prominent figure in every aspect of community life. At ninety-three years of age he is a living legend in Qosqo, a fascinating and inspiring Quechua gentleman. He continues to practice the ancient rituals and ceremonies of the Inkan religion and Andean cosmology with a genuine passion. His storytelling illustrates the interdependence of all elements of Andean life: the Kkechuwa language, work ethic, and how spirituality is incorporated into everyday life.

"My name is Faustino Espinoza Navarro. I was born on February 15, 1905, in Qosqo, at eleven o'clock in the morning, so my father told me.

"In Qosqo, I am referred to as the eldest living descendant of the Inkakuna through the lineage of both my parents, Antonio Espinoza Wampu and Elena Navarro Montegudo. My great grandparents carried the Inkan name Wampu, which means 'canoe' or 'boat' in Kkechuwa. The name comes from a culture called Orkkosuyu, a pre-Inkan civilization governed by the apukuna, the mountain deities.

"The *apu* is a mental domination of God, the strongest force of the cosmos. It is charged with the welfare and care of all people; thus, the apukuna created a procedure to govern mankind.

"My family was hated by the Spanish settlers for their blood connection to the Inkakuna. They were treated badly, as servants, and their wealth was removed. To avoid further degradation, they felt compelled to adopt Spanish names.

"My parents moved to Waroq where I spent my youth and entered elementary school. Luckily, I had a good teacher and gained knowledge that served me for the rest of my life.

"My parents suffered tremendous losses at the hands of robbers and suddenly became poor. When I completed my primary instruction, they could not afford to send me to high school. But I was not lazy. I understood my economic situation and did not allow myself to fall behind. I dedicated all my spare time to reading secondary school books and educating myself.

"The village campesinos were warm toward me and told me many things. They affectionately called me *waroq niñucha*, 'little boy of Waroq.'

"From the age of seven, I would spend time with Andean people who practiced the ancient ways of Andean cosmology. I was taught about

Andean cosmology from elderly pakkokuna from the nearby villages. I learned how to connect with the Pachamama and apukuna through singing and dancing in rituals and ceremonies.

"Always, I was meticulous and methodical, and faithfully repeated the invocations I had learned from the wise men. I have kept up the practice throughout my life, paying great attention to the teachings given to me in the Kkechuwa language.

"I am known in the administrative and political circles of this area, and I became secretary to the chief of the military. I was acknowledged for my abilities and the complete honesty instilled in me by my parents.

"Now at ninety-three years of age, I am registered in the 'University of Practical Life.' I am a student. I teach professors, students, everyone. My specialty is teaching the marvelous language of Kkechuwa. On occasion, I visit sacred sites and send offerings to Pachamama on behalf of others.

"I would like to tell you a couple of stories that happened to me when I lived in Andean villages many years ago.

"In 1928, when I was twenty-three years old, I worked on the advisory board of the municipality in Urcos. At night I slept in my office to ensure that no one would steal the machines and office equipment.

"In those days the victrola, or phonograph, was still unknown in Peru. I managed to buy one for my mother and proudly took it home to Waro, where it caused a sensation. No one in the Andes had ever heard such wonderful music. That day we played the two sides of the records over and over and over again. Then it was time for me to return to work.

"There was a full moon while I was walking to Urcos. About halfway there, I came to *unut'okquia*, 'the place where the water of the springs appears in great quantity.' Ahead of me on the path there appeared to be a large dark shape. I thought it was a special species of a tree that grew there, only thicker. But as I approached it, I saw that it looked more like a compact black sack.

"This sack-like shape was running in my direction, but did not seem to be a human figure.

"The dogs were howling in a terrible manner. 'What could it be? Is this a ghost?' The apparition came toward me, and was only twenty meters away when it moved aside on the path so that I could pass. As I approached it, it suddenly disappeared. My dog ran ahead barking. I sternly shouted to him '*Alqo*,' but he paid no attention. Ten meters ahead it appeared again, lifting up off the road and whistling like the wind.

"I ran into the village of Kaninkunka, where there is a chapel. All the village dogs began to howl and run in front of me toward the village of

Professor Faustino Espinoza Navarro performs a ritual of blowing the k'intu (three coca leaves) in the direction of the apukuna.

Urcos where I was heading. The dogs kept up their panicked barking. As I entered Urcos, the moon came out and the figure disappeared. My body felt tremendous in the light, and sparks came out of my eyes. But I was not frightened.

"Calmly, I walked to the commissioner's office at the village, reported the incident and went to sleep. I didn't think too much about it over the next few years.

"Ten years later, I was working in a community development program constructing schools in the heights of Kkollkkepata. I would get up at three o'clock in the morning and walk a long distance to the mountain communities.

"On one such walk, a heavy rain began to fall and I could not go on. I decided to try another route, and had to climb a steep hill covered in fog. A rainbow appeared across the sky. As I crossed the pass, I walked into a thick, white mist. I proceeded slowly, for it was drizzling heavily. Looking up, I saw a gigantic face in the mist ahead.

"It had a lively expression and unkempt hair. I said to myself, 'What can this be? It must be a ghost.' I continued to walk toward it, and it kept facing me the same distance away. As I proceeded to advance, the apparition stayed in front of me. I was curious to discover what it was.

"More of its body materialized, and at first I could not tell if it was male or female. It was not wearing clothes and appeared disheveled. The figure seemed to be a woman with well-developed breasts, coming from what appeared as a thick band of white clouds. It was still drizzling and I continued to follow the apparition mumbling, 'This is a ghost.'

"I had seen a *k'uychi* (rainbow) just before I had crossed the pass and walked into the mist. I wondered if the vision had something to do with the k'uychi.

"Just then an old man with a walking stick came by and I said, 'Greetings, *taytay*, old father, I have seen the strangest apparition.' I described the ghost and asked if it had anything to do with the rainbow.

"The old man replied, 'Yes, indeed. The place over there, from where you have just come, is called *k'uychiyok*, the place where the rainbow always appears. The female being appeared to you at the same place where k'uychi always appears. Because you were not scared and did not fear the being, or run or stumble and fall, it was a sign of good iu_k for you. See, now that the sun is coming out, a rainbow is forming in that precise spot.'

"Then he said, '*Kaymi k'uychi nispakka allinmi kkampak kausaynikipi kankka:* This is the rainbow appearing for you, and you will have a good future and life filled with the best of everything.'

"The old man invited me to *pikchar kuka* with him, and the two of us sat and chewed coca leaves. He told me many stories about k'uychi. The Quechua believe k'uychi represents the fertility of humankind. It is said that when young women who live in the countryside become pregnant, they often attribute the conception to the rainbow. A young woman would report that she was passing a place where water shimmered with the colors of the rainbow. The rainbow then would enter inside and impregnate her.

"When the baby was born, the mother would take the boy or girl to become baptized. When the priest asked what name the mother wanted the child to carry, she often would respond, 'Padre, my baby does not have a father because the rainbow entered me, and this is a child of the k'uychi. You can give him any name.'

"The priest would say, 'I can't, *nokkak sutillaytaña apachun:* The child must carry my name because it does not have a known father.' In this way, the priest perpetuated the name and surname of his own parents and ancestors.

"I arrived at the community and repeated to the villagers everything the old man had said. They all agreed that what he told me about the apparition and the rainbow was correct. They simply acknowledged that this is the way it is, in that place.

[The Quechua women continue to believe the rainbow can enter their bodies. They do not walk out in the countryside alone when it is raining, and they do not urinate next to a stream of water.]

"I believe that what happened to me that day, more than fifty years ago, was fortuitous. I felt no fear when the being appeared, and I am pleased that I had the ability to see those things.

"I still remember the teachings I received from Andean healers over eighty years ago as I traveled throughout the communities of Waroq, Andawaylillas, Urcos, and Oropesa.

"Throughout my lifetime, I have continued to honor Pachamama and send Her offerings on behalf of Quechua campesinos and city people alike who have needed Her help and protection."

I asked Professor Espinoza what message he would like to send to the Quechua people today. His reply:

"Man, like the animals, was born to work. A bird that flies but doesn't fly to look for food, dies.

"It is the same with man: a man who doesn't work in spite of knowing his obligations is a disgrace to the brotherhood of his fellow Quechua. He lives in misery and hunger. The man who works enjoys the gifts of nature. His life is filled with good luck.

"Discipline and work are most important. There are two ways to work. The first is physically, moving rocks. The other is with the mind, giving ideas to others who don't have this capacity. The two work together for the well-being of society.

"The Quechua campesinos maintain this philosophy, but they are lacking in the organization and total education of their teachers. Teachers today bear a sense of shame because they are uneducated in the Kkechuwa language. Honesty has been lost. We must return to the Inkan way of living because in those times, the Andeans respected the laws of *ama kkella,* don't be lazy; *ama sua,* don't be a thief; *ama llulla,* don't be a liar."

Appendix B:
Andean Map

The map on the following page was drawn by author Carol Cumes. All the main places discussed in the book are shown here, along with the major symbols and archetypes of the Andean cosmology.

Basically the map starts in the north at Salkkantay, the most sacred apu, and continues down the Aobamba valley, behind Machu Picchu, past the Sacred Valley and ends at P'isaq.

Through this map, you can almost visualize your own magical journey.

Legend

1. **Salkkantay**—Wild mountain Initiation at glaciers with three bolts of lightning. Altitude: 20,574 ft.

2. **Chakana**—Southern Cross constellation. Mythical foundation of entire universe.

3. **Apu Machu Picchu**—Old, male mountain.

4. **Apu Waynapicchu**—Young, feminine mountain.

5. **Kondor**—Messengers from mountain deities, representing hanakpacha, the upper world.

6. **Avalanche from Salkkantay** — Travels down Aobamba valley. Destruction of Lizárraga farm and hydroelectric plant.

7. **Apu Putukusi**—Happy skull, guardian of Machu Picchu.

8. **Inti**—Father Sun to the Inkakuna who were considered the children of the Sun.

9. **K'intu**—Three coca leaves, connection to the divine and used in offerings to Pachamama.

10. **Aguas Calientes**—Village with medicinal hot springs.

11. **Apu Wakaywillka**—Known as Veronica.

12. **Ollantaytampu**—Gigantic stone fortress.

13. **Puma**—Symbol of power representing the present world, Kaypacha. Mythical feline said to produce hail, storms, and rain.

14. **Apu Chicon**—Glacier and protector of the Sacred Valley.

15. **Willka T'ika**—"Sacred Flower," guest house with 500-year-old Lucma Tree.

16. **Urubamba**—Town in the heart of the Sacred Valley. Altitude: 9,000 ft.

17. **Chinchero.**

18. **Chicha**—Campesinos enjoying home-brewed chicha or akkha, corn beer.

19. **Urubamba River**—Real name is Willkamayu, also known as the river of stars in the sky.

20. **Sara**—Sacred corn, a gift from God.

21. **P'isaq**—Ancient city, guardian of the valley.

22. **Stone of three steps**—Representing the three worlds of the chakana. The serpent symbolizes the inner world, Ujhupacha.

23. **P'isaq market**—Filled with colorful hand-painted ceramic and woven goods.

24. **Qosqo**—Ancient capital city of the Inkakuna. Altitude: 11,000 ft.

Glossary

Words with Spanish origins have (Sp.) after them. All other words are in the Kkechuwa language. The plural forms of the Kkechuwa words are also included in some instances.

akkha: Type of beer made from maize. *Chicha* (Sp.).

aklla: Chosen woman.

akllay: To choose or select.

alpaka: Andean wool-producing animal.

alto misayoq: Andean healer or specialist.

amaru: Snake regarded as deity.

amau'takuna: Learned or wise men.

apachita, apachitakuna: Pebbles placed on mound as an offering.

apu, apukuna: Divine lords of the mountain.

Apu Yaya Jesucristo: Apu Jesus Christ.

Apurímakk: Qosqo shrine, the Lord who speaks.

Atawallpa: Inka ruler when Pizarro arrived in 1532.

ati: Power.

atichaw: Tuesday.

Awsankate: Sacred mountain near Qosqo.

Ayar Kachi: Founding brother of Qosqo.

Ayar Mankko: Founding brother of Qosqo.

ayawaska: Quechua for "vine of the dead." Hallucinogenic plant.

ayawaskeros: (Sp.) Healers who work with ayawaska.

ayllu: Andean community.

ayllu masi: Members of the community.

aylluruna: People from the community.

ayni: Reciprocal form of labor.

ayninakusunchis: Let us help each other.

ayninayukusun: Share with us.

brujería: (Sp.) Sorcery.

campesinos: (Sp.) Farmers, peasants.

cañazo: (Sp.) Cane spirits, alcohol.

cargo: (Sp.) Honor of being the host.

Carnaval: (Sp.) Festival.

cebada: (Sp.) Barley.

ceja de selva: (Sp.) The "brow" or beginning of the jungle.

ceque, cequekuna: Invisible lines of energy, ley network.

chahra: Farm or cultivated fields.

chahra llank'ak runakuna: Farm workers.

chahrachicuy: One who works the chahra.

chakana: Southern Cross.

ch'aki rayo: Dangerous dry lightning.

chakitaklla: Inka foot plow.

chaleco: (Sp.) Vest.

chalina: Woven scarf.

ch'allaskka: Ritual for beginning the harvest.

cháman: Medicinal plant.

chana wawa yachayniyuk: In Andean mythology, the last son with the gift of knowledge.

charango: Andean mandolin.

ch'arki: Dry.

ch'aska kuti: Sea Star.

Ch'aska mayu: Milky Way.

chayka: Spell or negative force.

ch'ekkche sara: Purple corn.

chicha morada: Non-alcoholic drink made from blue corn.

chijchi: Hail.

ch'illka paukar: Medicinal plant.

chirimuya: Fruit.

chiuchi piñi: Colored glass beads with holes.

chompa: A knitted sweater.

chokkllo: Andean maize or corn cob.

ch'ullpi sara: Corn for toasting.

ch'ullu: Multi-colored knitted hat.

ch'uñu: Freeze-dried potatoes.

ch'uspa: Woven pouch to hold coca leaves.

ch'usu: Unripe seed.

citua: Inka ritual to cleanse Qosqo of illness.

clavel t'ika: Carnation.

coca: (Sp.) kuka: Coca leaves.

concha: (Sp.) Sea shell.

curandero: (Sp.) Healer.

curvos: (Sp.) Machete.

doncella wallpakk runtun: First egg laid by a hen.

encomiendas: (Sp.) Andean tax tributes paid to the Spanish.

gringo, gringokuna: (Sp.) Slang, refers to Americans or foreigners. "Grin" refers to the green berets worn by American soldiers in Mexico. The people shouted: "Green go!"

hallpay: Ritual or everyday act of chewing coca leaves.

hampi: Medicine.

hampi kkatu: Traditional medicine market.

Hanakpacha: Andean world of higher consciousness.

hanka: Glacier.

hank'a: Toasted maize.

hanku kkañiwa: Raw cereal.

hanp'atu: Toad.

harawi, harawikuna: Andean songs.

haywarikuy: Offering, "to reach the earth."

haywaskka: Blessing or prayer.

huk'ucha: Rat.

illa: Pebble shaped like an animal.

inchis, inchiskuna: Peanuts.

Inka: Son of the Sun.

inti: Sun.

Intic Raymin: Festival of the Sun.

iwayllu: Supernatural, mythical animal.

K'achampa: Qoyllur R'iti dancing pilgrims from surrounding communities.

kachi: Salt.

k'akya: Clap of thunder.

Kallawayakuna: Healers from Bolivia.

Kaypacha: Andean world of humans, plants, animals, minerals.

k'eswa: Twisted rope made from straw.

khawa: Ceremony. Offering made to the apu to take care of animals.

khipu, khipukuna: System of tying knots. Inkakuna used it for counting, calculations and storing historical information.

killa: Moon.

Killapampa: Quillabamba.

killa raymi: October.

k'intu: Brief ritual to the apukuna, using coca leaves.

kinúwa: Quinoa.

kiska, kiskakuna: Thorns.

kiwicha: Andean cereal.

kollakuna: People from Titicaca region.

kuchunakuna: Machetes.

kuhuru: Guard who watches over seeds.

kuka: Coca leaf.

kuka akllay: Ritual to lay out coca leaves for divining purposes.

kuka k'intu: A ritual offering of coca leaves.

kukamama: Coca leaf mother.

kuka mukkllu: Seed of the coca leaf plant.

kumbi: Finely woven cloth for Inka lords.

Kurak akulleq: Highest level of initiated Andean master.

kutun: Men's shirt.

k'uychi: Rainbow.

k'uychipunku: Gate of the rainbow.

kkañiwa: Andean cereal.

Kkañaqway: Name of an apu.

kkarpay: Ritual to the apukuna. The healer receives his star.

kk'ata unu: Muddy water.

kkawa: Seven strands of colored wool.

kkaywa: Assistant.

kkechi: Mouse.

kkechuwa: Quechua language.

kkena: Andean flute.

kkeros: Large mugs.

kk'eperina: Carrying cloth.

kkéswa: Ravine or valley.

kkeswaa: Sound of boulders falling down Andean cliffs.

kkeswakuna: Early inhabitants of the Andean Valley.

kkeswaruna: Person from the valley.

kkeswarunakuna: People of the valley.

kkeswasimi: Believed to be correct name for Kkechuwa language.

kkeswaway'kko: Ravine.

kkhápakkuna: Ear decorations worn by Inka men. *Orejones* (Sp.).

kkhapákksimi: Language of the rich and powerful Inka lords.

kkhápak raymi or warachikuy: Ceremony for youths eligible to wear ear ornaments.

kkhayachonta: Medicinal plant.

kkhaya chonta: White quartz.

kkocha: Lake.

kkolkkampata: Palace of Mankko Kkhapakk.

kkolkke: Silver.

kkolkke botija: Sheet of silver paper.

kkolkke libro: Silver leaf.

kkolkke pinkuyllu: Silver flute.

kkolkke recado: Silver figurine.

kkollana: Man in charge of day's work.

kkora hampikuna: Common medicinal plants.

kkori: Gold.

kkori botija: Gold jug.

Kkorikancha: Enclosure of gold. Inka temple in Qosqo.

kkorikenki: Mythical bird of wisdom.

kkori libro: Gold dipped leaves.

kkori recado: Gold figurines.

kkowi: Guinea pig.

kkoya: Queen, wife of the Inka.

kkoyllor: Morning star.

kkoyllurchaw: Wednesday.

kkoyllur raymi: September.

lamperos: (Sp.) Laborers who use agricultural tools.

laykka: female pakko or healer.

llakjón: Edible root.

llakta alto misayoq: Andean healer serving the village.

llama ñawikuna: Eyes of the llama.

llank'ay: Work.

llank'aruna: Worker.

llank'ayniyukk: The one who has the gift of work.

llantén: Medicinal plant.

lliklla: Woman's shawl.

llipt'a: Piece of lime ash used to activate coca leaves. Lime ash is made from banana flower.

llo'ke: Left.

llo'ke seda: Left silk used in an offering.

llo'ke taku: Red and blue vermilion stone, placed on left in an offering.

lluth'u: Bird resembling a partridge.

mach'a mikhuykuna: Fruit from trees, such as avocado, chirimuya.

mach'akkway: Serpent.

machu incienso: (Sp.) Old incense.

machu, machukuna: Ancient beings.

machu wayra: Evil wind, negative force.

machula: Dancing pilgrims to Qoyllur R'iti from outer regions of Qosqo.

mallki: Ancestor, tree.

mamakuna: Caretakers of the chosen woman.

mamakuka: Mother of coca leaves.

Mama Okkllo: Founding woman born to the Sun and moon.

mamapapa: Chosen potato.

Mánkko Inka: Surviving son of Wayna Kkhápak.

Mánkko kkhápakk: Founding Inka.

Manturk'alla: Hill outside of Qosqo.

mayordomo: (Sp.) Head of the fiesta.

mayu: River, also referred to as the Milky Way, *ch'aska mayu*.

mazamorra morada: Purple jelly dessert.

Mesada: High grassland, 14,500 feet, near Machu Picchu.

melkkhay: Skirt.

mink'a: Ritual contract for reciprocal help.

miska: Harvest of the first crops.

misk'ikuna: Candies.

mokko mokko: Medicinal plant.

monte: (Sp.) Jungle.

montera: Brimmed hat worn by men and women.

moskkoykuna: Dreams.

munayniyuk: In Andean mythology, one with the gift of love.

munay phiwiwawa: In Andean mythology, first born with the gift of love.

mustaza: Sacrificial gift.

ñaupa machukuna: Ancient beings of the male sex.

nevados: (Sp.) Mountains.

ninapara: Firestorm.

ñust'a: Chosen woman, wife of the Inka.

Ollantaytampu: Ancient shrine at the end of the Sacred Valley of the Inkakuna.

oroya: Small platform with cable; transport across a river.

Pachakámak: Creator God.

Pachakútekk: Ninth Inka emperor, era of turning of time.

Pachamama: Mother Earth.

pakkarikktámpu: Inn of the dawn, place of origin.

pakkarina: Place of origin.

pákkay: Fruit of a tree.

pakko, pakkokuna: General name for Andean ritual specialists.

pampa misayoq: Andean herbalist or diviner of coca leaves.

paña: Right.

paña seda: Right silk used in an offering.

paña taku: Red and blue vermilion stone placed on the right side in offerings.

papamama: Mother of potatoes.

para: Rain.

parakkay sara: White maize.

pata patakuna: Andean terraces.

phukuy: To blow.

phututu: Spandolus shell.

picchar kuka: To chew coca leaves.

picchu: Peak or summit.

pinkuyllu: Andean flute.

pukllaytaky: Carnaval, "let's play."

puna: Grassland.

purutu: Legume, bean high in protein.

pujyu: Spring.

Putukusi: Apu across from Machu Picchu.

qhaskka sara: Speckled corn.

q'ello sara: Yellow maize.

Qosqo: Official name for Cusco.

Qoyllur R'iti: Star of the Snows. Annual sacred pilgrimage.

rakkacha: Sub-tropical edible root, similar to carrot.

raki: Earthenware tub.

rayo: (Sp.) Lightning, *k'akya*.

reducciones: (Sp.) Forced resettlement of Andean people by Spanish.

rit'i: Snow.

Ruak: Created the Sun.

ruda: Plant that removes negative energy.

rumu: Yuca, an edible root.

runa: Human being.

runa simi: Tongue of the people, language.

Runkurakkay: Ruin along the Inka Trail.

sabios: (Sp.) Learned men.

sach'a mikhuykuna: Fruit from a tree.

saksa kuti: Piece of curly nut.

Saksaywaman: Fortress where Spanish won final battle in Qosqo.

Salkkantay: Sacred Mountain. Wild mountain.

sankhu: Paste made from toasted maize.

San Nicolas T'anta: Bread used in offering.

saqueadores: (Sp.) Plunderers.

sara: Maize.

sara huñuy: Safe transfer of crops at harvest time.

saramama: Mother of the maize.

sara tarpuy: Sowing of maize.

sillukuy: Colored poncho worn on special occasion.

Sípan: Ancient royal tombs, recently excavated.

sirwanakuy: Unmarried couples formally living together. "To serve one another."

sok'a paya: Ancient beings of the feminine sex.

sok'a wasi: House of clay.

soltake solta: Medicinal plant.

sorokkch'e: Altitude sickness.

sullu: Fetus of llama or alpaka.

suyu alto misayoq: Andean healer who administers entire region.

suyunakuy: Cultivation of fields.

tákke: Special formation in corn stalk.

Tampumachay: Inn of rest, water fountains.

tarwi: Nutritious Andean lupin.

tawa: Four.

tawakkuchuy: wisdom of the four directions.

Tawantinsuyo: Four regions of the Inka Empire.

Taytanchis: Father, God.

Teksiwirakkocha: Creator God.

t'ika: Flower.

t'inkaskka: Ritual, to kiss and appreciate the earth.

tintu: Rope.

trago: (Sp.) Cane liquor.

Túpak Amaru I: Mánkko's son.

tupu: Decorative pin.

uchu: Peppers used as condiment.

uchukuta: Hot spicy sauce.

Ukhupacha: Andean inner world or the underworld.

ukuku: Spectacle bear.

ulluko: Small type of potato.

untu: Fat of llama or alpaka.

unu: Water.

unuchakuy: Andean ceremony for initiates.

Unu Raymi: Festival of Water.

unkhuña: Small cloth of beautiful colors.

usut'akuna: Sandals of rubber tires or leather.

uwija: Sheep.

uywakke: Creator, powerful being.

waka: Sacred shrine, object location.

wak'arumi, wak'arumikuna: Sacred stones.

wallpa: Chicken.

Wanakauri: Name of Apu.

wanako: Andean animal, guanaco.

Warachikuy: Festival of Kkhapak Rami, Inka youth becoming adults.

wañuy: Death.

warmi wañuskka: "Dead woman's pass" on Inka Trail.

wask'ha: Rope.

Waskar: Atawallpa's brother.

wawa: Baby.

Wayna kkápakk: Eleventh Inka, father of Atawallpa.

Waynapicchu: Young peak.

waynu, waynukuna: Andean songs.

Wayri ch'unchu: Wild ones from Paukartampu in the jungle.

wayruru: Seed from the jungle.

werakocha: Gentleman.

wijuju: Jungle vines.

wik'uña: Vicuña, produces the finest wool.

willka: Andean tree, hallucinogenic powder made from it.

willkamayu: Sacred river, Urubamba.

Willkapampa (Vilcabamba): Where Mánkko Inka fled after battle at Saksaywaman. Last stronghold of Inka.

Wirakkocha: Supreme Deity, Creator God.

wira q'oya: Medicinal herb.

wiru: Stalk of corn.

wisk'acha: Viscacha.

yachak: Man of knowledge.

yachay: To learn.

yachayniyukk: The one with the gift of learning.

yawar ch'onkka: Medicinal plant.

yerba de cáncer: Medicinal plant.

Bibliography

Agurto Calvo, Santiago. *La Traza Urbana de la Ciudad Inca*. Cusco, Perú: Proyecto PER-39 Unesco, Inc., 1980.

Angles Vargas, Victor. *Historia del Cusco Tomo 1*. Lima, Perú: Editorial Industrial Gráfica S.A., 1979.

Aranibar, Lizardo P. *Inkakunaq Mit'anpi Qelqay. La Gratificaion en La Època de Los Gobernantes*. Cusco, Perú: Amercar, 1990.

Arguedas, Jose María. *The Singing Mountaineers*. Austin, TX: University of Texas Press, 1956.

Arriaga, Padre José del. *Extirpación de la Idolatría en el Perú*. Lima, Perú: Imprenta y Librería San Martin y Cía, 1920.

Buck, Daniel. "Fights of Machu Picchu." South American Explorer, Number 32, Ithaca, NY: South American Explorers Club, 1993.

Bingham, Hiram. "In the Wonderland of Peru." Journal of National Geographic Society, Washington, D.C.: April 1913.

——."The Story of Machu Picchu." Journal of National Geographic Society, Washington, D.C.: February, 1915.

——. *Lost City of the Incas*. New York, NY: Atheneum, 1948.

Cobo, Father Bernabe, translated by Roland Hamilton. *Inca Religion and Customs.* Austin, TX: University of Texas Press, 1990.

Cooper, Mary Ann, edited by Paul S. Auerbach and Edward C. Geehr. *Physics of Lightning Stroke: Management of Wilderness & Environmental Emergencies.* St. Louis, MO: The C.V. Mosby Company, 1989.

Dalle, Luis. *El Despacho.* En rev. Allpanchis Phuturinga V.1 N.1 139–154, Cusco-Apurimac, Perú: Instituto Pastoral Andina, 1969.

———. *La Miska.* En rev. Allpanchis Phuturinga N.8 28–33, Cusco-Quispicanchis, Perú: Instituto Pastoral Andina, 1971.

Escobar, Rómulo. *Enciclopedia Agricola.* Lima, Perú: Universidad de San Marcos, 1981.

Girault, Louis. Kallawaya. *Curanderos Itinerantes de los Andes.* La Paz, Bolivia: UNICEF-OPS-OMS-PL-480, 1987.

Guenon, Renó. "La Pseudo Iniciación. El Reyno de la Cantidad y los signos de los tiempos." En rev. Gnossis, N 6 20–25. Qosqo, Perú: Gnossis, 1992.

Herrera Tamayo, José. *Algunos Conceptos Filósóficos de la Cosmovisión Andina del Indígena Quechua.* En rev. Allpanchis Phuturinqa N.2 245–254. Cusco, Perú: Instituto Pastoral Andina, 1970.

Intosh, Eduardo. *La Apachita y su Función Religiosa en el Mundo Quechua.* Lima, Perú: N 52 Perú-Cusco-Anta, 1987.

Lanning, Edward P. *Peru Before The Incas.* New York, NY: Prentice-Hall, Inc.,1967.

Leon, Gorge. *Fundamentos Botánicas de los Cultivos Tropicales.* San Jose, Costa Rica: Servicio Editorial I.I.C.A.(Instituto Interamericano de Cooperacion para la Agricultura), 1987.

Lira, Jorge. *Fundamentos de la Lengua Kkechuwas.* En rev. Waman Puma V.3 N 15.43.48. Cusco, Perú: Instituto Pastoral Andina, 1943.

———. *Diccionario Kkechuwa-Español* 2nd Edition. Bogota, Colombia: Convenie Andres Bella, Secretaría Ejecutiva Instituto International de Integración IADAP. 1982.

Lizárraga Valencia, Luis. *Evaluación del Contenido de Fibra en Semillas de Colección.* Qosqo, Perú: Universidad de San Marcos, 1981.

MacCormack, Sabine. *Religion in the Andes.* Princeton, NJ: Princeton University Press, 1991.

Mannheim, Bruce. *The Language of the Inka Since the European Invasion.* Austin, TX: University of Texas Press, 1991.

Mayta Medina, Faustino. *La Cosecha del Maiz en Yucay.* En rev. Allpanchis Phuturinqa N.3. Cusco-Urubamba, Perú: Instituto Pastoral Andina, 1971.

McIntyre, Loren. *The Incredible Incas and Their Timeless Land.* Washington, D.C.: The National Geographic Society, 1975.

Meisch, Lyn. *A Traveler's Guide to El Dorado and The Inca Empire.* New York, NY: Penguin Books, 1977.

Métraux, Alfred, translated by George Ordish. *The History of the Incas.* New York, NY: Schocken Books, 1970.

Montaldo, Alvaro. *Cultivo Tropicales de Raices y Tubérculos.* Lima, Perú: Grafico Pacific Press S.A., 1972.

Nuñez del Prado, Juan V. *El Mundo Sobrenatural de los Quechuas del Sur a través de la comunidad de Qatabamba.* En rev. Allpanchis Phuturinqa N.2: 57–120. Cusco, Perú: Instituto Pastoral Andina, 1987.

———. "Contenidos Implicitos en el Hatun Kkarpay, Ritual de iniciación Superior Andina." En rev. Gnossis N6 20–25. Qosqo-Machupicchu, Perú: Gnosis 1992.

Roersch, Carlos. *Plantas Medicinales del sur Andino del Perú.* En rev. Allpanchis Phuturinqa N.9 Cusco, Perú: Instituto de Pastoral Andina, 1976.

Sanchez, M. Marino O. *De las Sacerdotistas, Brujas y Adivinas de Machupicchu.* Cusco, Perú: Editora Cotental Perú S.A., 1989.

Urton, Gary. *At the Crossroads of the Earth and Sky: An Andean Cosmology.* Austin, TX: University of Texas Press, 1981.

Van der Hoogte, Liesbeth. *Centro de Medicina Andina.* Cusco, Perú: Instituto de Pastoral Andina, 1980.

Van Gennep, Arnold. *The Rites of Passage.* Chicago, IL: Chicago Press, 1972.

Wagner, Catherine. *Coca y Estructura Cultura, en los Andes Peruanos.* En rev. Allpanchis Phuturinqa N. 9 103–223 Cusco, Perú: Instituto Pastoral Andina, 1976.

West, John Anthony, Dr. Robert Schoch, and Dr. John Kutzbach. "The Mystery of the Sphinx." NBC television program, 1993.

Zuidema, R. Tom, translated by Jean-Jaques Decoster. *Inca Civilization in Cuzco.* Austin, TX: University of Texas Press, 1986.

Index

☽ REACH FOR THE MOON

Llewellyn publishes hundreds of books on your favorite subjects! To get these exciting books, including the ones on the following pages, check your local bookstore or order them directly from Llewellyn.

ORDER BY PHONE
- Call toll-free within the U.S. and Canada, 1-800-THE MOON
- In Minnesota, call (651) 291-1970
- We accept VISA, MasterCard, and American Express

ORDER BY MAIL
- Send the full price of your order (MN residents add 7% sales tax) in U.S. funds, plus postage & handling to:

    Llewellyn Worldwide
    P.O. Box 64383, Dept. K186-4
    St. Paul, MN 55164–0383, U.S.A.

POSTAGE & HANDLING
(For the U.S., Canada, and Mexico)
- $4.00 for orders $15.00 and under
- $5.00 for orders over $15.00
- No charge for orders over $100.00

We ship UPS in the continental United States. We ship standard mail to P.O. boxes. Orders shipped to Alaska, Hawaii, The Virgin Islands, and Puerto Rico are sent first-class mail. Orders shipped to Canada and Mexico are sent surface mail.

International orders: Airmail—add freight equal to price of each book to the total price of order, plus $5.00 for each non-book item (audio tapes, etc.).

Surface mail—Add $1.00 per item.

Allow 2 weeks for delivery on all orders.
Postage and handling rates subject to change.

DISCOUNTS
We offer a 20% discount to group leaders or agents. You must order a minimum of 5 copies of the same book to get our special quantity price.

FREE CATALOG
Get a free copy of our color catalog, *New Worlds of Mind and Spirit*. Subscribe for just $10.00 in the United States and Canada ($30.00 overseas, airmail). Many bookstores carry *New Worlds*— ask for it!

Visit our web site at www.llewellyn.com for more information.

Sacred Sites of the West

Bernyce Barlow

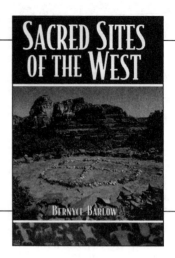

Stroll through a forest of the world's oldest living trees, explore secret healing caves, or take a midnight dip in the hallowed waters of Big Sur! *Sacred Sites of the West* takes you on an exciting journey of enchantment and explains how the earth's energies can heal you, rejuvenate your inner energies, and effect your dreams. Investigate ley lines and grid networks, vortexes, and energy wellsprings—all here in the United States! Visit the "Lourdes of America" in New Mexico, tour the inner temple of a Hawaiian heiau, then raft the most treacherous rapids on the North American continent. See the never-before-documented Albino Redwood of California and the Child Nest Rock of Nevada.

Dream spots, healing centers, goddess and warrior sites, temples, and vision caves are just a few of the places you'll encounter. Plus, color photographs, holy history, earth physics and legends become an integral part of each site narration, leaving you with a clear understanding of just what makes these sites so captivating.

0-87542-056-6, 240 pp., 6 x 9, 12-pp. color insert $19.95

Mother Nature's Herbal

Judith Griffin, Ph.D.

A Zuni American Indian swallows the juice of goldenrod flowers to ease his sore throat…an East Indian housewife uses the hot spices of curry to destroy parasites…an early American settler rubs fresh strawberry juice on her teeth to remove tartar. People throughout the centuries have enjoyed a special relationship with Nature and her many gifts.

Now, with *Mother Nature's Herbal*, you can discover how to use a planet full of medicinal and culinary herbs through more than 200 recipes and tonics. Explore the cuisine, beauty secrets and folk remedies of China, the Mediterranean, South America, India, Africa and North America. The book will also teach you the specific uses of flower essences, chakra balancing, aromatherapy, essential oils, companion planting, organic gardening and theme garden designs.

1-56718-340-9
400 pp., 7x10, 8-pp. color insert, softcover $19.95

To order, call 1-800-THE MOON
Prices subject to change without notice

Shapeshifter Tarot

D. J. Conway and Sirona Knight

Illustrated by Lisa Hunt

Like the ancient Celts, you can now practice the shamanic art of shapeshifting and access the knowledge of the eagle, the oak tree or the ocean: wisdom that is inherently yours and resides within your very being. The *Shapeshifter Tarot* kit is your bridge between humans, animals and nature. The cards in this deck act as merging tools, allowing you to tap into the many different animal energies, together with the elemental qualities of air, fire, water and earth.

The accompanying book gives detailed explanations on how to use the cards, along with their full esoteric meanings, and mythological and magical roots. Exercises in shapeshifting, moving through gateways, doubling out, meditation and guided imagery give you the opportunity to enhance your levels of perception and awareness, allowing you to hone and accentuate your magical understanding and skill.

1-56718-384-0
Boxed kit: 81 full-color cards, 6x9, 264-pp. illus. book $29.95

Animal-Speak

The Spiritual & Magical Powers of Creatures Great & Small

Ted Andrews

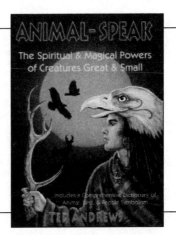

The animal world has much to teach us. Some are experts at survival and adaptation, some never get cancer, some embody strength and courage while others exude playfulness. Animals remind us of the potential we can unfold, but before we can learn from them, we must first be able to speak with them.

In this book, myth and fact are combined in a manner that will teach you how to speak and understand the language of the animals in your life. *Animal-Speak* helps you meet and work with animals as totems and spirits— by learning the language of their behaviors within the physical world. It provides techniques for reading signs and omens in nature so you can open to higher perceptions and even prophecy. It reveals the hidden, mythical and realistic roles of 45 animals, 60 birds, 8 insects, and 6 reptiles.

Animals will become a part of you, revealing to you the majesty and divine in all life. They will restore your childlike wonder of the world and strengthen your belief in magic, dreams and possibilities.

0–87542–028–1
400 pp., 7 x 10, illus., photos, softcover $17.95

The Intimate Enemy

Winning the War Within Yourself

Guy Finley and Ellen Dickstein, Ph.D.

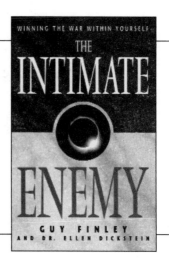

Within each of us lurk invisible psychological characters that inhabit our inner beings and make choices for us—choices that repeatedly cause us pain on some level. Now, best-selling self-help author Guy Finley and psychologist Dr. Ellen Dickstein expose these characters for what they really are: our mechanical, unconscious reactions and misperceptions that create a threatening world.

The Intimate Enemy will introduce you to astounding parts of yourself that you never knew existed. You will observe the inner dramas that control your life without your knowledge. Best of all, you will awaken to a higher awareness that provides the only true strength and confidence you need to walk into a fearless future. As you uncover the exciting truth about who you really are, you will gain an unshakable understanding of the human struggle and witness proof of a higher world, free from all strife.

1-56718-279-8, 256 pp., 5 ³⁄₁₆ x 8 $9.95